Acta Universitatis Upsaliensis
Studia Uralica Upsaliensia 35

D1935296

André Hesselbäck

Tatar and Chuvash Code-copies in Mari

UPPSALA 2005

Dissertation for the degree of Doctor of Philosophy in Finno-Ugric languages presented at Uppsala University in 2001.

Abstract

Hesselbäck, A. 2005: Tatar and Chuvash Code-copies in Mari. Acta Universitatis Upsaliensis. Studia Uralica Upsaliensia 35. 180 pp. ISBN 91-554-6125-5.

The Finno-Ugric language Mari is considered to be among the most turkicized of the Finno-Ugric languages. The impact of the two Turkic languages Tatar and Chuvash on Mari is considerable and concerns every part of the Mari language: lexicon, phonology, morphology and syntax. The factors underlying this impact are both social and structural. Among the social factors are the cultural, political and numerical dominance relations between the Mari and the Turkic peoples that have led to complex language-contact situations. Among the structural factors of importance is the typological similarity between Mari and the Turkic languages which has further increased the Turkic impact on Mari. In this thesis, some aspects of this complex language-contact situation are investigated. Social and structural factors are of importance for understanding the outcome of the Tatar and Chuvash impact on Mari. The Turkic elements in Mari are analyzed as code-copies, elements of another linguistic code copied into Mari. Since copies can establish themselves as parts of the language they are copied into, the thesis furthermore aims to show the extent to which the copies of Tatar and Chuvash models in Mari can be analyzed as habitualized or conventionalized.

Key-words: Mari, Tatar, Chuvash, Middle Volga region, language contact, social factors, structural factors, code-copying, global copies, mixed copies, selective copies, morphological influence, syntactic influence.

André Hesselbäck, Department of Finno-Ugric Languages, Uppsala University, Box 527, SE-751 20 Uppsala, Sweden.

The figure on the cover is based on an original photograph of a Khanty female from Vakh with bow and arrow. It was taken by U. T. Sirelius towards the end of the 19th century, and is now in the possession of the National Museum of Finland.

Cover lay-out: Jerk-Olof Werkmäster

© André Hesselbäck 2005

ISSN 1101-7430
ISBN 91-554-6125-5

Distributed by Uppsala University Library, Box 510, SE-751 20 Uppsala, Sweden

Printed in Sweden 2005 by
Textgruppen i Uppsala AB

Table of contents

List of tables, and maps

Foreword

This book is the English version of my thesis "Tatariska och tjuvasjiska kodkopior i mariskan". It is the result of my interest in Mari, a Finno-Ugric language spoken by approximately 500 000 persons in the eastern parts of Russia, and its contacts with two neighbouring Turkic languages, Tatar and Chuvash. Many people to whom I am deeply grateful have contributed to this book and since they generally received acknowledgement in the Swedish edition, I will only mention those who have contributed to the English version. My deepest thanks go to Professor Lars-Gunnar Larsson, Uppsala university, who has shown a never ending trust in me and my work. Professor Sirkka Saarinen, University of Turku, Finland, has made invaluable comments and suggestions for which I am very grateful. I am also forever in debt to Rodney Bradbury who revised my English. I am fully responsible for all errors and shortcomings as far as form and content is concerned. However long the distance between the Volga Region and Africa might seem, large parts of this work were actually carried out in Kenya and Ethiopia. I am deeply obliged to many people in both countries for making it possible to conduct research in Finno-ugric languages in an East African setting. Last but no least, I am very grateful to my wife Penja and my son Beniam for their patience during these all too many years. In the end, there was a book after all.

Uppsala, October 2004

André Hesselbäck

1 Introduction

1.1 Background

1.1.1 The Volga

The Volga is the longest river in Europe. It has its sources in the Valday mountains, 400 kilometres north-west of Moscow, and when it finally flows into the Caspian Sea at Astrakhan, the river has covered a distance of more than 3,500 kilometres. The Volga and its tributaries drain a vast area and, with the building of several large canals, the flow of the river has been connected with both the Baltic and the Black Sea. The Volga is one of the most important waterways not only in Russia but also in the whole of Europe. In its entire length, the Volga flows through the so-called Russian Lowland which occupies a large part of European Russia. Topographically this area is characterised by small differences in altitude and the relief of the river is gently sloping. The river valley of the Volga is also characterised by the higher and steeper right bank, whereas the left bank is flatter and lower. From its sources in Valday, the Volga flows in a north-eastern direction until it turns south-west at Rybinsk. From here the river flows past the cities of Jaroslavl and Kostroma, Nizhny Novgorod and Kozmodemyansk. When the river reaches the city of Kazan in Tatarstan it bends off to the south. Between Kazan and Ulyanovsk the river Kama, originating in the Ural Mountains, flows into the Volga and the river changes its course once again. It flows to the south-west until it reaches the Caspian Sea. Due to its length, the Volga flows through several nature types and connects the large coniferous forests in the north, the taiga, with the vast steppes in the south. The areas around the central parts of the river's flow constitute what can be labelled as a transitional area between the taiga and the steppes, and the area is characterised by the presence of mixed forests and fertile soils of different types. The climate is continental with cold winters and warm summers.

In historic times, the Volga has been one of the most important contact ways between the western, Christian cultures of Europe and the Moslem world in Central Asia. Arabian, Persian, Slavonic and Scandinavian traders have all travelled along the Volga, as well as merchants belonging to various Turkic peoples. On these trade routes, new thoughts and ideas have been promoted. The Middle Volga region is thus a transitional area not only in a geographical sense but also historic-political, economical, cultural and ethnical. Several centralised states have emerged in the Middle Volga region, and although the river today flows within the borders of present-day Russia, trade along the river has, at times, been controlled and dominated by peoples and states which have preceded the Muscovite empire, the Soviet Union and modern Russia. The Middle Volga region has been, and still is, inhabited by different peoples speaking Turkic or Finno-Ugric languages. Among the speakers of Turkic languages there are Tatars, Bashkir and Chuvash whereas the Mari, the Udmurt and the Mordvin peoples speak Finno-Ugric languages. The—at times—intensive contacts between the Finno-Ugric and Turkic languages of the area have resulted in large-scale structural changes especially in the Finno-Ugric languages, particularly in Mari. Bartens (1997: 334) claims that "für einen Sprachkontaktforscher ist ja das Tscheremissische [Mari] ein direktes Paradebeispiel". Saarinen (1997b: 388) states that "The Volga-Kama region of Russia can be described as a treasure house for areal and contact linguistics".

Mari has been influenced by the Turkic languages of Tatar and Chuvash in the most profound way and the influence concerns every part of the Mari language system: lexicon, phonology, morphology and syntax. The reasons for this can partly be found in the social relations between the Mari and the Turkic peoples where the Tatar and the Chuvash have been the politically, economically, numerically, and culturally dominating peoples. The contacts between the languages concerned have also been long and intensive, and the structural closeness between Mari and the Turkic languages has further enhanced the influence. The widespread bi- and in some cases also multilingualism has been of importance for the structural changes in Mari (Isanbaev 1978: 177). The contacts between Mari and the Turkic languages have received much attention among many scholars in different times and countries and the literature on the subject is extensive. In later years, research on the contacts between Finno-Ugric languages and other languages has become more concentrated on the contacts with various Indo-European languages and some scholars see the contacts between Turkic and Finno-Ugric languages as something belonging to the past. Volodin (1997: 35) describes the situation in the following way: "Alle frühere Kontakte mit anderen Sprachen (z.B. mit Turksprachen) sind jetzt Vergangenheit; einige Spuren davon sind in uralischen Sprachen geblieben, aber eine weitere Entwicklung dieser Kontakte ist heute kaum möglich."

1.1.2 Language contact

Language is the primary means of communication between humans. It is not static, however, but undergoes systematic changes over time, changes that can have language-internal causes. But languages can and do change for reasons other than purely language-internal, even as a result of conscious planning (Raag 1998). Language contact too leads to linguistic changes and the influence that languages can exert on each other in a contact situation is a frequently discussed theme in linguistics (Johanson 1992: 169). The research on language contact can be described as a discipline within linguistics where radically different views are expressed, not least when it comes to the question of which the factors are that can promote contact-induced changes. In Weinreich's *Languages in Contact* (1953), the importance of social and structural factors for linguistic changes in language contact situations are emphasized and after the publication of Weinreich's book, a number of scientific works on language contact have been published, many of them with similar basic assumptions. Which of these factors is going to be considered to be the most important is still being debated, as is the question of the relation between social and structural factors. Other often discussed questions are what it is that can change, how deep the changes are and which factors promote or impede structural changes in language contact situations (Johanson 1992: 169). With the basic assumption that contact-induced change is the result of a complicated interaction between social and structural factors, many different theories have been proposed in recent years. One such theory is developed by Sarah Grey Thomason and Terrence Kaufman who in their *Language Contact, Creolization and Genetic Linguistics* (1988) have developed a framework for the analysis of linguistic change as a result of language contact. The theory has received widespread attention among scholars studying the contacts of Finno-Ugric languages with other languages. The theory is discussed by Pugh (1999) in a book dealing with the incorporation of Russian verbs in Baltic-Finnic languages and—among other theories—also by Sarhimaa (1999) in a study on the contacts between a Baltic-Finnic language, Karelian, and Russian. In the model of analysis of Thomason and Kaufman, the importance of social and structural factors is emphasized and also the questions of what it is that can change and how deep these changes can be, are explicitly dealt with. Thomason and Kaufman base their model on a large linguistic material and a number of case studies. Of particular interest to Finno-Ugric lingustics is their case study of possible Uralic influence on Baltic and Slavic languages (Thomason & Kaufman 1988: 238–251). The theory, which is not presented in detail here, has a basic assumption that can be said to be what was going to be proven. Thomason and Kaufman assume that what they call *mixed languages* exist, languages that have emerged as a result of language contact and which can not be ascribed a common origin with other languages. Thomason & Kaufman (1988: 3–4) distinguish two different types of language contact that can lead to such extensive structural changes that a mixed language emerges. The first type is the case when a language changes as a result of large-scale *borrowing*; the language is maintained but in a new form. The second type is when speakers of a given language adopt the language of another people and in the process of language-shift carry over features of the language they abandon to the language to which they shift, a phenomenon traditionally labelled *substratum influence*. For my purposes, the model is not applicable because it can be assumed that Mari, although having undergone major structural changes because of its contacts with the Turkic languages, does not constitute a "mixed language". In spite of the large-scale structural changes, Mari is still a language with very much in common with other Finno-Ugric languages. That Mari is a Finno-Ugric language is easily observed in lexical correspondences between Mari and other Finno-Ugric languages in the basic vocabulary. Numerals and personal pronouns in Mari, for instance, are of an unmistakably Finno-Ugric character. Also the case endings are with some exceptions of high age, such as the accusative ending *-m* (Collinder 1960: 284). To describe the structural changes that Mari has undergone as a result of its contacts with Turkic languages, another theory is thus needed.

1.2 Theoretical background

The turcologist Lars Johanson has elaborated a model for the analysis of structural changes in language contact situations labelled *the Code-copying Framework*. The basic assumptions underlying this model are fully accounted for in the paper *Strukturelle Faktoren in türkischen Sprachkontakten* (Johanson 1992) and the model is also presented in a more concentrated form in the paper *The dynamics of code-copying in language encounters* (Johanson 1999). The Code-copying Framework is a model aiming at a coherent analysis of language contact phenomena and is based on the characteristic features of the contacts between Turkic and other languages.

As is the case with Thomason & Kaufman, Johanson assumes that social and structural factors are decisive for the outcome of contact-induced linguistic change, and Johanson too distinguishes two different types of language contact leading to such changes. It is assumed that a language can be socially dominant over another and exert a structural influence on that other language. This type of change corresponds to what Thomason & Kaufman call change as a result of borrowing. The socially dominated language can, however, also exert an influence on the dominant language and this kind of change corresponds to what Thomason & Kaufman label change as a result of substratum influence. A third possibility according to Johanson, is that the socially dominated language finally has so few social functions left that it is abandoned completely in favour of the dominant language. Among the social factors of importance according to Johanson (1992: 172) are political, economical, cultural and numerical dominance. The length and intensity of the contacts are of decisive importance since they are an important prerequisite for the emergence of a qualified bilingualism, and the direction, kind, extension and depth of the structural changes correlate with the length and intensity of the contacts. Social and structural factors are concurrent, but social factors can overcome the structural factors. Contact-induced change can occur even if the contact languages in question have very little in common structurally. On the other hand, structural changes can be very extensive if the contact languages are typologically close to each other. In contrast to Thomason & Kaufman (1988: 4) who claim that the two types of language contact have radically different effects, Johanson (1992:170) states that it is a question of two different but interacting kinds of language contact that can lead to very complicated structural changes. The social relations governing the process can change over time: a socially dominated language can become a dominant one and there may even be language contact situations with more than one socially dominant language.

1.2.1 Code-copying

There are other aspects in which the theory proposed by Johanson differs from the theory of Thomason & Kaufman, especially when it comes to the analysis of contact-induced changes. Johanson does not use the terms borrowing or substratum influence. The central concept of the theory is rather what Johanson labels *code-copying*.

According to Johanson, contact-induced structural changes can be analysed as *code-copies*. The language from which models are copied constitutes what Johanson calls the *model code* while the language into which copies are inserted is the *basic code*. If a socially dominant language influences a socially dominated language, the copies are said to be *taken over* or *adopted*. If the socially dominated language influences the dominant one the copies are said to be *carried over* or *imposed*. According to Johanson, borrowing is not a suitable term, since the model code is not deprived of anything and the basic code does not adopt anything identical to the original (Johanson 1992: 175). The term substratum influence is equally unsuitable because of its negative connotation, and according to Johanson (1999: 40) code-copying does not have any effects that can be valued as positive or negative.

Code-copies can be of different kinds. They can be units made up of free or bound morphemes or morpheme sequences constituting what Johanson (1999: 40) calls blocks of material, combinatorial, semantical or frequential properties. Free lexical units are for instance substantives, adjectives and verbs while bound lexical units include derivative morphemes. Non-lexical units can be functional ones such as case endings. Copies of units are labelled as *global copies* (Johanson 1999: 41). Another type of copies is not made up of units but rather of properties of a material, combinatorial, semantic and frequential nature. These copies are labelled *selective copies*. In global copying, both form and function of a unit are copied, while selective copying does not concern morphemes but extrapolated structural properties and patterns applied to units of the basic code. According to Johanson (1999: 41), global and selective copying are closely related and should be treated in the same way.

1.2.1.1 Global copies

In global copying, the copied elements are segmental—phonological, morphological, lexical and phraseological. Lexical units are often part of more complex units such as idiomatic expressions and can later be copied in isolation. According to Johanson (1999: 43) this is normally the case with derivative endings: first, they are parts of complex global copies but can later on be copied in isolation and used productively. Global copies are inserted into the basic code in a position reserved for an indigenous item, an equivalence position (Johanson 1999: 43) and can complement or replace this indigenous item. Global copies are inserted into the morphology of the basic code, but this way of inserting copies into the grammatical structure of the basic code is not to be confused with code-switching, the use of several codes in the same phrase. The copied elements are not foreign elements and do not belong to any other system than that of the basic code other than in an etymological sense (Johanson 1999: 39).

A model for a global copy possesses certain defined material, combinatorial, semantic and frequential properties. When inserted into the basic code, the copies are always modified with respect to these properties so that they better fit in with the basic code. This can mean an adaptation to the phonology of the basic code or morphological restructuring to integrate the copies in the morphological system of the basic code. Other kinds of adaptation can entail a restructuring of combinational properties. Semantic restructuring is very common (Johanson 1999: 44). Not even copies that fill lexical gaps in the basic code are totally identical with the models. Another important form of restructuring concerns frequential patterns: a copy may for instance have a higher frequency in the basic code than in the model code.

1.2.1.2 Selective copies

Selective copying does not concern every aspect of a unit but only certain properties of material, combinatorial, semantic or frequential nature. This type of copying often produces what has been called *loan sematics, loan phonology* and *loan syntax* (Johanson 1999: 44). An example of selective copying in Finnish is *kovalevy* 'hard disc': *kova* 'hard', *levy* 'disc'. Certain segments and properties, typical for those in the model code, can be copied onto equivalents in the basic code, a case ending for instance may develop new functions. Frequential copying may lead to changing structures in the basic code so that the use of certain functional units may increase or decrease. A very common type of selective copying is, according to Johanson (1999: 45), a change in word order.

1.2.1.3 Mixed copies

Apart from global and selective copies, the Code-copying Framework also accounts for the existence of so-called mixed copies (Johanson 1999: 45). These are made up of at least one global copy and a selective copy, for example in the form of a combinatorial pattern. This type of copy has been labelled *loan blend* when occurring in the lexicon but there are also other kinds of mixed copies. An entire phraseological pattern may be copied if it contains a copy of a subordinate conjunction. As an example, the Mari subordinate conjunction *jesli* 'if', of Russian origin, can be mentioned. This conjunction sometimes occurs parallel to the Mari conjunction *γə̑n* with the same meaning, e.g. *mə̑jat tuγe ə̑štem, jesli tuδo toleš γə̑n* 'I too will do so, if he comes' (Saarinen 1994: 213). The copying of the Russian subordinate conjunction *jesli* 'if' has changed the Mari word order, normally SOV (c.f. Saarinen 1994: 213), in which the relative clause normally precedes the main clause, e.g. *tuδo toleš γə̑n, mə̑jat tuγe ə̑štem* 'If he comes, I too will do so'. A similar example is given by Galkin (1977: 110), *jesli tə̑j čoδə̑raš kajet γə̑n, mə̑jat kajem* 'If you go to the forest, I too will go'. In this example the order between the main and the subordinate clauses is unchanged. Mixed copies may be highly creative formations in the sense that both the global and selective copies differ from the original in the model code as a result of adjustment to the basic code, and mixed copies often constitute a transitional stage between global copying and a large-scale selective copying.

A large amount of global copies seem to make way for mixed and selective copying, but it is not necessary. In principle, the entire lexical material of a language may be copied without any structural change of the basic code. This is the case with classic Osman Turkish with a large number of Persian and Arabic lexical copies (Johanson 1999: 42).

1.2.2 Momentary, habitualised and conventionalised copies

Even if the entire lexical material of a language may be copied without any structural change of the basic code, code-copying normally contributes actively to linguistic change (Johanson 1999: 47). The copies may develop in two different ways that should be distinguished. On one hand, copies can develop from structurally less integrated copies to copies with a high degree of structural integration, with respect to their phonological and morphological adjustment to the basic code. On the other hand, copies can develop from *momentary* to *habitualised* and *conventionalised* copies. Momentary copies are instances of sporadic copying, often the result of an individual's use of a copy. These copies can become habitualised and conventionalised and have long-term effects for changes in a given language and for the emergence of new linguistic norms. Habitualised copies occur often, regularly and normally in the speech of individual speakers or in a language community (Johanson 1999: 47). The way from a momentary copy to a conventionalised one is according to Johanson (1999: 47), a process of increased acceptance of the copy. Conventionalisation of copies is a normal phenomenon and momentary and habitualised copies can establish themselves and even replace equivalents in the basic code. Conventionalised copies can occur in a variety of the basic code or in the whole language community and in this be used also by non-bilingual individuals. Code-copying is therefore an ongoing and dynamic process and every structurally changed basic code is open to further copying and new processes of conventionalisation. In contact situations where several dominant codes exist side-by-side, there may be very complicated processes of code-copying.

1.2.3 Convergence

Global and selective copying both lead to a situation where the basic code and the model code converge with each other, which means that they will become more similar to each other structurally. The basic code is gradually adjusted to the model code with respect to morpho-syntactic and semantic structures. Countertendencies exist, since every copied item will become a part of the basic code and as such it is subject to the normal internal processes of the code (Johanson 1999: 52). Long-term copying processes can lead to a situation in which the basic code is changed so that new equivalence positions occur, which will lead to further morpho-syntactic convergence (Johanson 1999: 53). An increased similarity between the basic and the model code can favour and accelerate convergence and it can become difficult to distinguish between conventionalised copies and non-copied indigenous elements (Johanson 1999: 53). Code-copying processes of this kind can lead to a situation where one language differs radically from other languages of the same language family. A basic code can nevertheless often be defined by elements that are less inclined to be replaced by copies. Among these elements are, for instance, postpositions and affixes with a generalised meaning such as case and tense markers.

1.2.4 Contact settings

Code-copying and the development the copies undergo is dependent on certain socio- and psycholinguistic aspects which in their turn are connected to structural factors (Johanson 1999: 38). The development of the copies is dependent on the surrounding, the contact setting in which the code-copying process occurs. Social and structural factors are in any case not reasons for code-copying. The reasons are rather psycholinguistical ones, an "inclination to say something the way it comes most naturally or is most easily expressed" (Johanson 1999: 39).

A typical setting for code-copying is, according to Johanson (1999: 54), a dominated non-monolingual speech community with strong bonds to a dominant speech community. It is often a diaspora variety, which for some reason has become separated from other speakers of the language in question. Asymmetrical dominance relations lead to unilateral processes where the plurilingual situation causes speakers to adopt new linguistic habits. According to Johanson (1999: 54), dominated codes of this kind become more heterogenous and show greater variation than the ones that develop in speech communities with weaker external bonds. Important variables for the outcome of contact-induced changes are, for instance, the degree of competence in the dominant and the dominated code, the degree of social asymmetry in the contact situation and the strength of the internal bonds within the dominated speech community.

Johanson (1999: 48) states that knowledge about earlier processes of code-copying and the outcome of these processes is of vital importance for the analysis of current processes. Experiences from different contact situations can shed light upon the development in modern diaspora varieties. Cases of established loans can be useful in the discussion of present-day code-copying since the processes of conventionalisation that have led to the use of these copies must have once started in momentary copying.

As regards Mari, the Eastern dialect of Mari is a particularly interesting object of study. This dialect is spoken by approximately 100 000 persons in the republic of Bashkortostan and it can be viewed as a diaspora variety which has been separated from the main part of the speakers of Mari. In this respect, Eastern Mari is comparable to an immigrant language: it is spoken by small, geographically separated groups of speakers with partly different linguistic backgrounds (Bereczki 1985: 192), surrounded by numerically superior groups of speakers of other languages. The contact between Mari and Turkic languages that Volodin (1997: 35) sees as something belonging to the past has continued up to the present day in Bashkortostan. According to Saarinen (1997a: 193), apart from in Bashkortostan, there are also villages in Tatarstan where Mari and Tatar live side-by-side and the population is completely bilingual (see also Bereczki (1994: 70) regarding bilingualism among the Mari in Tatarstan).

The so-called Mountain and Northwest dialects of Mari are also examples of different kinds of contact settings. Unlike Eastern Mari, these dialects do not constitute diaspora varieties since they have been, and still are, spoken in the vicinity of the largest dialect of Mari when it comes to the number of speakers, Meadow Mari. But it might possibly be claimed that their bonds to the rest of the language community are varied. The speakers of Mountain Mari have earlier than the rest of the Mari come in close contact with Russian, and the areas they inhabit became a part of the Russian sphere of interest at an earlier stage in history. At the same time, Mountain Mari has, according to many scholars, undergone a more profound change as a result of its contacts with Chuvash (Róna-Tas 1988: 772; Johanson 2000: 168), while its contacts with Tatar have been less important. The Northwest dialect of Mari is spoken by small, scattered groups and is an interesting dialect because of its close contacts with Mountain and Meadow Mari, and with Russian.

1.2.5 The applicability of the Code-copying Framework

The Code-copying Framework has up to now mostly been used by turcologists and has been applied in scientific works dealing with the contacts between Turkic and other languages, c.f. Menz (1999). Johanson (1999: 37), however, sees his model as generally applicable on all types of language contact. Code-copying is seen as a natural development process, a universal tendency in the human language, the characteristic features of which can be compared with the mechanisms that regulate second language aquisition and the emergence of so-called pidgin and creole languages. The aims of the theory are given in Johanson (1999: 37–38).

For my purposes, the model has several advantages. It is based on the contacts between Turkic and other languages, and the linguistic changes resulting from language contact are analysed in a more thorough way than in the theory of Thomason & Kaufman. This makes the Code-copying Framework a good starting point for the presentation and analysis of the structural changes that Mari has undergone due to its contacts with Turkic languages. Since Mari, in the opinion of many scholars, is the Finno-Ugric language most profoundly influenced by the Turkic languages, it is a suitable language to try the model on.

1.2.6 Theories related to the Code-copying Framework

The Code-copying Framework aims to be a descriptive apparatus for the analysis of language contact phenomena, but many of the theoretical assumptions underlying the Code-copying Framework have older roots and build upon similar thoughts presented by earlier scholars. Among them, Haugen seems to have been studying language contact phenomena based on assumptions similar to those of Johanson. These assumptions are thoroughly examined in a paper called *The Analysis of Linguistic Borrowing* (1950). In the paper, Haugen (1950: 210) points to the fact that all borrowings from one language to another are dependent of a certain amount of bilingualism in the languages involved. According to Haugen is it necessary to reckon with the existence of considerable groups of bilinguals in every instance of what he refers to as "large-scale borrowing". Haugen also tries to define the terms used and to formulate hypotheses about borrowing processes. The idea that the term "loan" is less appropriate in the description of the process that takes place when a language adopts features of another apparently comes from Haugen (1950: 211) who is of the opinion that "the metaphor implied is certainly absurd, since the borrowing takes place without the lender's consent or even awareness, and the borrower is under no obligation to repay the loan." According to Haugen, even the term "stealing" would have been more appropriate, had it not been for the fact that the owner (the language) is not deprived of anything, and does not feel obliged to take it back. Haugen still uses the term since it according to him is relatively unambiguous in linguistic discussions and since none more accurate term has been proposed. Haugen also discusses the term "mixing" and is of the opinion that the instances in which a speaker uses two languages at the same time are abnormal cases. Speakers can switch rapidly between languages, "but in at any given moment they are speaking only one, even when they 'resort to the other for assistance' " (Haugen 1950: 211). According to Haugen, the introduction of an element from one language to another only means a change of the other language, not a mixing of the two. The term "mixture" implies the emergence of something completely new and that both constituents disappear and that it is of what he refers to as a "haphazard nature".

Haugen (1950: 211) defines the term loan in the following way: "(1) We shall assume it as axiomatic *that every speaker attempts to reproduce previously learned linguistic patterns* [the capital letters in the original have been replaced by italics: A.H.] in an effort to cope with new linguistic situations. (2) *Among the new linguistic patterns which he may learn are those of a language different from his own*, and these too he may attempt to reproduce. (3) If he reproduces the new linguistic patterns, *not in the context of the language in which he learned them*, but in the context of another, he may be said to have "borrowed" them from one language into another. The heart of our definition of borrowing is then the attempted reproduction in one language of patterns previously found in another." Haugens definition corresponds well with what Johanson refers to as code-copying.

There are other resemblances between Johanson's Code-copying Framework and Haugen's analysis of borrowings. Haugen (1950: 213–14) distinguishes three different types of loans, "loanwords", "hybrids" and "loan translations" and these correspond to Johanson's global, mixed and selective copies. Haugen (1950: 217ff) also deals extensively with how loanwords are inserted into utterances in another language. According to Haugen, loanwords must be adapted to the grammatical structure of the other language, e.g. “be assigned by the borrower to the various grammatical classes which are distinguished by his own language”. This is in accordance with Johanson’s view that code-copies are always adapted to the grammatical morphology of the basic code. Other resemblances between the theories will not be further dealt with here. It is evident, though, that the Code-copying Framework is based on assumptions that form the basis for Haugen’s analysis but that the terminological apparatus has been redefined and developed. Evidently, social factors are of greater importance to Johanson than to Haugen.

1.3 Aim

The aim of this thesis is to show that the structural changes in Mari as a result of its contacts with the Turkic languages are not only extensive, but that they also are systematic and that the Mari language does not constitute a mixture of different languages. The thesis further aims to show that the changes are possible to analyse with the help of the Code-copying Framework by means of applying the model on a non-Turkic language. The thesis will show that lexical, phonological, morphological and syntactic changes in Mari due to its contacts with the Turkic languages of the Middle Volga region can be analysed as code-copies of various kinds: global, selective and mixed copies. It is also the aim of the thesis to show to what extent social and structural factors have promoted structural changes or exerted a restrictive influence. To be able to show the role of social factors in Mari-Turkic language contacts, I investigate if the social factors Johanson sees as vitally important for structural change in a language—political, economical, cultural and numerical dominance—are, or have been, present. The length and intensity of the contacts, assumed to be of importance for a widespread bilingualism, are discussed. The social factors are discussed with an emphasis on the historic-political, cultural and demographic factors. Structural factors are assumed to combine with social factors, producing structural changes in a language. These changes can be expected to increase in extent if the structural resemblances between the contact-languages in parts or in the whole of the language system are great, for which reason I investigate the structural features of the Finno-Ugric and Turkic languages.

1.4 Material

There is extensive linguistic material on Mari in the dialect texts collected in the late 19th and early 20th century by scholars working in Hungary and Finland. Some texts have been collected also by native speakers of Mari, such as the texts of Timofej Jevseev. There is a difference between the material published in Hungary and the material published in Finland, in the sense that the text material of the

Finnish scholars was collected during field work in various parts of the Mari language area. The texts published by Beke on the other hand are based on material collected among Russian prisoners of war in Hungary after World War I. In my opinion, this difference has no importance for the way the texts have been analysed.

A large part of my linguistic material from Mari has been taken from these dialect text collections. The most important of the collections are the ones by Beke (1951; 1957; 1961a; 1961b: 1995) and Yevseev, published by Alhoniemi & Saarinen (1983). Some examples have been taken from the collections of Paasonen (1939), Ramstedt (1902) and Wichmann (1931). Apart from this, I have taken examples from modern texts from the modern Mari literary languages, the most important sources being Izhboldin (1994) and Petukhov (1994). Material for comparing the Mari examples has been taken from the Chuvash texts collected by Paasonen (1949) and the Tatar examples have been taken from the Kazan and Mishar Tatar texts collected by Kúnos and published by Kakuk (1980; 1989; 1996). To some extent, Tatar examples have also been taken from the Mishar Tatar texts collected by Paasonen (1953).

To be able to show the nature of the language contacts in a correct way, the choice of the material is of decisive importance. Since the direction, kind, extent and depth of the influence the Turkic languages have exerted on Mari can be assumed to vary in different parts of the Mari language area, the linguistic material from Mari has been taken from sources representing the different dialects of Mari. Regarding the internal division of Mari dialects, see section 2.3.1.1.1.

1.5 Method and delimitation

When choosing the examples, I have tried to obtain as large a variety as possible as far as the Mari dialects are concerned. The reason for this is that it gives me the possibility to show the direction, kind, extent and depth of the influence the Turkic languages have exerted on Mari. It is my assumption that the Mari dialects differ from each other in this respect. The reason why the examples from the texts collected around 1900 are compared to examples taken from modern texts is partly connected to the fact that these texts can be assumed to represent an older stage of the Mari language. But the main reason is that by comparing older and newer examples, it is possible to show how global, selective and mixed copies have been conventionalised and now form integrated parts of the Mari language system.

In this thesis, I will exclusively deal with the contact-induced changes Mari has undergone as a result of its contacts with the Turkic languages. According to Johanson, a socially dominated language can influence the dominant one, and Johanson (1992: 174; 1999: 58; 2000: 168) makes frequent mentions of Chuvash as a language influenced by Finno-Ugric languages. It is my intention to return to this question on another occasion. Suffice it to say that in my opinion it is probably not just Mari that can be held responsible for possible Finno-Ugric features in Chuvash; speakers of Permian languages have in all likelihood played an important role in this process. In this thesis, thus, it is mainly such structural features in Mari that with certainty can be ascribed a Turkic origin that will be discussed and I have tried to refrain from speculation about dubious cases. Certain structural features of Mari that have been put in connection with the influence of Turkic languages will not be dealt with here. This concerns, for instance, the use of possessive suffixes to express definiteness, compound tenses and the question of whether the word order in Mari has changed as a result of its contacts with Turkic languages. The reason for this is that an analysis of these features would demand a very large material for comparisons. For the interested reader there is a certain amount of literature on the influence of Finno-Ugric languages on Chuvash. One of the most ardent supporters of this idea is the turcologist Adamovič who in a number of articles has dealt with this question (c.f. Adamovič 1983a; 1983b; 1985). Agyagási (1998) has discussed possible Mari influence on Chuvash, and in Agyagási (1997) the possibility of making a chronological interpretation of words of Mari origin in Chuvash is considered. Isanbaev & Arslanov (1984) deal with the question of Mari lexical items in Tatar and Fedotov (1965) discusses Mari lexical elements in Chuvash.

Tatar and Chuvash have exerted a certain influence on other Finno-Ugric languages spoken in the Middle Volga region. To some extent, Mordvin has been influenced by Tatar and Chuvash, the influence being mainly of a lexical nature. More far-reaching structural changes as a result of contacts with the Turkic languages have occurred in Udmurt, changes that in some ways are comparable to those in Mari. In this thesis, a detailed analysis of these contacts would take up too much space and for this reason I leave them out of the discussion. Udmurt, however, is an interesting object of comparison since certain structural features of Turkic origin are present also in Udmurt. In case Udmurt offers interesting comparable material I will discuss this explicitly.

1.6 Transcription

If the examples given have German or English translations, I have chosen to keep these translations, whereas examples with Hungarian, Finnish, Russian or Norwegian translations have been translated into English by me. The same applies to examples taken from either one of the Mari literary languages. As for the Mari examples, I have transcribed them using the system in use in Finno-ugric linguistics. They have been standardized to some extent so that some diacritic marks have been omitted. I have also taken the liberty of replacing some of the so-called reduced vowels of certain dialects with full vowels, mainly because they are rare in occurrence and because the standardization does not affect the meaning of the examples. The Chuvash examples taken from Paasonen (1949) have been standardized following the system used in Krueger (1961) which means that diacritics generally have been omitted.

The Tatar examples, as opposed to the Chuvash ones, come from different sources each with its own system of transcription. I have not been able to treat them in the same way as the Mari and Chuvash examples and therefore they have been kept fairly unchanged. However, I have taken the liberty of omitting some diacritics also in these examples.

1.7 Earlier research

Mari is among the more well-known and best described of the languages in the Finno-Ugric group. A number of scholars of various nationalities, working in different times, have contributed to this. One of the first to notice the resemblance between Mari and other Finno-Ugric languages was Philip Johan von Strahlenberg who was taken as prisoner of war after the battle at Poltava. In his book *Das Nord- und Ostliche Teil von Europa und Asia* (1730), von Strahlenberg gives examples of Mari words. Another Swedish officer who was captured at Poltava was the second lieutenant Anders Pihlström who kept a diary during his forced stay in Russia. In his diary, Pihlström describes rites and customs among the Mari, and he is probably the first Swede who has written down a Mari place-name. The earliest purely linguistic work is a grammar published in St Petersburg in 1775, which was followed by the grammars of Castrén (1845) and Wiedemann (1847). From the late 19th century and onwards, the study of Mari in Hungary is connected with scholars such as Budenz and Beke, and in more recent times in particular with Bereczki. In Finland, scholars like Wichmann, Paasonen, Ramsted and Räsänen were among the pioneers. In the 20th century, scholars like Kangasmaa-Minn, R. Bartens, Alhomiemi and Saarinen are among the more prominent, and in the new generation of scholars devoted to the study of Mari, Luutonen and Moisio can be mentioned. In Germany, Lewy published a grammar of Mari in 1922 and more recently H.-H. Bartens has published material on Mari. In Russia and the former Soviet period there is also a considerable number of scholars who have dealt with Mari, often (but far from always) native speakers of the language. Among these, Serebrennikov, Galkin, Pengitov, Isanbaev, Fedotov and Aduganov can be mentioned. In the United States, quite a lot has been published on Mari, especially by Sebeok and finally there are also in Japan scholars who have studied Mari, for example Matsumura. It should be stressed that the list of names only represents a selection and that it is not exhaustive. There are many scholars with a good knowledge about Mari in the world.

Many of these scholars have dealt with the contacts between Mari and the Turkic languages. The earliest sources in which Mari-Turkic parallels are discussed are listed in Räsänen (1923: 1–10). Among these is the above mentioned grammar by Castrén in which words of Tatar or Chuvash origin in Mari are marked with a "tat." (Räsänen 1920: 2). Räsänen's *Die tschuwassischen Lehnwörter im Tscheremissischen* (1920) and *Die tatarischen Lehnwörter im Tscheremissischen* (1923) are among the first scientific works that systematically treat the contacts between

Mari and the Turkic languages on the lexical field. More recently, Serebrennikov, Bereczki and Isanbaev have dealt with subject in an exhaustive way. A considerable amount of material on the contacts between Mari and the Turkic languages has been published in the journal Sovietskoe Finno-ugrovedenie (SFU) between 1965 and 1989, and also after the journal changed its name to Linguistica Uralica (LU). As far as research on contacts between Mari and the Turkic languages is concerned, scholars working in Russia both during and after the Soviet Union are well represented. Particularly the way in which Isanbaev treats the problem is based on assumptions similar to those that form the basis for the present thesis, namely that social and structural factors have contributed to the intensity and extent of the language contacts. More recently, in Finland, Saarinen has taken an interest in the contacts between Mari and the Turkic languages of the Middle Volga region, and Saarinen has explicitly dealt with the subject in a number of publications (Saarinen 1997a; 1997b; 1999). More comprehensive works on the contacts between Mari and Tatar and Chuvash have been published by Bereczki (1983) and Wintschalek (1993), both with a basis in areal linguistics. The work of Bereczki is characterised by a profound knowledge of Mari and deals with features that will be discussed in this thesis, but the description is at times somewhat brief. Wintschalek's work is devoted to the study of syntactic resemblance between Finno-Ugric and Turkic languages of the Middle Volga region. The study is characterised by a multitude of data and is an ambitious effort but is also questionable in certain aspects (c.f. Hesselbäck 1996).

2 Factors in language contact

Johanson (1992) repeatedly emphasises the importance of the interplay of social and structural factors for contact-induced changes in a language. Among the social factors of importance are social, political, economic and numerical dominance. The length and intensity of the contacts are vital for the direction, kind, depth and extension of the contacts and length and intensity are also important for the emergence of a qualified bilingualism. Another condition for the emergence of bilingualism is mixed settlements (Johanson 1992: 172). The social and structural factors work together. Where there is a great structural resemblance between the languages and the contacts are long and intensive, it is reasonable to expect wide- spread structural changes. In many cases, these changes can be said to result from language contact, but at times it can be quite difficult to distinguish contact-induced changes from changes resulting from inner development in a socially dominated language. Social factors can apparently overcome structural factors, so that a language may change structurally as a result of contacts with a language with which it has very little in common structurally. A contact setting, in which the languages in contact have much in common structurally, and in which the contacts have been long and intensive and are characterised by social asymmetry, can display structural changes not only in one language but in several, depending on how the dominance relations change over time.

2.1 Social factors

2.1.1 Geographical delimitation

The Middle Volga region, Srednee Povolzhe in Russian, is a term which occurs frequently in Russian sources. The exact extent of the area, however, is a question on which opinions differ (Kappeler 1982: 4). Kappeler makes a delimitation of the area at the rivers Chepcha in the north-east, Vetlyuga, Okna and Cna in the west, a line running from Tambov in the north-east via the cities of Penza and Samara to the river Samara and the rivers Ik, Belaya and Kama in the east. The areas immediately to the west of the Ural mountains fall outside of this delimitation and are not part of the area according to Kappeler. However, he emphasises the fact that these areas have been important immigration areas for the peoples of the Middle Volga region in historic times. Kappeler (1982: 5) sees the term "Middle Volga region" as a dynamic term that can be defined with the use of historic, political and ethnical criteria. For my purposes, this dynamic use of the term is suitable. The main part of the Mari population inhabit an area which lies within the geographical delimitation of Kappeler, but the large populations of Mari living outside the area can be said to belong to the Middle Volga region for historic and ethnical reasons.

2.1.2 History of the Middle Volga region

The Middle Volga region has been inhabited for a long time. The archaeological material shows that several different cultures have left their mark on the area, from the third millennium B.C. and onwards (c.f. Hajdú 1987: 296ff). At times the carriers of these cultures have been identified with various Finno-Ugric peoples, but the time-spans during which the cultures have flourished can be said to have been characterised by complex ethnical processes and large migrations (Hajdú 1987: 298). At the end of the third and in the beginning of the second millennium B.C. there were significant changes in the ethnical and cultural processes in as much as the so-called Kama-culture expanded westwards and developed into the culture which has been called the Volosovo-culture. The Volosovo culture was characterised by the use of advanced stone tools, the use of bronze and richly ornamented pottery. A common motif was birds. The Volosovo culture had connections with Indo-Iranian peoples and cultures, both pastoral and sedentary. In the middle of the second millennium B.C. the Volosovo culture split in an eastern and a western branch: the Podznyakovo and Kazan cultures. Out of the Podznyakovo culture emerged the Dyakovo and Gorodec cultures which, according to Hajdú (1987: 299) were the ancestral cultures of the present-day Mari and Mordvin. The Kazan culture was replaced by the Ananino culture whose descendants are said to be the Udmurt and the Komi. It can be assumed that the Finno-Ugric peoples—particularly the Udmurt—have long been settled close to the areas they presently inhabit. As far as the Mari are concerned, it is according to some scholars possible on the basis of toponymes to draw the conclusion that they earlier were living to the west of the areas they inhabit today (Kangasmaa-Minn 1998: 219), and apparently also further to the south (Bereczki 1994: 16). On the other hand, there are also scholars who claim that the Mari always have lived in their present-day settlement areas (c.f. Agyagási 1999).

2.1.2.1 The Volga Bulgar empire

In the same way the western parts of Europe during a few centuries in the beginning of our time were characterised by large-scale migrations, the eastern parts of the continent were also the scene of big population movements. It might be said that while these migrations in western Europe led to the decline and fall of a large empire—the Roman—the processes in the eastern parts of the continent had the opposite result. The first East Slav empire emerged during the closing years of the Great migrations, and at the same time, at the end of the 10th century, the Volga Bulgar empire was founded. The Volga Bulgar empire was to develop into a world power with its centre in the Middle Volga region. The history and development of this empire has been described comprehensively by Kappeler (1982: 22–31) and Rorlich (1986: 10–16) and the brief sketch outlined here is based mainly on these sources. According to Kappeler (1982: 23), the Bulgars, a Turkic-speaking people culturally influenced by Iranian steppe pastoralists, advanced from their earlier settlements north of the Caspian Sea in the late seventh century. One part of the people drew west where they were to become the founders of the Danube Bulgar empire, the ancestor of modern Bulgaria. In the course of time, they were to be assimilated by the Slavic-speaking majority of the empire. Other Bulgars, under the chief Batbay, wandered north from the Azov steppes (Rorlich 1986: 10) until they reached the Volga where they founded the Volga Bulgar empire which soon was to become one of the most important commercial and cultural centres in eastern Europe (Kappeler 1982: 23). At the turn of the 12th century, the borders of the Volga Bulgar empire were established. During the 10th century Islam become the state religion of this empire, but apparently Islam was established even earlier in the region (Rorlich 1986: 11). Evidence for this can be found in books by Arab travellers from the 10th century which give detailed accounts of the existence of mosques. By accepting Islam, the Volga Bulgars established religious, political and cultural connections with the rest of the Islamic world and even later on the region was visited by Arab travelers, for instance by Ibn Battuta. Kappeler (1982: 24–25) stresses the fact that the Volga Bulgar empire is less known than the Russian principality of Kiev, mainly because of the fact that, apart from tomb inscriptions, no written documents have been preserved. This has meant that the importance of the Volga Bulgar empire for the history of Europe has been underestimated.

Various Bulgar people constituted the bulk of the population of the empire. According to Rorlich (1986: 11) there were in all five different peoples. Apart from the proper Bulgars, there were also the Suvar, the Esegel, the Bersula and the Barandzhar. The relationship between these peoples was characterised by rivalry and it was not until the 11th century AD that the power of the Bulgars was consolidated. The Middle Volga region, with its rich and fertile soils was suitable for agriculture, and the originally nomadic Volga Bulgars gradually shifted to a sedentary way of life and agriculture became one of the cornerstones of the economy of the empire. Another important part of the economy was trade, and in the empire Slavic and Scandiavian merchants traded with Persian, Arabian and Byzantian merchants. The Volga Bulgar empire developed into a connecting link between the Orient and Europe. Volga Bulgar merchants traded both within the borders of the empire and outside it, and they were able to take control over the transit trade and even to monopolise it (Rorlich 1986: 14). From Caucasus, Central Asia and Persia there was a flow of spices, precious stones, carpets, gold and silver, while the Russian principalities contributed with furs and weapons (Rorlich 1986: 15). Merchants from western Europe offered cloth and amber while the Volga Bulgars traded in wax, leatherwork and furs.

Trade and the existence of agriculture—in the Volga Bulgar empire one of the most advanced agricultural implements of that time was invented, an iron plough called *saban*—(Kappeler 1982: 23) made way for the establishment of large market places in different parts of the empire (Rorlich 1986: 15). These marketplaces can perhaps be seen as both a cause for and a consequence of the emergence of the great cities in the empire. The largest of these cities was Biliar but equally important was the capital, Bulgar, situated to the south of present-day Kazan, the capital of the autonomous republic of Tatarstan. Craft skills were an important feature of these cities, but also of the villages, where artisans like carpenters, blacksmiths and potters produced goods of such a high quality that they became known far outside the borders of the empire (Rorlich 1986: 13).

Islam became the centre of spiritual life in the Volga Bulgar empire and the original Turkic runic script—of the same type that is used in the runic inscriptions in Orkhon—was replaced by the Arabic script. Some of the Muslim scholars, *ulama*, in the Volga Bulgar empire became famous also in other parts of the Islamic world. Very little of the written material the Volga Bulgars produced has been preserved, except for the grave inscriptions, the majority of which can be found within the borders of present-day Tatarstan. There are a few inscriptions also in the Udmurt republic but none in the republics of Chuvashia and Mari-El (c.f. Róna-Tas & Fodor 1973; Erdal 1993). The Volga Bulgar empire was a centralised state, with an economy based on trade and agriculture. The tax system was well developed and essentially any kind of product was subject to taxation (Rorlich 1986: 15). It is important to emphasise that although Islam was the official religion of the empire, it is highly unlikely that this was the religion of all citizens. It can be assumed that Islam—as was later to be the case in the Khanate of Kazan—was a religion concentrated to the urban centres of the empire and that the population in the rural areas had other religious values. Both the Mari and the Chuvash have preserved their animistic religion up to the present century. It has been proposed that the Chuvash are the descendants of a part of the Volga Bulgar population that never converted to Islam. The animistic religion of the Chuvash has many features in common with that of other Turkic peoples and has also been influenced by—and in its turn influenced—the animistic beliefs among the Finno-Ugric peoples of the area.

The spread of Islam has taken various shapes in different parts of the world, but at least in Africa Islam was spread along the major trade routes. In West Africa, Islam spread rapidly along the caravan routes across the Sahara and became the dominant religion in the large kingdoms of Ghana, Mali and Songhay. A conversion to Islam was necessary for any one who wished to benefit from this trade (Levzion & Pouwels 2000: 3). In East Africa, Islam was introduced along the ancient trade routes across the Indian Ocean and on the East African littoral, Islam was for a long time concentrated to the city states of the Swahili. Levzion & Pouwels (2000: 6) claim that "the Swahili Islamic civilization was quintessentially urban". According to Nurse & Spear (1985: 95), the influence of Islam among the Swahili was restricted to the contacts between local and foreign merchants, applying Islamic law and ethics to facilitate trade between the peoples in question. The spread of Islam in the Volga Bulgar empire is thus comparable to the spread of the religion in Africa. The river Volga was the most important of all the trade routes in the empire, and since trade was carried out mainly in urban centres such as Bulgar and Biliar, it is not surprising that Islam was a religion restricted to the commercial centres of the empire.

The Volga Bulgar empire was a multi-ethnic empire with several ethnic groups within its borders. The trade led to intensive contacts with other peoples and languages in the area, which is evident from the words of Volga Bulgar, or Chuvash, origin in the Finno-Ugric languages Komi and Udmurt. It can be assumed that many of the peoples resident in the Volga Bulgar empire participated actively in this trade and that they in many cases produced the goods they traded with. It can also be assumed that many of these peoples contributed to the formation of the Volga Bulgar people (and also to the formation of the Volga Bulgar language, c.f. Johanson 2000: 168, 176–177). According to Rorlich (1986: 14), the Volga Bulgar potters developed a style of their own. Birds were a common motif, especially ducks, which were a symbol of life in Volga Bulgar mythology. This is perhaps a common theme among many peoples in the eastern parts of Europe, but birds were a common motif on pottery also during the period when the Voloso culture flourished. If Kappeler (1982: 23) is right in stating that the Volga Bulgars originally were culturally influenced by Iranian pastoralists, it is highly likely that they later on were influenced in this respect as a result of their contacts with various Finno-Ugric peoples among which birds—especially water birds—are a common theme in mythology.

It can seem far-fetched to give the history of the Volga Bulgar empire this much attention since it existed only from the late 10th century to the early 13th century. The historical roots of the empire, however, go much further back in time. And, which will be discussed further below, not even the revolutionary events in the middle of the 13th century meant that the influence of the Volga Bulgar language and culture came to an end. Kappeler (1982: 24–25) is certainly right in saying that the scant sources about this state have led to its importance being underestimated. The Volga Bulgar empire was a world power, whose economic strength and political and cultural vitality continued to exert an influence even after the time when its political independence had ended.

The Volga Bulgar empire originated in the large migrations in eastern Europe in the early years of the Middle Ages. The direct reason was, according to Rorlich (1986: 6), Arab expeditions of war directed towards the Azov steppes inhabited by the ancestors of the Volga Bulgars. During the first centuries following these expeditions, the Volga Bulgars were dependants of the Kazar empire. They were able to free themselves from Kazar superiority in the early years of the 10th century. During the time it existed, the Volga Bulgar empire had close contacts with other peoples and states and the contacts with the Russian principalities in the west were characterised by several skirmishes and expeditions of war, as a result of conflicts over the control of trade and trade routes. On several occasions in the 12th and 13th centuries the empire was invaded by Russian forces (Kappeler 1982: 26). The hostilities were interrupted by periods of peace and co-operation, mainly due to the fact that well-functioning trade and commercial ties were of vital importance for both parties (Rorlich 1986: 12). As was indicated above, the Volga Bulgar empire had connections with other peoples and empires also in the east, but it was its encounter with one of the largest and most diverse empires in world history that was going to have a great importance for the continued history of the Volga Bulgars. This empire is known as the Golden Horde.

2.1.2.2 The Golden Horde

The Golden Horde is the Russian name of the state that was founded by Batu, the grandson of Dzhingis Khan. The heartland of the Golden Horde was situated in the Middle Volga region, and the name is said to originate in the impression the Mongol encampment on the banks of the Volga made on contemporary eye-witnesses. There is an extensive literature on the Golden Horde, not least because its importance for Russian history is vital. The history of the Golden Horde and its characteristic features have been described by Kappeler (1982: 31–39) and Rorlich (1986: 17–23) but apart from these short overviews there are more substantial historic descriptions, with an emphasis on the importance of the Golden Horde for Russian history, by Halperin (1985a; 1985b) and Spuler (1965). The Golden Horde had its centre in the Middle Volga region but it exerted a considerable influence far outside its borders. The Mongols, who constituted the political, cultural and military elite, and their allies had connections with both Western Europe and Central Asia.

Already in the early years of the 13th century, the Volga Bulgar Empire had attracted the attention of the Mongols and in 1229, the first military encounters took place in which Volga Bulgar outposts in the Ural Mountains were captured (Rorlich 1986: 17). In the spring of 1236, Batu launched an attack on the Volga Bulgar empire with an army of more than 600,000 men. The land of the Volga Bulgars was conquered and devastated. The army then continued westwards and the areas inhabited by the Mordvins shared the same fate in 1239. A year later, Kiev fell and in 1240 and 1241 the Mongol army plundered Hungary, an event which in Hungarian history is known as *a tatárjárás*, 'the Tatar invasion'. The conquest of Hungary was never completed. The news of the death of the Mongol khan reached Batu who withdrew to Bulgar where he had better opportunities to lay claims to the throne (Rorlich 1986: 18). The history of Hungary—and the rest of Europe—would probably have taken a different course had it not been for the death of the Mongol khan.

Bulgar was the first capital of the Golden Horde, but there were several other large cities in the empire and Bulgar's position as capital was later taken over by Saray. Kappeler (1982: 32) claims that the Golden Horde, in spite of its flourishing cities and the well-developed agriculture, remained a nomadic empire. This view is challenged by Rorlich (1986: 19), who claims that the Golden Horde was unique in the way it combined the characteristic features of the pastoral and sedentary societies ruled by the khan. The ethnic and cultural variation and the differences in socio-economic development, as well as the differences in the political and administrative systems the Mongols encountered were of importance for the way in which the Mongols treated and administrated the conquered areas (Rorlich 1986: 20). The Volga Bulgar empire had possessed a highly developed administration and was ruled indirectly by the Mongols, whereas the Russian principalities were treated differently. There are apparently differing opinions in this respect since other scholars claim that also the Russian principalities were ruled indirectly by the Mongols (c.f. Kappeler 1982: 33). There was in all likelihood a shift in the way the Mongols were administrating the Russian principalities, so that a system of direct rule gradually was replaced by one of indirect rule (Halperin 1985a: 39). The system of indirect rule probably contributed to the quick recovery of the former Volga Bulgar empire, which led to a time of prosperity during the late 13th and early 14th centuries (Kappeler 1982: 35). The centre of the empire, however, shifted to areas north of the river Kama.

The Golden Horde was an empire concentrated on trade, just as the Volga Bulgar empire before it and the Volga Bulgar empire became a part of the new world power. Trade in the Golden Horde recovered quickly, although it was re-orientated in some areas. An empire such as the Golden Horde, in which several types of societies and ethnic groups co-existed, did however possess an inner instability. Many of the cities originally established as military outposts developed into economic centres out of which semi-autonomous principalities grew. These principalities or petty khanates were a cause for the disintegration of the Horde that was soon to come. There were of course counter-tendencies: Under the rule of Ozbek, Islam was adopted as the official religion of the Golden Horde, a fact that according to Rorlich (1986: 19) led to the Volga Bulgars—already moslem—coming to view themselves as part of a larger political entity. They also enjoyed a considerable degree of autonomy and were allowed to deploy a foreign policy of their own.

During the second half of the 14th century, the Golden Horde gradually disintegrated, partly because of conflicts between the khan and the military aristocracy (Kappeler 1982: 33). This process began under the rule of Murid who was khan between 1362 and 1364. Under the rule of Toktamysh, between 1376 and 1391, the situation stabilised temporarily but after his death the disintegration process accelerated and at the end of the 14th century several khanates had emerged, such as the Siberian khanate, the Astrakhan khanate and the Crimean khanate. The last of the states leading its origins back to the conquest of Batu, was the Kazan khanate.

2.1.2.3 The Kazan khanate

In a period between the late 1430s and the late 1440s the khanate of Kazan, the last of the independent states in the Middle Volga region before the area was incorporated into Russia, was formed. Its pre-Russian history has been described by Rorlich (1986: 25–31) and Kappeler (1982: 39–66). The Kazan khanate was founded by Ulu Mehmet, or Muhammed, previously the khan of the Golden Horde. Different years have been proposed as the date of its foundation. According to Pelenski (1974: 23), the foundation of the khanate was a process which started in 1438 and ended in 1445. Rorlich (1986: 24) points to the fact that 1437, the year in which Muhammed was deposed as a khan in Saray and established himself as a ruler of Kazan, by some scholars is seen as a turning point. Others claim that 1445 should be seen as the founding year of the khanate, because this was the year in which Mahmut, the son of Muhammed ascended to the throne. Kazan had grown into an economic centre on the river Kazanka under the Golden Horde and was one of the cities in which a local prince ruled. It is significant that the importance of the Volga Bulgars did not end with the Mongol invasion, because the original rulers of Kazan belonged to the Volga Bulgar ruling dynasty (Rorlich 1986: 19). The fact that Kazan originally was founded by Volga Bulgars can be traced in the contemporary Udmurt and Mari terms for Tatars, Udm *biger* 'Tatar' (lit. 'Bulgar') and Ma *suas* 'Tatar' (lit. 'Chuvash').

A couple of Muhammed's other sons went into Russian service in Moscow under Vassily II, resulting in the foundation of a Tatar khanate in Kasimov, named after Muhammed's son Kasim. The khanate in Kasimov was a dependant of Moscow and this is decisive for the future relations between Moscow and Kazan, since Moscow from time to time tried to influence the succession to the throne in Kazan. During most parts of its history, from the foundation to the Russian conquest in 1552, however, Kazan was an independent state, politically and military superior to Moscow. The relations between Moscow and Kazan were never straightforward and uncomplicated: at times Kazan was a Muscovite protectorate and occassionally Moscow interfered directly in the domestic politics of Kazan (Rorlich 1986: 26). The conflicts between Moscow and Kazan were not simply due to the fact that Moscow considered itself in a position to dictate the succession order in the khanate. It was also due to the fact that the Muscovite empire expanded to the northeast, thus intruding into the Kazan sphere of interest. The relations between the two states was also conditioned by the trade, and Moscow was in this respect dependent on Kazan which continued to occupy the position of the former Volga Bulgar empire. Kazan, however, had expanded these trade contacts considerably (Rorlich 1986: 27).

Territorially, the Kazan khanate was also the successor of the Volga Bulgar empire, but its exact borders can not be established with certainty (Kappeler 1982: 42; Donnelly 1968: 13). Its capital, Kazan, was—and still is—situated on the river Kazanka and in the Middle of the 16th century the city had somewhere between 20,000 and 30,000 inhabitants, making it one of the largest cities in Eastern Europe at this time (Kappeler 1988: 43). Apart from the link back to the Volga Bulgar empire in the form of an earlier ruling dynasty of Volga Bulgar origin, Kazan had a Volga Bulgar heritage also in other respects. The economy was based on agriculture, craft, and trade. The cultivable lands were in the hands of a landowning nobility, of the khan and of various religious congregations. On lands in the hands of the nobility, the so-called three-field technique was in extensive use (Rorlich 1986: 30), whereas land owned by peasants liable to taxation was less advanced agriculturally with smaller harvests. With regard to craft skills, the Volga Bulgar tradition of leather-work and pottery was continued. Kazan became a centre of transit trade where merchants of different nationalities exchanged their goods (Rorlich 1986: 30) and Kazan developed into a prosperous state on the basis of trade and taxation. The cultural life, with education and literature, flourished on the basis of Islam. The population was made up of merchants and craftsmen in the cities and peasants of Kipchak Turkic, Volga Bulgarian or Finno-Ugric origin in the countryside. At the bottom of society were servants and slaves and the slave-trade was—as in the Volga Bulgar empire—an important part of the economy (Rorlich 1986: 29). The khan was sovereign and there was also an upper class in the form of a land-owning nobility with a varied ethnic background, for instance Chuvash or Mari.

The relationship between Moscow and Kazan changed dramatically after the coronation of Ivan IV in 1547 (Rorlich 1986: 28) and became more and more hostile as the expansionist aspirations of Moscow increased. The hostilities came to an end with the conquest of Kazan in 1552. The factors behind the fall of Kazan have been described by Pelenski (1974). In Russian history and folklore the fall of Kazan has taken almost mythical proportions and the conquest of the city symbolized "the destruction of the powers of the enemies of the Russians" (Donnelly 1968: 13). The military and political powers of the Kazan khanate had long been weakening and according to Donnelly, the city was defended by an army of 30,000 men, mainly armed with bows and arrows. The Russians, on the other hand were more than 150,000, which makes the fall of Kazan something unavoidable rather than something miraculous.

Even after the Russian conquest, the Volga Bulgar empire and the Golden Horde continued to exert an influence. The state that was incorporated into Russia possessed its own well-developed political, economical and social structures that to some extent were taken over by the Russians. This concerns for instance the taxation and administrative system and the fall of the khanate does in this respect not mark the end of its importance for the region. The conquest of Kazan did not mean that Moscow secured its superiority over the territory and the peoples inhabiting it. The incorporation of the Kazan khanate in the Muscovite empire was a gradual one, characterised by at times contradictory aims and methods, including large-scale military expeditions and the foundation of military outposts on strategically important locations. In areas inhabited by the Mari, cities or forts were founded in Kokshaysk 1574, Kozmodemyansk 1583, Tsarevokokshaysk (present-day Yoshkar-Ola) 1584 and in Yaransk, probably around 1594. On several occasions in the late 16th century there were armed rebellions against Muscovite authority, for instance the so-called Cheremis War (Kappeler 1982: 142). For a very long period, the Middle Volga region constituted a frontier area at the margins of the Russian Empire. It was not until the Russians finally took control over Bashkortostan in the middle of the 18th century that the Middle Volga region was definitely integrated into the Muscovite State.

2.1.3 Demographic factors

The comparatively lengthy sketch of the historic processes which have formed the Middle Volga region may seem to be somewhat beside the point but they are of fundamental importance for the understanding of the contact-induced changes in Mari that will be analysed in this thesis. It is even the case that certain aspects of the historic processes that have not been discussed above deserve further attention, this especially concerns the demographic factors and their importance. Beside other social factors—political, economical, cultural and numeric superiority—the demographic factors have contributed directly to the contacts between Finno-Ugric and Turkic peoples of the Middle Volga region. It can be assumed that already the arrival of the Volga Bulgars in the region caused migration flows with effects on the relations between the peoples. That the Volga Bulgars had contacts with the ancestors of the Udmurt and the Komi, is evident from the words of Volga Bulgar or Chuvash origin in the Permian languages. The words have been examined by Wichmann (1903). According to Róna-Tas (1988: 760), the words of Chuvash origin common to both Permian languages are representative of different dialects of a Chuvash type. To what extent these words have entered the common Permian language as a result of large-scale migration or casual trading contact is hardly possible to determine. The establishment of the Golden Horde in the area on the other hand caused migration flows and changes in the ethnic composition in the area to a much larger extent. Rorlich (1986: 18) states that "the immediate impact of Batu's conquest of the Bulgar state was a massive population dislocation". The Mongol conquest caused a demographic shift to the north, north-east and north-west. The reason for this was probably not only connected to the fact that the population wanted to escape from the Mongol and Turkic conquerers. It can also be assumed that the well-developed agriculture of the Bulgar state went through a period of stagnation following the conquest, a fact that caused massive migration. This was especially the case with parts of the Volga Bulgar population that migrated to the north to areas today inhabited by Chuvash and where the first large-scale contacts with speakers of Mari took place. Agyagási (1999) has discussed the ethnogenesis of the Mari and the differing opinions that exist on the question of whether the Mari have always lived in their present areas of inhabitation or if they have arrived in these areas at a later time. Bereczki (1994: 16) claims that it is not possible to conclude that the Mari have been present in the areas they inhabit today before the 12th century.

There was also a considerable flow of different Turkic-speaking peoples to the area from the steppes in the south (Kappeler 1982: 38). The disintegration of the Golden Horde in the 14th and 15th centuries also had far-reaching consequences for the demographic conditions. Large-scale military campaigns and plundering expeditions were devastating and emptied large areas of their population. After the Russian conquest of Kazan there were also considerable changes in the demographic situation. The Tatar population of Kazan was expelled from the city that became inhabited mainly by Russians. Russian peasants had started to colonize certain areas of the Middle Volga region even prior to the conquest of Kazan, and there was even a Russian-speaking population within the borders of the Kazan khanate before the conquest. After the fall of Kazan, the processes of colonisation acquired larger proportions.

An apparent consequence was that the political and economical power passed into Russian hands. When the Tatar population was expelled from Kazan, the urban, moslem culture of the Tatars became a culture with a rural basis (Kappeler

1982: 101). One consequence of this was in all likelihood that its importance among other ethnic groups in the area increased. The Russian conquest of Kazan, and the sometimes shifting policies towards the Finno-Ugric and Turkic peoples of the region, were also a cause for migrations. Remote areas such as Bashkortostan became important areas of immigration for many of the peoples of the Middle Volga region. A sizeable group of Mari today inhabit various areas in the republic of Bashkortostan and these Mari are the descendants of Mari who migrated there in the late 17th and early 18th century. There were different reasons for such migration, one being that the Mari wanted to escape Russian orthodox mission. The Mari that migrated to Bashkortostan did not form a homogenous group since they came from different parts of the Mari-speaking area (Luutonen 1997: 58). During the same period, the first Chuvash, Tatar and Mordvin settlements in Bashkortostan were established.

2.1.4 Numerical, political and cultural conditions

The relations between the Finno-Ugric and Turkic peoples in the Middle Volga region are characterised by a high degree of asymmetry. The Volga Bulgars and later also the Chuvash have in all likelihood constituted a numerically dominant group that assimilated or pushed aside the Finno-Ugric peoples. It is, according to Bereczki (1994: 16), on the basis of place-names, possible to conclude that about half of the Chuvash language area originally was inhabited by Mari, who were finally assimilated during the first half of the 15th century. The Volga Bulgars possessed a highly developed spiritual and material culture as a consequence of their religious, economical and cultural connections with Central Asia and the Arab world. The Volga Bulgar empire was further characterised by the existence of large cities that had grown in size and importance from trade. The Volga Bulgar empire also embraced many of the areas presently inhabited by Mari, Udmurt, Tatar and Chuvash (Bereczki 1994: 14). The social, political, and economic elite was made up of Volga Bulgars and later on perhaps also by Chuvash. The historic processes during the reign of the Golden Horde and in the Khanate of Kazan were in the same way characterised by a considerable degree of asymmetry in the social relations between the different peoples. In the Golden Horde, the Mongols were the economically and culturally dominant part of the population, but the Kipchak Turkic peoples allied with them were numerically dominant. In the time during which the khanate of Kazan existed, the Kipchak Turkic-speaking peoples were in majority and Mongols as well as Volga Bulgars and various Finno-Ugric peoples became assimilated and gradually switched to a Turkic language. It has been suggested that the Mishar Tatars originally spoke a Finno-Ugric language and the same applies to the so-called Karatay-Mordvin, presently speaking a Kipchak Turkic language. In their language, the Karatay have preserved a number of Mordvin words, especially terms for kinship and female dresses (Róna-Tas 1988: 768). For a detailed description of the Karatay Mordvin, see Paasonen (1902). There are possibly also examples of Turkic peoples switching to a Finno-Ugric language. The so-called Bessermen Tatars today speak an Udmurt dialect but have been assumed to be the descendants of an originally Volga Bulgar speaking group that has been assimilated by the Udmurt. For a detailed discussion of possible Volga Bulgar features in Bessermen, see Teplyashina (1975). According to Kelmakov (1985), however, the Besserman are the descendants of a southern group of Udmurts who have migrated northwards and there are no Volga Bulgar substratum influences in their dialect.

Culturally, the Mari and other Finno-Ugric peoples of the Middle Volga region are strongly influenced by their Turkic-speaking neighbours. This is evident in, for instance, the religious beliefs. Although the Mari today are at least nominally Christians and adherents of the Russian orthodox faith, they have preserved elements of an earlier animistic religion up to the present day. In the end of the 19th century, a new-founded religion called *Kuγu šorta* 'the Great (Wax)candle' flourished. A considerable part of the religious terminology of the Mari religion is of Turkic origin. For a detailed description of the animistic religion of the Mari, see Holmberg (1914) and Paasonen (1939: 181–215).

The moslem culture of the Tatars and its religious terminology have left fewer traces in the Mari culture and language but there are exceptions such as the term *mulla* 'priest' < tat *mulla* 'id'. Many of the prayers directed to native gods and spirits are often begun with words such as *rakmat* 'thanks' < tat *räχmät* 'Dank', *βə̂smə̂lla, βə̂smə̂llä* 'bless' < tat *bismilla* 'im Namen Gottes (Gebet)'.

Also in the field of fairy-tales, riddles and proverbs there is considerable similarity between the Mari and the Turkic peoples, compare, e.g., the following Mari and Tatar fairy-tales:

MaMe *pire aδak βütküc lekteš ta kaja nur βokten. Nur βokšalne šolγa oš βülö. Pire ojla βülülan: "mə̂j tə̂ńə̂m kockam" maneš. βülö ojla pirə̂lan: "mə̂ńə̂m ot tošt kockaš, mə̂ńə̂m pilet ulo," maneš. Pire ojla: "oncə̂kto, maneš, moγańe piletet!" βülö kutanə̂m kaδə̂rten šoγaleš, pocə̂šə̂m küš nöltaleš. "teβə, lut!" maneš. Pire tolə̂n šə̂nzeš βülö kutan tök. βülö pirə̂m cumal γolta*

'Der Wolf kommt (wieder) aus dem Wasser heraus und läuft feldaus, feldein (eig. [quer; Ö. B.] übers Feld). Inmitten des Feldes steht eine Schimmelstute: "Ich fresse dich" (sagt er). Die Stute antwortet: "Du wirst es nicht wagen, mich zu fressen, ich habe einen Pass" (sagt sie). Der Wolf spricht: "Zeig mir, wie dein Pass aussieht!" Die Stute wendet dem Wolf die Kruppe zu (eig. steht im die Kruppe zuwendend), hebt den Schweid [und sagt; Ö. B.]: "Da hast du ihn, lies!" Der Wolf nähert sich der Kruppe (eig. kommt zur K.) der Stute und setzt sich nieder. Die Stute [schlägt aus und; Ö. B.] stösst den Wolf um' (Beke 1957: 268)

tatM *älige zamanda ber büre ać ďürgän. ocoragan ber biyä. büre: "min sine ašïm, biyä" digän. "sin mine ašï almasïñ". "nik ašamïm?" büre digän. biyä ätkän: "minem pašpurtïm bar", digän. büre ätkän: "kaya?", digän. "artkï yakïmda čïgïp kara" digän. büre "pašpurt ukïm" diyep artïna čïkkan. biyä awïzïna tibep tešlären kuzgatkan*

'In alter Zeit lief einmal ein Wolf hungrig umher. Ihm begegnete eine Stute. Der Wolf sagte: "Stute, ich will dich fressen." "Du kannst mich nich fressen." "Warum könnte ich dich nicht fressen?" fragte der Wolf. Die Stute sagte: "Ich habe den Reisepass." Der Wolf fragte: "Wohin?" "Er ist an meinem Hinterteil, geh und beschaue ihn" sagte sie. "Ich will den Reisepass durchlesen", dachte der Wolf und ging hinter die Stute. (Da) versetzte die

Stute ihm einen Schlag gegen das Maul, dass ihm die Zähne losgingen' (Paasonen 1953: 80).

The Mari fairy-tale is taken from Beke's (1957: 64–363) collection of linguistic material from the dialect spoken in the village of Turšo-Mučaš. Linguistically, this dialect represents a transitional dialect between Northwest and Meadow Mari (c.f. Bereczki 1985: 190). The Tatar fairy-tale is included in Paasonen's collection of Mishar Tatar fairy-tales and songs, collected in the region of Samara in 1899. Apparently, a similar fairy-tale has been told also among the Chuvash since it is included in the material of Ahlqvist (Ahlqvist, manuscript) kept in the archives of the Finno-Ugric Society in Helsinki.

The culture of the Mari has been influenced by the conditions in the neighbouring Turkic languages also in other respects. Ayplyatov (1965: 90–93) has demonstrated that Mari personal names were formed with Tatar personal names as a model, while Russian personal names were more rare.

2.2 Structural factors

Structural factors are of decisive importance in language contact situations and they combine with social factors. Structural factors may impede or promote structural change in a language contact situation and some structural factors can apparently be described as relatively attractive so that they are more easily transferred from one language to another (c.f. Johanson 1992: 202ff). If there is a great typological resemblance between the languages involved, the structural changes in one or more languages can be very large.

2.2.1 Structural features of the Finno-Ugric languages

Together with the Samoyedic langauges, the Finno-Ugric languages form the Uralic superstock of languages. According to Abondolo (1998: 1), there are more than 30 Uralic languages. Other scholars have reached other conclusions concerning the total amount of Uralic languages. This difference in opinions is probably connected to the problem of how languages are to be distinguished from dialects and also to whether literary languages are used as a basis to estimate the total number of speakers of Uralic langauges (c.f. Larsson 1999: 70–71). Mari is an example of the problem of distinguishing languages from dialects, since some scholars are of the opinion that Mountain and Meadow Mari constitute two different languages and not two dialects (c.f. Kuznetsova 1996).

There are more Finno-Ugric than Samoyedic languages and the Finno-Ugric group has in all likelihood always been the larger of the two (Abondolo 1998: 2). When counting the total amount of speakers, Hungarian with 14 million speakers is by far the largest of the Finno-Ugric languages. Hungarian is spoken in Hungary and neighbouring countries. Finnish, with more than 5 million speakers is spoken in Finland but also by minorities in Sweden and Norway. Estonian, with well over 1 million speakers is one of the largest of the Finno-Ugric languages whereas languages like Votic and Livonian probably will become extinct in the near future. The Finno-Ugric languages have been divided internally in different ways at different times, for a detailed discussion of this, see for example Abondolo (1998: 1–8) and Sinor (1988: xiii-xx).

According to Comrie (1988: 451), Finno-Ugric languages as a whole are a lot more homogenous than the Indo-European langauges, but rather less so than the Turkic languages. Somewhat surprisingly, not much has been published on the structural features of Finno-Ugric languages, and the body of work that does exist (see for instance Comrie 1988; Abondolo 1998) is not only concerned with the structural features of the Finno-Ugric languages, but tries to give as comprehensive an overview as possible of the structure of Uralic languages, including the Samoyedic ones.

Like the Turkic languages, Finno-Ugric languages possess a predominantly synthetic structure with an—in most languages—agglutinative morphology. In cases where the languages have vowel harmony, it is mainly of the palatal type. Finno-Ugric languages are also characterised by an aversion to consonant combinations in an initial position. With a few exceptions, Finno-Ugric languages possess highly developed case systems and complex verbal systems with several tenses and modes. Finno-Ugric languages are also characterised by the possibility of expressing the causativity and momentanity of the verb morphologically by using a number of deverbal derivational endings. Finno-Ugric languages make an extensive use of postpositions rather than prepositions, and finally many of the languages possess several enclitic particles to express emphasis, identity and probability. Finno-Ugric languages lack a grammatical gender and generally also definite articles. In many Finno-Ugric languages, the most common word order is subject—object—verb (SOV) and for this reason postpositions are used instead of prepositions. Definiteness can be signalled by accusativity of the object and finally, adjectives are not morphologically distinct from substantives.

2.2.2 Structural features of the Turkic languages

Turkic languages are spoken by well over 100 million persons in an area extending from Eastern and South-eastern Europe to Siberia, Central Asia and China. In spite of their vast geographical distribution, the Turkic languages are a lot more homogenous in their structure than the Finno-Ugric languages, and have certain structural features in common. The short description below contains just a selection of such common features; for more detailed descriptions of the structure of the Turkic languages, see Johanson (1992: 184–194; 1998: 30–66).

Characteristic for Turkic languages is a highly synthetic structure. The Turkic languages possess a large number of morpheme categories in word formation, declination and conjugation. These morphemes generally have a strongly generalised content. To nominal stems plural, possessive and case morphemes are added. A high number of morphemes are added to verbal stems to express actionality, causativity and diathesis. Turkic languages are characterised by juxtaposition, the morphemes are added to stems but retain clear boundaries between them. The suffixes show a limited predictable variation with few allomorphs. They are successively added to each other so that each morpheme modifies the preceding one with respect to its content. Certain suffixes are what Johanson (1992: 187) refers to as "locker angefügte Suffixe", which means that they define the content of a whole sequence of morphemes. Turkic languages make frequent use of enclitic particles, free grammatical units with highly generalised functions. In Turkic languages, adjectives are not morphologically distinct from substantives, and normally there is only a distinction between nominal and verbal stems. Adjectival attributes seldom concord with the main word in Turkic languages. The common word order in Turkic languages is subject—object—verb and consequently Turkic languages are characterised by the use of postpositions instead of prepositions. In older stages of Turkic, there are few free junctors such as conjunctions. Turkic languages are further characterised by case systems with broad uses, the locative case can indicate both place and movement. Turkic languages have complex verb systems with several grammatical categories. The use of so-called inferential forms in narratives and post-verbs that expresses actionality is a distinctive feature of Turkic languages. Anaphora are rare in Turkic languages which makes sentences lacking a formal subject possible. Turkic languages are further characterised by the use of an interrogative suffix *-mV* which is added to the sentence constituent which is questioned. Turkic languages lack grammatical genders and definite articles. Definiteness is signalled by the accusativity of the object or in certain cases by the genitive of the subject. Turkic languages are characterised by echolali and reduplication and the difference between short and long vowels is not distinctive. Many Turkic languages lack liqiuds in an initial position and fricatives in the same position are rare. Other structural features of Turkic languages are palatal vowel harmony and aversion to consonant combinations in an initial position.

2.3 The languages of the Middle Volga region

2.3.1 Finno-Ugric languages

Several Finno-Ugric languages are spoken in the Middle Volga region today besides Mari, for instance Mordvin and Udmurt. Udmurt and the closely related language Komi belong to the Permian group of the Finno-Ugric languages and like Mari, Udmurt too has been influenced by the Turkic langauges in the area. The contact-induced changes in Udmurt are, however, not as extensive as those in Mari and are mostly concentrated to areas where Tatar is spoken. If certain features of Mordvin and Udmurt provide interesting material for comparisons, this will be dealt with in the following sections.

2.3.1.1 Mari

Mari is a Finno-Ugric language. Traditionally, it has been classified as a Volga Finnic language together with Mordvin which is also spoken in the Middle Volga region. However, Mari and Mordvin differ from each other in several respects. There are considerable differences in the lexicon, phonology, morphology and syntax of the languages and structurally Mordvin has more in common with the Baltic Finnic languages. According to Bereczki (1994: 11), it is not possible to assume that Mari and Mordvin have a common origin and it is likely that the criteria that were used for the classification of Mari and Mordvin as Volga Finnic languages were based more on geography than on linguistics. The structural characteristics of Mari have been described by Alhoniemi (1988), Saarinen (1991) and Kangasmaa-Minn (1998). The history of Mari is described in Bereczki (1994).

As to its structure, Mari is an agglutinating suffigating language with few morphophonological variations (Luutonen 1997: 11). Mari lacks grammatical gender and definite articles. Mari words can be made up of one single morpheme but are in most cases made up of at least two morphemes (Kangasmaa-Minn 1998: 224). There are three morpheme classes: bases, suffixes and clitics. The bases are divided into three groups: nouns, which can take case endings and possessive suffixes; verbs, to which tense and modal suffixes are added, and finally particles which normally occur in a final position. Adjectives are not morphologically distinct from nouns in Mari and adjectives are only inflected when they function syntactically as nouns (Kangasmaa-Minn 1998: 225). There are a large number of derivative endings used in the creation of new words and also a rich and varied verbal system with several tenses and modes. There are two different verb conjugations, the *am*- and *em*-conjugations, the terms deriving from the ending of the first person singular in the present tense.

There are approximately 670,000 Mari and about 80% of them speak Mari as their first language. A little more than 300,000 Mari live within the borders of the Republic of Mari-El where they are in minority since more than 50% of the population are Russians. In Mari-El, the 320,000 Mari made up 48% of the total population in 1989 (Kangasmaa-Minn 1998: 219). Apart from Mari and Russians, there are also smaller groups of Tatar and Chuvash living in the republic. The rest of the Mari live in adjacent areas, for instance around the cities Nizhny Novgorod and Perm and also in Tatarstan. A large number of Mari live separated from other Mari in the republic of Bashkortostan, mainly around the cities of Birsk and Ufa. There are approximately 100,000 Mari living in Bashkortostan where they are in minority, the largest ethnic groups being Russians, Tatar and Bashkir.

2.3.1.1.1 The dialects of Mari

Mari has been divided into dialects by different scholars in different times, but the bases for these divisions have been varied. Wichmann and Beke for instance, when dividing the language into dialects in the beginning of the last century, used administrative borders in Tzarist Russia rather than linguistic differences as their main criteria (Bereczki 1985: 187). This has confused matters, and Beke sometimes uses different terms to designate what in reality is one and the same dialect. In Mari linguistics, there have been other principles for the division of the language into dialects. Gruzov (1969: 46) differs between four main dialects of Mari: Meadow Mari, Mountain Mari, Eastern Mari and North-west Mari. According to Bereczki (1985: 187) this division is far more realistic, but also based more on the geographical distribution of the speakers of Mari, than on linguistic differences. As far as Mari linguistics is concerned, the reportedly best monograph on Mari dialects, *Mari dialektologij* by Ivanov (1985) has unfortunately not been at my disposal.

Bereczki (1985) divides the language into dialects by use of a number of criteria. On the basis of these criteria, Bereczki distinguishes two main dialects of Mari, one Eastern and one Western. The two main dialects are then further divided into subdialects and varieties of these. The criteria that are used are differences in the vowel systems of the dialects as well as stress patterns. In the field of morphology, the use of different plural markers in different dialects is emphasised as a distinguishing feature. Of less importance, according to Bereczki, are differences in the consonant systems and the existence or lack of vowel harmony. According to Bereczki, lexical differences in the dialects are not a decisive criterion when dividing Mari into dialects.

Saarinen (1985) divides the Mari language into dialects by use of a number of criteria that are similar to those used by Bereczki. On the basis of these criteria, she divides the language into two dialect groups, one Eastern and one Western. To the Western group belong the Mountain dialect, by Saarinen called the West dialect, and the North-west dialect. To the Eastern dialect group, the Meadow dialect and the proper Eastern dialect belong. In accordance with Bereczki, Saarinen sees the vowel system as important for the classification of dialects, but also the consonant systems and morphological differences such as the use of different plural markers in the dialects are considered to be of importance. Stress patterns too are of vital importance in distinguishing the Eastern and Western dialect groups from each other according to Saarinen. Lexical differences, on the other hand, are not important in this respect, although Saarinen points to the fact that the lexical stock of Eastern Mari has undergone systematic changes as a result of Tatar influence. In a later published paper, Saarinen (1994: 222) points to the fact that there are variants of Eastern Mari—which in this context probably refers to the varieties of Mari spoken in Tatarstan and Bashkortostan—in which as much as 80% of the lexicon is of Tatar origin but the morphology is Mari. However, she does not describe this in detail.

It can be added that there are other differences between the Mari dialects than the ones mentioned above. Kuznetsova (1996) discusses whether Meadow and Mountain Mari are to be considered two different languages or not, and gives further examples of the differences between the two. According to Kuznetsova (1996: 235) there are nine cases in Meadow Mari and ten in Mountain Mari. The cases are the same in both dialects but Mountain Mari also makes use of a caritive case with the ending *-te, -δe*. There are certain differences in the use of these cases. Some of the functions of the dative case in Meadow Mari are filled by the lative case in Mountain Mari, and in some contexts the functions of the inessive case of Meadow Mari are filled by the genitive case of Mountain Mari. There are also differences in the verbal systems, and the differences concern both infinite forms and personal endings. The conditional is a productive mode in Mountain Mari, beside the indicative, the imperative and desiderative, but not in Meadow Mari. Judging from what Kuznetsova (1996: 235–236) writes about lexical differences, these are apparently greater than what has been assumed earlier. Bereczki (1999: 67) claims that there are about 500 words of Finno-Ugric origin in Mari. In the Western dialects, there are according to Bereczki 11 words occurring only in these dialects, whereas there are 24 words in the Eastern dialects that lack equivalents in the western dialects. According to Bereczki, this is due to the fact the Volga Bulgar and Chuvash—and later also the Russian—impact on the Western dialects has been greater.

Differences between two or more dialects can be the result of contact-induced change but it is also a fact that language-internal processes are of importance. It is therefore interesting to note that many of the criteria used in the classification of the Mari dialects can be said to be examples of differences caused mainly (but certainly not only) by language contact. This mainly concerns the stress patterns in the different dialects, the vowel systems and the existence or lack of vowel harmony. Since the language contact processes show differences as far as the direction, kind, extension and depth in different parts of the Mari language area is concerned, I will follow the Mari linguistic tradition and reckon with the existence of four different dialects of Mari; Mountain Mari, North-west Mari, Meadow Mari and Eastern Mari. For these, the abbreviations MoMa, MaNw, MaMe and MaE will be used. The geographical distribution of the Mari dialects is shown in map 1.

Mountain Mari is spoken in the western parts of the republic of Mari-El, on both sides of the Volga, which in this respect does not constitute a dialect boundary. According to Bereczki (1985: 189), Mountain Mari is spoken in an area extending from the left bank of the Volga to the northern border of the Mari republic. These Mari call themselves *kožla mare* 'forest Mari'. North-west Mari is spoken by a small group of people in scattered settlements in an area immediately to the north of the republic. According to Saarinen (1985: 197), North-western Mari is the dialect of Mari with the largest amount of lexical items of Russian origin. Meadow Mari is the largest dialect of Mari when it comes to the total number of speakers, and this dialect extends from an area between the cities of Kozmodemyansk and Yoshkar-Ola in the west to the eastern border of the republic. Eastern Mari, finally, is spoken in areas immediately to the east of the republic and in several, geographically separated areas in Tatarstan and Bashkortostan.

The four main dialects of Mari have become separated from each other during the last centuries. According to Bereczki (1999: 71), there were only minor phonetic and morphological differences between the dialects in the middle of the 13th century, and the lexical differences were insignificant. If this is true—it would probably be hard to present solid evidence—the conclusion that can be drawn is that the Mari dialects started to separate from each other at a time when the most extensive contacts with the Turkic languages started.

2.3.1.1.2 The literary languages of Mari

Today, two different literary languages are used for written Mari, one eastern and one western. In both cases, the Cyrillic script is used. There are several reasons for the existence of two different literary languages and a comprehensive description of this can be found in Ivanov & Moisio (1998). Unfortunately, Ivanov's (1975) book on the history of the literary language has not been at my disposal. The first Mari grammar, published in 1775, apparently had, according to Ivanov & Moisio (1998: 9), the object of establishing a single literary language for Mari since it contained an alphabet especially developed for this and made use of lexical material from all dialects. To some extent, the grammar was also normative in the sense that it gave basic rules for the use of these words and it was also used as a school-book. In 1804, the first Mari catechism was published, written in Mountain Mari. It was followed by the first catechism in Meadow Mari, published in 1808. In 1867, the first Mountain Mari ABC-book was published and in 1870 the first one in Meadow Mari. In the end of the19th century, two different literary standards had thus been established.

Out of these two literary standards, the two literary languages in use today were formed. There are various reasons for this. The fact that two different ways of writing Mari already had been established was of great importance. Apart from this, the so-called dialect patriotism, according to which one's own dialect is the only one suited to become the basis of a literary language had a great impact (Ivanov & Moisio 1998: 20). Another contributing factor was the somewhat self-contradictory efforts by a linguistic commision, which at the same time as it was trying to promote the establishment of a single literary language, also continued to promote the publishing of dialect texts until the literary language had been established. Linguistic isms in the Soviet Union also contributed to the formation of two different literary languages. In the end of the 1920s, the Soviet scholar N.J. Marr, based on his rather wilful linguistic theory, claimed that Mountain and Meadow Mari were not one but two different languages and as a result of Marr's intervention, the efforts to establish a single literary language were abandoned.

The literary languages of Mari are of interest not because there are two of them, but mainly because the creation of them includes the establishment of standardised orthography and a standardised lexicon. The latter means that words and derivational endings used in a dialect can be chosen as standard forms of a literary language. The largest dialect of Mari when it comes to the total number of speakers is Meadow Mari and the heartland of the Mari language and culture is situated in the Morki area in the republic of Mari-El (Ivanov & Moisio 1998: 29). A considerable number of the leading figures in Mari linguistics and literature during the 1920s and 1930s, a period during which the literary languages were created, came from the Morki area and the Morki variety of Meadow Mari is the basis for the present Eastern literary language. According to Ivanov & Moisio (1998: 29), also many Mari from Bashkortostan were active participants in the cultural life in the Mari republic in the time during which many words and derivational endings originally restricted to dialects became part of the standard literary language. This means that a speaker of a particular dialect can exert a considerable influence on the not-yet standardised literary language, either as a linguist or a writer, or in some cases both. This is of importance in this thesis because it means that words and derivational endings, which in reality are code-copies, can be integrated into the literary language and thus spread also to other dialects. What can be labelled as habitualised copies in a dialect could in this way gain acceptance and were more easily conventionalised. Among the words chosen as literary norms in the 1920s and 1930s there are several examples of code-copies. From the Meadow dialect in the Morki area, words like *tamə̂k* 'hell' and *aru* 'clean' (Ivanov & Moisio 1998: 30) were taken. Both are of Tatar origin, cf. TatM *tamïk* 'Hölle' (Kakuk 1996: 173) and TatK *aru* 'clean, in good health' (Poppe 1963: 200). The same applies to words chosen as standard forms from the Eastern dialect in Bashkortostan, for instance *paγə̂t* '(period of) time', *sare* 'yellow' and *kök* 'grey (of horses)' (Ivanov & Moisio 1998: 31). These words are also of Tatar origin, cf. TatM *wakït* 'Zeit, Zeitpunkt' (Kakuk 1996: 184), TatM *sarï* 'gelb' (Kakuk 1996: 166), TatM *kük* 'blau' (Kakuk 1996: 155).

The choice of copied elements as standard forms of the literary language is not restricted to global copies of words but applies to mixed and selective copies as well. In the period between 1918 and 1937 a considerable number of new words were formed in Mari and this was done by creating new compound words, by using morphological means as derivational endings or by modification of the semantics of already existing words (Ivanov & Moisio 1998: 33). The rapid development of the literary languages of Mari in the period 1918–1937 is closely connected to the fact that the use of indigenous languages was encouraged in the Soviet Union during this time.

2.3.2 Turkic languages

Several Turkic languages have been spoken in the Middle Volga region in historic times, among these languages are Volga Bulgar and Pecheneg. Volga Bulgar has probably exerted an influence on Mari, but according to Räsänen (1923: 90) there are also words of Turkic origin in Mari which are not of a Volga Bulgar or Chuvash type. Some of these words can thus be quite old. Today, three different Turkic languages are spoken in the Middle Volga region. Two of them are Kipchak Turkic languages and one is an Oghur Turkic language.

2.3.2.1 Kipchak Turkic languages

2.3.2.1.1 Tatar and Bashkir

Tatar and Bashkir are closely related languages, belonging to the so-called Kipchak Turkic or North-western group of the Turkic languages (Berta 1998b: 283). The Kipchak Turkic group includes several other languages and can be further divided into sub-groups. Tatar and Bashkir constitute a northern Kipchak or "Volga-Ural group" (Johanson 1998a: 82). Both Tatar and Bashkir originate in the

Kipchak Turkic dialects spoken in southern Russia and Asia between the 13th and 16th centuries, usually labelled “Middle Kipchak” (Berta 1998a: 158). According to Rorlich (1986: xiv), there are over 5 million Tatars in total, but only 1,5 million of them live within the borders of the Tatar republic. There are also considerable groups of Tatars in Bashkortostan, and in the areas around Perm, Nizhny Novgorod, Samara, Saratov and Orenburg. In western Siberia there are several groups of speakers of Tatar (Johanson 1998a: 82), such as the so-called Baraba Tatars. Tatar is divided into three main dialects: the Central dialect or Kazan Tatar, the western dialect or Mishar Tatar and West Siberian Tatar, or eastern dialect. The literary language of Tatar developed during the second half of the 19th century. Its phonetic system is based on the Kazan dialect whereas its morphology is based on the Mishar dialect (Berta 1998b: 283). At present, Tatar is written with cyrillic characters, but earlier other scripts too have been used (c.f. Baldauf 1993).

Bashkir is closely related to Tatar and differs from it mainly in (morpho)phonology (Poppe 1964: 3). According to Berta (1998b: 284), the phonetic differences between Tatar and Bashkir mainly concerns their consonant systems. There are approximately 1.5 million Bashkirs and in the republic of Bashkortostan they are in minority in a population mainly consisting of Russians and Tatars. Bashkir is divided into three main dialects and several sub-dialects (Berta 1998b: 300; Poppe 1964: 3). The main dialects are the Mountain or Eastern dialect, the North-west dialect and the Steppe dialect. The literary language of Bashkir uses the cyrillic script like that of Tatar, but there are differences in orthography. The literary language of Bashkir was developed only after the proclamation of the Bashkir republic in the 1920s (Poppe 1964: 3)

In this thesis, the term Tatar will be used for both Tatar and Bashkir. There are several reasons for this. It can be assumed that the contacts between Mari and these languages started before the two Kipchak Turkic languages had become separated from each other. It can also be assumed that words of Bashkir origin are more frequent in the dialects of Mari spoken in Bashkortostan, but since also Tatar is spoken in the republic, the importance of Tatar in this respect can not be neglected. The possibility of distinguishing Tatar lexical material in Mari from Bashkir lexical material is discussed in Isanbaev (1988).

2.3.2.2 Oghur Turkic languages

2.3.2.2.1 Chuvash

Chuvash is a language in the Oghur group to which also Volga Bulgar and possibly also Khazar belonged. The only living language in this group is thus Chuvash. Its contacts with other languages, especially with Finno-Ugric languages, and the changes it has undergone tend to obscure its Turkic character (Clark 1998: 434). According to Krueger (1961: 56) some turcologists, such as the notable scholar Radloff, have held the view that Chuvash is a turkicised Finno-Ugric language and the Chuvash have at times been described as a Finno-Ugric rather than a Turkic people. This view has been put forward also in modern scientific works. Donnelly (1968: 9), in a monograph dealing with the Russian conquest of Bashkortostan, states that "the Mordvinians, Mari (Cheremises), Chuvashes and Udmurts (Votiaks), lived mostly between Nizhny Novgorod [and] were largely the descendants of indigenous Finnish inhabitants [...]". The Finnish linguist August Ahlqvist was early of the opinion that Chuvash was a Turkic language. This opinion is explicitly expressed for instance in the material kept in the archives of the Finno-Ugric Society in Helsinki. Ramstedt (1922) has demonstrated the Turkic character of Chuvash. Chuvash has retained most of a Common Turkic morphosyntax and lexicon (Clark 1998: 434). The innovations in the language are characterised by a series of sound changes and replacements (Clark 1998: 434). According to Johanson (2001: 32) Chuvash is "of eminent importance for the reconstruction of earlier stages of Turkic".

In Finno-Ugric linguistics, Chuvash is often directly connected with Volga Bulgar and Bereczki (1994: 14–15) makes the following periodic division of the Volga Bulgar language: 1. Proto-Bulgar (1st –9th centuries AD), 2. Middle Bulgar (9th-15th centuries AD) and 3. Chuvash (15th century AD and onwards). Both Chuvash and Volga Bulgar are Oghur Turkic languages, but according to Boeschoten (1998: 7), no direct evidence for diachronic development between the two has been established. It is probable, that the Chuvash are the descendants of one of several Oghur Turkic speaking groups in the Middle Volga region. The ethnonym *suvar* which according to Rorlich (1986: 11) was used to designate a group of speakers of a Volga Bulgar language is interesting in this respect. It is unlikely, however, that any direct conclusions can be drawn from this. Volga Bulgar words have been preserved in a number of grave inscriptions from the 13th to the 14th centuries AD and they are mainly to be found in present-day Tatarstan. As was stated above, there are also a few inscriptions in the republics of Bashkortostan and Udmurtia, but none in the Mari and Chuvash republics. This is probably connected to the fact that the major part of the area inhabited by Volga Bulgars was conquered by the Golden Horde and that the population there became assimilated. It is probably also of importance that the grave inscriptions are the work of moslems, whereas the Chuvash have preserved their animistic religion up to the present day. Today there are less than 1.5 million Chuvash and the majority live within the borders of the Chuvash republic, where they constitute a majority of the population. There are also Chuvash settlements in Tatarstan and Bashkortostan, and around the cities of Samara and Ulyanovsk. Chuvash is divided into two major dialects, the southern dialect, or Anatri-dialect, and the northern, Viryal dialect (Clark 1998: 451; Krueger 1961: 64). The Chuvash living outside of the republic all speak varieties of the Anatri dialect. The literary language of Chuvash is based mainly on the Anatri dialect and the script is cyrillic. Like Mari, Chuvash too is heavily influenced by Tatar. This influence is most easily observed in the Anatri dialect (Johanson 1999: 58). I have not had access to texts from the Viryal dialect. The text material collected by Paasonen (1949) represents the Anatri dialect.

2.4 Bilingualism

Bilingualism occurs for instance in language contact situations and the degree of bilingualism is closely connected to social factors like political, economical, cultural and numeric dominance. Bilingualism can be seen as the result of an adaptation to changing social conditions. In many of the scientific works on the linguistic contacts between Mari and the Turkic languages, the question of bilingualism is touched upon but its extent is rarely defined. Today, most Mari are bilingual in Mari and Russian. One of the more comprehensive descriptions of bilingualism among the Mari and other Finno-Ugric peoples can be found in Ariste (1969: 245–254). According to Ariste, trilingualism is a characteristic of certain groups of Mari. A Mari-Russian-Udmurt trilingualism exists in the districts of Mari-Turek and Paranga in the republic of Mari-El (Map 3), and in the district of Malmyzh in the Kirov region, to the east of the Mari republic. A Mari-Chuvash-Russian trilingualism exists in the district of Mari-Turek and also among the Mountain Mari in areas bordering on the Chuvash republic. There is a similar trilingualism in Mari, Chuvash and Russian also in other areas where there is a mixed population of Mountain Mari and Chuvash. There is also, according to Ariste, some villages in the district of Mari-Turek where the population speak Mari, Russian, Tatar and Udmurt. Ariste further claims that trilingualism is characteristic of the middle and younger generations of Mari. Mari is used among representatives of all generations, whereas Tatar, Udmurt and Russian is used for conversation with representatives of each language but also sporadically between speakers of Mari (see also Bereczki 1994: 69–70). According to Ariste, what he refers to as switching, or the use of several codes in a single utterance, occurs in areas where the Mari population is trilingual. Ariste (1969: 250) gives the following example from the district of Kukmor in Tatarstan:

ma *Volostnoj starsjina* (russisch) *din* (tatarisch) *βaštareš šoγen əš kert* (marisch) 'der Gemeindeälteste konnte der Gemeinde nicht widerstehen'

It is evident that the linguistic contacts between Mari and the Turkic languages are not entirely finished and that the considerable plurilingualism in parts of the Mari language area can shed light over previous processes. The earlier contacts between Mari and the Turkic languages can in a similar way be of importance for the understanding of current processes of contact-induced change. From Ariste's description, it is possible to draw the conclusion that the processes today are concentrated to the margins of the Mari language area. This means that the analysis of Turkic code-copies in Mari not just will be an analysis of processes that have come to an end, but also can contribute to the analysis of processes of code-copying presently going on in various parts of the Mari language area.

3 Lexical and phonological code-copies

3.1 Lexical code-copies

The Mari vocabulary, like that of any other language, contains elements of foreign origin. Words of foreign origin are essential parts of the vocabulary of all languages and these words are important for the identification and description of contacts between languages. To some extent, words of foreign origin in a language can be distinguished from each other chronologically, and this applies also to Mari. Among the oldest layers of words originating in another language in Mari are the Indo-Iranian words. The Indo-Iranian words in Mari form a small group of words and contain among others the self-designation *mari* 'a mari, human, man'. There are indo-Iranian words also in other Finno-Ugric languages, such as Hungarian. The question of the exact nature of the contacts between Finno-Ugric and Indo-Iranian is complicated by several factors which are of comparatively little interest in this study but have been dealt with by Korenchy (1988). There is considerable disagreement on the subject of possible contacts between Mari and the Baltic languages and some scholars, for instance Mägiste (1959), are of the opinion that the vocabulary of Mari contains no words of Baltic origin, with the possible exception of one single word. Other scholars however, claim that lexical parallels make it possible to conclude that speakers of the Volga Finnic languages—in any case at least the Mordvins—have had direct contacts with speakers of Baltic languages (Suhonen 1988: 614). The Mari vocabulary has been enriched also as a result of contacts with other Finno-Ugric languages. Bereczki (1977) has presented evidence for the existence of words of Permian origin in Mari and there are also examples of Permian influence in the phonology and morphology of Mari (Bereczki 1999: 68).

It can also be assumed that Mari has had sporadic contacts with other languages as well. Larsson (1990) discusses the possibility of finding evidence for contacts between Mari and Romany. Since there are a number of Mari legends, see for instance Beke (1995: 29–30), in which the main characters are Romany, this possibility cannot be excluded. There is also a great number of words of Mongolian origin in Mari, but these words have in all likelihood entered the language via the Turkic languages, especially Tatar. In more recent times, the contacts between Mari and Russian have been extensive, and this is particularly the case with Mountain and North-west Mari. The Russian influence on Mari is considerable, especially in the lexical field, but Russian has also exerted a phonological, morphological and syntactic influence. The contacts between Mari and Russian began after the Russian conquest of Kazan—with the exception of the western parts of the Mari language area, which were drawn into the Russian sphere of interest even earlier—but became intensified and extended after the Russian revolution. The

Turkic languages however, have left more permanent traces in the Mari vocabulary and other parts of the language system. The contacts between Mari and the Turkic languages place themselves chronologically between the contacts with Indo-Iranian languages (and the possible contacts with Baltic languages) and the contacts with Russian.

There is a large amount of lexical items of Tatar and Chuvash origin in Mari. The Tatar and Chuvash words in Mari have been thoroughly examined by Räsänen (1920; 1923) and also by Isanbaev (1989). According to Räsänen (1923: 90, footnote 1), there are also words of Turkic origin in Mari that are neither Tatar nor Chuvash and some of these words can be very old. The works of Räsänen are very comprehensive and show that the lexical material of Turkic origin has penetrated the Mari vocabulary deeply and that the Turkic words are not restricted to a particular semantic field, see for instance Räsänen (1923: 95–97). There are lexical items of Turkic origin in most word categories in Mari. The exact number of words of Turkic origin in Mari however, is a frequently debated question, and there are differing opinions in this respect, see for instance Saarinen (1997a; 192); Bereczki (1994; 16); Räsänen (1923: 90) and Gordeev (1976). Saarinen (1997a: 193) states that Mari and Tatars in many areas in Tatarstan and Bashkortostan live in the same villages and the population is entirely bilingual. According to Saarinen (1997a: 193), this means that "in speech especially, words from the other language can be used as sorts of quotations, but they should not be considered as real loanwords". This use of words of another language as sorts of quotations can be described as code-copying.

My point of departure in the discussion of Tatar and Chuvash lexical elements in Mari is to see them as lexical code-copies. It is possible to classify these copies as global, mixed or selective copies and also to some extent to determine whether they constitute momentary, habitualised and conventionalised copies. The lexical code-copies of Tatar or Chuvash originals are so many that almost all word categories have been influenced. Apart from global copies of substantives, there are also global copies of verbs, adjectives, adverbs, postpositions, interjections and particles.

As was mentioned above, there are two different verb conjugations in Mari, the *am-* and the *em*-conjugations, the names deriving from the ending for the first person singular in each conjugation. The reasons for the development of two different conjugations are uncertain. Ravila (1938: 13), who has written a detailed study of the two verb conjugations in Mari, claims that all verbs of foreign origin are conjugated in the *em*-conjugations. Here, two remarks can be made: First, it is not correct that all verbs of Turkic origin are conjugated in the *em*-conjugation, the verb *sižam* 'fühlen < Tat *siz* 'empfinden, fühlen' (Räsänen 1923: 64) is an exception. Secondly, the fact that a majority of the verbs of Turkic origin are conjugated in the *em*-conjugation is in all likelihood an indication that this conjugation was the most productive one at the times during which the verbs were incorporated into Mari.

Lexical code-copies of Tatar and Chuvash originals in Mari are characterised by both phonological and semantic restructuring. Phonological restructuring can take many shapes. The Chuvash phoneme *χ* is treated in different ways in Mari. In an initial position it is often absent, for instance MaMe *ola* 'city' < Chuv *χala* 'id'. According to Räsänen (1920: 21) this phoneme has been preserved in MaMo, c.f MaMo *χala* 'city', but it is far more likely that the existence of a phoneme *χ* in MaMo is due to the fact that this dialect has maintained its contacts with Chuvash longer than the other dialects. The existence of a phoneme *χ* is not necessarily to be interpreted as something preserved in MaMo but rather as a phoneme that has been habitualised and conventionalised.

3.1.1 Global copies

There are a large number of global copies of Turkic lexical originals in Mari, but it is not only the specifications of their exact number that show variation. There are considerable differences also in their geographical distribution. It is often claimed that the eastern dialects are under a strong Tatar influence, and the western dialects are more heavily influenced by Chuvash (Róna-Tas 1988: 772; Johanson 2000: 168). Saarinen (1997a: 191–195) points to some interesting facts in this respect. Judging from Saarinen's description, the number of Tatar lexical items in Mari vary a great deal in different dialects and the number of Tatar lexical items is indeed higher in the eastern dialects, but considerably smaller in the western dialects (Saarinen 1997a: 193). Saarinen refers to the Atlas Linguarum Europae (ALE) in which words of Tatar origin in the basic vocabulary of Mari is said to be 153 all in all, out of which only five occur in all dialects. As to words of Chuvash origin, the picture is different. According to Saarinen (1997a: 192) the Mari material in ALE shows that there are 154 words of Chuvash origin in the basic vocabulary of Mari. Of these, no less than 51 occur in all dialects, including the one spoken in Bashkortostan. Such figures raise the question of whether all dialects of Mari first have undergone a large-scale Chuvash influence, followed by a later Tatar influence in just some dialects. Below, a list of global copies of Turkic originals in Mari is given. The examples have not been specified with respect to dialects, since the purpose is to show that copies of Turkic originals occur in all word categories.

3.1.1.1 Substantives

Ma *ak* 'price' < Tat *ak* 'id'
Ma *aka, äkä* 'elder sister' < Chuv *akka* 'id'
Ma *akə̑l* 'reason, mind' < Tat *akıl* 'id'
Ma *araka* 'vodka' < Chuv *ereke* 'id'
Ma *azap* 'worry, trouble' < Tat *azap* 'torment, anguish'
Ma *el* 'surroundings, village, land, kingdom' < tat *il* 'people, villager, village'
Ma *ešak* 'donkey' < Tat *išäk* 'id'
Ma *jal* 'village' < Chuv *yal* 'id'
Ma *jalə̑k* 'cloth' < Tat *yaulık* 'id'

Ma *jazu* 'writing, script' < Tat *yazu* 'id'
Ma *kalpak* 'cap' < Tat *kalpak* 'a kind of cap'
Ma *kalə̂k* 'people' < Tat *kalık* 'id', Chuv *χalăk* 'id'
Ma *kapka* 'gate' < Tat *kapka* 'id'
Ma *kara* 'ink' < Tat *kara* 'black, ink'
Ma *karbə̂z* 'water melon' < Tat *karbız* 'id'
Ma *kijar* 'cucumber' < Tat *kıyar* 'id'
Ma *kuat* 'strength' < Tat *kuat* 'id'
Ma *namə̂s* 'shame' < Tat *namıs* 'honour, reputation'
Ma *nörep, müγrep* 'cellar' < Chuv *nüχrep* 'id'
Ma *nasta* 'gadget, thing' < Tat *nästä* 'id'
Ma *oksa, okśa* 'money' < Chuv *ukśa* 'id'
Ma *olma* 'apple' < Chuv *ulma* 'id'
Ma *orol, orolə̂* 'guard < Chuv *χural* 'id'
Ma *ölaksa* 'corpse, body' < Tat *üläksä* 'id'
Ma *patə̂r* 'hero, brave, strength' < Tat *batır* 'hero, brave'
Ma *pölek* 'gift' < Tat *bülek* 'id'
Ma *tam, täm* 'taste' < Tat *täm* 'id'
Ma *oβer, uβer* 'news' < Chuv *χıpar* 'id'
Ma *urem* 'street' < Tat *uram* 'id'

3.1.1.2 Verbs

In the list of verbs of Turkic origin in Mari, the form of the first person singular present tense is given in the Mari verbs. For the Turkic verbs, the stem form of the verb is given.

Ma *jöratem* 'to love' < Chuv *yurat* 'id'
Ma *kalasem* 'to say, talk' < Chuv *kala* 'to tell, to say'
Ma *kə̂čkə̂rem* 'to howl, to cry' < Tat *kıckır* 'to cry, to shout, to croak'
Ma *ondalem* 'to lie, to deceive' < Chuv *ultala* 'to deceive'
Ma *örkanem* 'to laze, to idle' < Chuv *ürken* 'id'
Ma *palem* 'to know' < Chuv *palla* 'id'
Ma *pölem* 'to divide, to separate' < Tat *bül* 'to divide'
Ma *šižam* 'to feel' < Tat *siz* 'id'
Ma *tarβanem* 'to move' < Chuv *tapran* 'to move'

3.1.1.3 Adjectives

Ma *akmak, okmak* 'stupid' < Chuv *uχmaχ* 'id', Tat *akmak* 'id'
Ma *äjβat* 'good' < Tat *äybät* 'id'
Ma *kazak* 'unmarried' < Tat *kazak* 'free person, kosack'
Ma *kök* 'grey' < Tat *kük* 'blue'
Ma *motor* 'beautiful' < Chuv *motor* 'id'
Ma *saj* 'good' < Tat *say* 'clean, ready'

Ma *taza* 'healthy' < Tat *taza* 'clean, healthy'
Ma *türlö* 'different', *târlâ* 'sort, category' < Tat *törlö* 'different'

3.1.1.4 Adverbs

Ma *aδak* 'again' < Chuv *tata, tataχ* 'again, too'
Ma *keneta* 'suddenly, quickly' < Tat *kinät* 'id'
Ma *βara* 'then, later, afterwards' < Chuv *vara* 'id'

3.1.1.5 Postpositions

Ma *köra* 'because of, according to' < Tat *körä* 'according to, in view of'
Ma *pârľa* 'together with' < Chuv *pĕrle* 'id'
Ma *posna, pasna* 'except, without' < Chuv *puśne* 'id'

3.1.1.6 Interjections

Ma *ajδa* 'well! Let's go! < Tat *äydä* 'id'

3.1.1.7 Conjunctions

Ma ala...ala... 'either...or...' < Tat *ällä...ällä...* 'id'
Ma *ja...ja...* 'either...or...' < Tat *yä...yä...* 'id'
Ma *ta...ta..., tä...tä...* 'either...or...' < Chuv *ta...ta..., te...te...* 'id'

3.1.1.8 Particles

Ma *γâna* 'if, only' < Tat *gınä* 'id'
Ma *laj, läj* 'in the way of, as if' < Tat *-lEy, -lÄy* 'in the way of, as if'

3.1.2 Mixed copies

There are also examples of what can be classified as mixed copies in the Mari vocabulary, or copies consisting of at least one global copy and a selective copy. As for Mari, the Tatar and Chuvash influence on the morphological system plays an important part in this respect and particularly important are the derivational endings of either Tatar or Chuvash origin. An example of one such derivational ending of Turkic origin in Mari is the suffix *-lâk*, used in the formation of, among others, abstract nouns. For a more detailed discussion of *-lâk,* see section 4.4.2.1. Another example is the adjective forming suffix with the allomorphs *-le, -lo, -lö, -lâ* and *-lə* (see section 4.4.3.1). Both suffixes are frequently added to Mari stems and are according to Saarinen (1999: 251.251) examples of productive suffixes in Mari. Other scholars too are of the opinion that these suffixes are productive in Mari, although the term productivity is seldom properly defined. Isanbaev (1979), in an article about word formation in Mari, states that derivational endings originating in the Turkic languages have been abstracted away from the Turkic words and added to Mari stems. There are other examples of such derivational endings besides the two mentioned, such as the suffix *-kala*, used in the formation of iterative verbs. According to Kangasmaa-Minn (1998: 245) this is a suffix "originally occuring only in Chuvash borrowing, e.g. *jamdəl=kalə̂* 'prepares repeatedly', but available now for (F)U roots, as well: *lüj=kalə̂* 'shoots repeatedly' from *lüjə̂* 'shoots'".

In this context, productivity should probably be interpreted so that the suffix *-lə̂k* in Mari now is such an integrated part of the language that it can be used freely with Mari stems. Although I do not doubt that this can really be the case, most of the examples given to support this opinion leave a lot to wish for. The productivity of this suffix in Mari is actually to a certain extent regulated by the combinatorial properties of the, in all likelihood, Tatar original. In section 4.4.2.1 I will discuss this suffix extensively and for this reason I will only give a short overview here. Isanbaev (1979: 77) stresses the productivity of the Mari suffix *-lə̂k* and gives among others the following examples: *nerlə̂k* 'nose-ring', *šinčalə̂k* 'eye-glasses, spectacles'. The derived substantives are *ner* 'nose' and *šinča* 'eye'. Saarinen (1999: 251) too gives *šinčalə̂k* as an example of a productive use of the suffix *-lə̂k*, and also the example *porə̂lə̂k* 'benevolence, kindness' whereas Ivanov &Moisio (1998: 41) gives the example *arulə̂k* 'cleanness'. A few comments can be made on this. According to Ivanov & Moisio, *arulə̂k* is an example of a recently formed word, created in the period between 1918 and 1937 during which several new words were formed by use of morphological means such as derivational endings. The word *arulə̂k*, however, is not a well chosen example of a recently formed word in Mari, and certainly not a good example of the productive use of the suffix *-lə̂k*, namely because it is purely Tatar. In Tatar, the word *arulık*, just like its Mari equivalent, means 'cleanness' (VTD I 284). As for the productive use of the suffix *-lə̂k* in the sense that it is freely added to Mari stems, the examples given by Saarinen and Isanbaev are characterised by another kind of productivity. In the word *porə̂lə̂k*, the suffix *-lə̂k* is added to the adjective *poro* 'good' which makes it comparable to Tatar *yaχšılık* 'Gutes; Wohltat', in which form the suffix *-lık* is added to the adjective *yaχšı* 'gut; recht; in Ordnung'. It could be argued that the productivity rather lies in that a Tatar stem is substituted with a Mari stem, i.e. this is a case of selective copying in the form of semantic copying. The same applies to examples of a productive use of other suffixes as well, e.g. *-le,-lo,-lö*, *-lə̂*, *-lə* and *-kala*. The words formed with the use of these suffixes can be described as mixed copies. Below, examples of abstract substantives, verbs and adjectives in Mari formed with suffixes of Turkic origin are given, and these are compared to equivalents in the Turkic languages. In my opinion, these words in Mari should be analysed as mixed copies: they combine selective copying in the form of semantic copying with the global copying of Tatar and Chuvash derivational endings.

3.1.2.1 Substantives

Ma *sinčalə̑k* 'eye-glasses, spectacles' ← *šinča* 'eye'; Tat *küzlek* 'Brille' ← *küz* 'Auge'
Ma *porə̑lə̑k* 'goodness' ← *poro* 'good'; Tat *yaχšılık* 'Gutes; Wohltat' ← *yaχšı* 'gut; recht; in Ordnung'
Ma *kornə̑lə̑k* 'for the road, food etc. ← *korno* 'road'; Tat *yullık* 'für den Weg (Geld, Proviant)' ← *yul* 'Weg'
Ma *kečə̑lə̑k* 'sufficient for a day' ← *keče* 'day'; Tat *könlek* 'für einen Tag' ← *kön* 'Tag'
Ma *ulə̑lə̑k* 'wealth, well-being' ← *ulo* '(there) is)'; Tat *barlık* 'Dasein; Existenz; Bestehen; Vorhandensein' ← Tat *bar* 'ist; es gibt; es existiert; vorhanden'

3.1.2.2 Verbs

Ma *βozgalem* 'to write (often)' ← *βozem* 'to write'; Chuv *śırkala* 'to write a bit' ← *śır* 'to write' (Krueger 1961: 231)

3.1.2.3 Adjectives

Ma *lümlö* 'known, famous' ← *lüm* 'name'; Chuv *yatlă* 'with the name of, famous' ← *yat* 'name'

3.1.2.4 Compound copies

In the Mari vocabulary, there are examples of copies consisting of a Mari stem combined with a copied stem with the same meaning: *βij-kuat* 'strength, power' < Ma *βij* 'strength, power, Tat *kuat* 'id', *uš-akə̑l* 'reason, sense' < Ma *uš* 'reason, sense', Tat *akıl* 'id' (Galkin 1977: 109). These examples are interesting in the discussion of the characteristic features of the Turkic code-copies in Mari because they have parallels also in other respects to which I will return below. Parallel instances of a Mari and a Turkic item are not restricted only to nouns but can also concern particles and plural morphemes.

3.1.2.5 Copies in areas with several dominant codes

In an area where several codes can fill the role of a model code, the identification of different types of copies can be very difficult. In the Middle Volga region, both Russian and the Turkic languages have been dominant codes and several dominant codes can exist side by side. According to Kappeler (1982: 496), Tatar maintained its position as "zweite Umgangssprache neben dem Russischen" in the south-eastern parts of the area and in the Urals up to the middle of the 19th century. It can be assumed that even a dominating code has copied elements from other languages, items that in their turn can be copied into other basic codes as a result of other instances of language contact. One example, which will discussed below in sections 5.1.1.2 and 5.1.1.3 are the disjunctive conjunctions *ja...ja...* 'either...or...' and *ta...ta...* 'id'. In Mari, they are copies of Turkic conjunctions, which in their turn are copies of what most likely are Indo-Iranian originals. In the case of the Mari disjunctive conjunctions, it is quite clear that the Indo-Iranian influence is secondary and that the model codes are the Turkic languages. In cases where two or more dominant codes exist side by side and both can constitute a model code, it can be very hard to identify the basic code. Wintschalek (1992: 454), in an article on language contact in the Volga-Kama area discusses what he refers to as "die Übernahme von Derivationssuffixen, [die] in die Wortschöpfung einer Sprache eingreifen, wie das tatarische Bildungssuffix -lik". Apart from Mari, this suffix exists also in Udmurt and was according to Wintschalek (1992: 454) "zunächst auf tatarische Lehnwörter beschränkt, wurde schliesslich allgemeingültig, wotj *geroj* 'Held' - *geroj-lik* 'Heldentum' ". Here, it can be argued that this is in reality a copy of a copy. In Mari too there is a word *gerojlək* with the same meaning as the Udmurt word, but also forms like *gerojla* 'in the way of a hero', *gerojlanem* 'to become a hero', *gerojlo* 'hero-like' (Moisio 1994: 45). Since all these words have been formed by use of a Tatar derivational ending, it is quite likely that they in Mari are global copies of Tatar originals, in their turn the result of the copying and incorporation of a Russian original in the model code, in this particular case the Tatar *geroj* 'hero' (Poppe 1963: 210). In my opinion, the same applies to Udmurt.

3.1.3 Selective copies

Selective copying does not concern morphemes but rather properties of a material, combinatorial, semantical or frequential nature. In cases where the copying concerns lexical material, it produces what has been labelled "loan semantics" (Johanson 1999: 44). Other terms used in this context are "translation loans", "calquing" and "mirror translations". Bereczki (1983: 209–210) gives a detailed description of what he refers to as mirror translations in the Finno-Ugric and Turkic languages in the Middle Volga region. Below, a few of these examples are quoted, the Udmurt and Mordvin examples excluded.

'Parents': Chuv *atte-anne* (*atte* 'father', *anne* 'mother'): Tat *ata-ana* (*ata* 'father', *ana* 'mother'): Ma *ača-aβa* (*ača* 'father', *aβa* 'mother')

'Wednesday': Chuv *yunkun* (*yun* 'blood', *kun* 'day'): Tat *kankün* (*kan* 'blood', *kün* 'day'): Ma *βürγeče* (*βür* 'blood', *keče* 'day')

'Sunrise': Chuv *χĕveltuχăś* (*χĕvel* 'sun, day', *tuχăś* 'rising, leaving'): Tat *künčıγıš* (*kün* 'sun, day', *čıγıš* 'rising, leaving'): Ma *kečəlekmaš* (*keče* 'sun, day', *lekmaš* 'leaving')

Bereczki also points to the existence of phraseological units common to the Finno-Ugric and Turkic languages of the regions, e.g. the expression 'to marry': Chuv *χĕr il* (*χĕr* 'girl', *il* 'to take': Tat *χatın alu* (*χatın* 'woman', *alu* 'to take'):

Ma *üδər nalaš* (*üδər* 'girl', *nalaš* 'to take'). This particular example, however, is not a phraseological unit common only to the languages in the Middle Volga region, but exists also in other languages, c.f Swe *ta sig en hustru* 'to take a wife, i.e to marry'

3.1.4 Momentary, habitualised and conventionalised copies

Momentary copies are according to Johanson (1999: 47) sporadic instances of copying, the result of an individual's use of a copy. A possible example of this in the material that I have examined is the use of the Tatar word *kitap* 'book', in the following sentence: *Jüsüp mollan kitapse oγəl* 'Sie ist nicht das Gebetbuch des Molla Jussuf' (Beke 1961b: 317). Momentary copies can be assumed to be regularly and frequently occurring in language contact situations, but most of them do not have any effects on the linguistic norms in the way the habitualised and conventionalised copies do. The way from a momentary copy to a habitualised or conventionalised one is a process characterised by an increased acceptance of the copy in the linguistic community. Lexically, it can sometimes be hard to distinguish between a habitualised and a conventionalised copy, and in my opinion, the Code-copying Framework is not quite clear in this respect. The question is also connected to the problem of whether Mari is to be considered one or several languages and is dependent on the situation in the dialects. A copy can be habitualised in one dialect and conventionalised in another. An example of a habitualised copy in Mari is perhaps the word *nästä* 'gadget, thing', frequent in the texts from Bashkortostan. In Moisio (1994: 181) this word—in the dictionary given in the form *nasta*—is described as a word restricted to the colloquial language.

3.2 Phonological code-copies

A large number of lexical code-copies make way for other types of copies: phonological, morphological and syntactic. These copies can be global, mixed or selective copies of different kinds, momentary, habitualised and conventionalised. The Tatar and Chuvash impact on the phonological system of Mari, as well as the obvious lexical influence, is a subject that has been given due attention in many studies. Several scholars have dealt explicitly with the problem, among them Räsänen (1920; 1923) and Róna-Tas (1988: 768–770) can be singled out for mention. The discussion of the phonological impact the Turkic languages have made on Mari is often connected with a discussion of the lexical influence, such as the works of Räsänen referred to above. A comprehensive study of this problem can be found also in Bereczki (1994). Since the emphasis of my study is on morphological and syntactic influence, only the main characteristics of the Tatar and Chuvash influence on Mari in the field of phonology will discussed. The opinions sometimes differ rather dramatically from each other when it comes to the question of what is to be considered as Tatar or Chuvash influence—this is especially the case concerning the origin of reduced vowels in the first syllable in Mari. The Turkic impact on the phonological system in Mari is an interesting problem area in which several interpretations sometimes are possible. A few questions, however, are more frequently debated than others, such as the emergence of new vowel and consonant phonemes, stress patterns and vowel harmony.

3.2.1 New vowel and consonant phonemes

The copying of lexemes of foreign origin means, at least in earlier stages of language contact, that the copied lexemes undergo some kind of restructuring to better fit into the basic code. Phonological restructuring is very common. A characteristic feature of both Finno-Ugric and Turkic languages is an aversion to groups of consonants in an initial position. This means that words with such consonant clusters in an initial position will have a different phonological shape when inserted into a basic code of the Finno-Ugric or Turkic type. An example of this is the Russian word *svoboda* 'free, freedom' which has been copied into both Hungarian and Finnish. In Finnish, it has the form *vapaa* 'free' since the initial *s* has not been copied. In Hungarian, on the other hand, it has the form *szabad* 'free' and in this language, it is the consonant *v* in the Russian word that has not been copied (see Honti 1992). In certain cases, phonological restructuring can mean that there can be difficulties in identifying the model code. The Finnish word *ranta* 'beach', for instance, can be a copy of either the Swedish *strand* 'id' or of a Baltic word, c.f. Lithuanian *krantas* 'id' (Larsson 2001: 251).

In Mari, many of the copied lexemes display a considerable phonological restructuring. An example is the originally Tatar word *albasta* 'devil, darned! (interjection) which in the material that I have examined occurs also in the metathetic form *lə̂βasta* 'devil'. In more advanced stages of bilingualism, the phonological restructuring is less pronounced, since a qualified bi- or plurilingualism will include a better knowledge and competence in the phonological system of the model code, and in this way also vowel and consonant phonemes originally not occurring in the model code can be copied.

3.2.1.1 Vowel phonemes

The vowel systems in the two main varieties of Mari, eastern and western Mari, differ from each other in some instances. In the eastern literary language of Mari, there are eight vowel phonemes and in the western literary language there are 10 (see table 1). In the dialects, even more vowel phonemes occur. In MaNw, there are 12 vowel phonemes, whereas MaE has the eight vowel phonemes of the eastern literary language + *ä* (Alhoniemi 1985: 15).

3.2.1.1.1 Reduced vowels in the first syllable in Mari

A characteristic feature, perhaps the most characteristic, of the vowel system of Mari is the existence of what is commonly referred to as reduced vowels in the first syllable. These vowels have been discussed at length by Bereczki (1994: 65–84). In a strictly phonological sense, these vowels are not characterised by being reduced but rather by being shortened, that is not fully articulated (Bereczki 1994: 65). In this respect, Mari does not differ from the Turkic languages of the area, in which similar vowels exist. In the western literary language of Mari, there is an opposition between a front and a back reduced vowel, MaWL *ə* and *ə̂*. In the eastern literary language there is only one reduced vowel, MaEL *ə̂*. In the dialects, other reduced vowels can occur in the first syllable. This feature is most notable in MaNw where four different reduced vowels occur, and where there is an opposition not only between front and back reduced vowels but also between rounded and unrounded reduced vowels, MaNw *ə*, *ə̂*, *n̤* and *ŭ*. Also in the Turkic languages in the area, the distribution of these vowels to some extent differs between the dialects. In Tatar and Bashkir, there are four reduced vowels: a front unrounded *ĕ*, a front rounded *ö̆*, a back unrounded *ı̆* and a back rounded *ŏ* (Johanson 2000: 166). In the northern dialect of Chuvash, Viryal, there are also four reduced vowels, *ă*, *ĕ*, *ö̆* and *ŏ*. In the southern dialect of Chuvash, Anatri, and in the Chuvash literary language, there are only two reduced vowels, *ĕ* and *ă* (Johanson 2000: 173). The so-called reduced vowels in the first syllable in Mari and the question of their origin is one of the most frequently discussed problems in Finno-Ugric linguistics and the discussion is likely to go on in the future.

There is a sizeable literature on the problem of reduced vowels in the first syllable in Mari. Bereczki has given the problem due attention on many occasions, see for instance his *Grundzüge der Tscheremissischen Sprachgeschichte* (Bereczki 1994: 65–84). Strictly speaking, there are two different traditions within Finno-Ugric linguistics when it comes to the origin of the reduced vowels in Mari, and one of them assumes that this was a characteristic feature already of Proto-Mari.

In two of the most famous theories of the vocalism of the Finno-Ugric languages, the ones proposed by Steinitz and Itkonen, the reduced vowels in Mari are at the heart of the discussion. Although there are considerable differences between the theories, they share a common basic assumption since both Steinitz and Itkonen assumed that reduced vowels in the first syllable occurred already in Proto-Mari. Steinitz (1944) compared the vowel system of Mari to that of Khanty, a Ugric language spoken in western Siberia, and was of the opinion that the systematic correspondences between the MaMo reduced vowel phonemes *ə* and *ə̂* in the first syllable and the Khanty equivalents could not be the result of chance. They were a feature common to MaMo and Khanty. As for the full vowels in the first syllable in Mari, Steinitz assumed that they had developed from reduced vowels. E. Itkonen (1954), on the other hand, argued that the early Proto-Finnish vowel system, in which an opposition between short and long vowels existed, was the original one. The short vowels in the first syllable in Mari had, according to Itkonen, developed into reduced vowels in Proto-Mari, whereas the long vowels had developed into short full vowels. The reduced vowels in Mari could in this way be seen as the result of an inner development (for the vowel theories, see also Wickman 1962).

A representative for the second tradition is Bereczki, who claims that the reduced vowels in the first syllable in Mari are of Kipchak Turkic origin. Bereczki (1994: 65–84) argues for the secondary character of the reduced vowels in the first syllable in Mari, and sees them as a result of Tatar (and Chuvash) influence. Bereczki points to the fact that reduced vowels occur as independent phonemes in Tatar, Bashkir and Kazakh, in Bashkir even in all dialects. According to Bereczki, the correspondence between the languages is too large to be the result of a parallel development and the Turkic languages are too numerous and have such a wide distribution that a Finno-Ugric substratum influence is unlikely (Bereczki 1994: 67).

The existence of reduced vowels in the first syllable in Mari has attracted the attention of scholars specialising in Turkic languages, and the problem has been discussed at length by Róna-Tas (1975). Johanson (2000) has recently given a detailed account of the question and the differing opinions expressed concerning the origin of these reduced vowels, by Johanson (2000: 166) referred to as "lax vowels". Johanson discusses the explanation given by Steinitz but also other explanations. According to Johanson (2000: 173), the opposition between the "tense" and "lax vowels" is a comparatively old feature in the Kipchak Turkic languages of the Middle Volga region. Johanson states that some scholars have assumed a Kipchak Turkic origin of the phenomenon, while others have argued in favour of a Volga Bulgar origin (c.f. Róna-Tas 1975). Johanson (2000: 174) also points to the fact that some scholars find it impossible to say anything with certainty about the origin of the vowels in question and ascribe them a common origin in what is called "areal relations". From this point of view, the reduced vowels of the first syllable in the languages of the Middle Volga region, are a common feature for which none of the languages in question can—as Johanson (2000: 174) puts it—"be held responsible".

In what follows, Johanson makes a deeper study of the problem by example of the different vowel systems in the Kipchak Turkic languages and in Chuvash. At the heart of the discussion stands the notion that there is little sense in focussing on individual reduced vowels, without taking into consideration the roles they play in the sound systems of the languages. Johanson claims that the Kipchak Turkic languages and Chuvash represent two different cases with respect to the role the reduced vowels play in the sound system (Johanson 2000: 174). The discussion is based on a detailed account of the vowel changes in the Kipchak Turkic languages and Chuvash. The subject of these changes and their origin is controversial and frequently debated and I will not go into details here. Suffice it to say that Johanson (2000: 175) arrives at the conclusion that the changes in the Kipchak Turkic languages are systematic, and governed by internal principles in the phonology of the Turkic languages, whereas the changes in Chuvash are not, although these changes in Chuvash and Kipchak Turkic languages are often described as being basically identical (Johanson 2000: 175). In Chuvash, the old opposition between high and non-high vowels has not been preserved and the opposition between reduced and non-reduced vowels does not fill the same phonological purpose in Chuvash as in the Kipchak Turkic languages. According to

Johanson (2000: 176), it is not sufficient to state that the vowel changes in question are a local phenomenon occuring also in the Finno-Ugric languages of the area. Johanson is of the opinion that the changes in Chuvash are a result of what we, using the terminological apparatus of the Code-copying Framework, can call the imposition or carrying over of copies. Johanson claims that speakers of Proto-Mari (and most likely also Permian) carried over their pronounciation habits to the variety of Volga Bulgar they started to speak. The reduced and non-reduced vowels were kept and reorganized under what Johanson calls "Finno-Ugric substratum influence".

The question of the origin of the reduced vowels in the first syllable in Mari is thus far from being solved. It is evident, though, that the opinion expressed by Bereczki that these vowels originate in the Turkic languages to some extent lacks support from turcologists. I share Johanson's opinion that the discussion of the reduced vowel must take the role they play in the over-all sound systems of the languages in the area into consideration. Bereczki is probably right in assuming that it is not possible to reckon with Finno-Ugric influence on all the Turkic languages in the area, but we can assume that this is possible to reckon with as far as Chuvash is concerned. This question, however, will not be dealt with in detail here.

3.2.1.1.2 Full vowels

Bereczki (1994: 100–104) has shown that a PFU vowel phoneme **ä* has changed into several other vowels in Mari. Therefore, it can be claimed that the phoneme *ä* occurring in MaE is secondary and that it is a copy of a Tatar vowel phoneme *ä*. The emergence of a secondary vowel phoneme *ä* in this dialect is closely connected to the copying of another phonological feature of Tatar, i.e. the vowel harmony of a palatal-velar type, see further in section 3.2.3.2.

But a vowel phoneme *ä* occurs also in the western dialects and the differences in the vowel systems of MaMo, MaNw and MaMe, their age and origin, have been frequently discussed. The discussion focusses on the words of Chuvash origin in Mari, and the time during which the contacts between the languages began. Wichmann (1924: 53) is of the opinion that these contacts began already in the 8th century AD. Räsänen (1920: 94) on the other hand, claims that the majority of the words of Chuvash origin in Mari entered the language sometime after the 12th century AD. Róna-Tas (1988: 769–772) gives a detailed account of the problem. In Mari, the words of Chuvash origin fall into two categories with respect to vocalism. In the first of these categories, Category I, the phonemes *a* and *ä* in the western dialects correspond to *o* and *a* in the eastern dialects:

MaMo *päläš* 'to know', MaMe *palaš* 'id'; MaMo *χala* 'city, town', MaMe *ola* 'id'

In the second category, Category II, the vocalism in words of Chuvash origin is the same in both dialect groups:

MaMo *oń* 'father-in-law', MaMe *oń* 'id'

The problem of the differences in the vocalism of the Mari dialects is closely connected to changes in the Chuvash vocalism. Several scholars, among them Wichmann (1924: 44), are of the opinion that the western dialects of Mari have better preserved an original Chuvash vocalism. Others (Räsänen 1920: 79–80; Bereczki 1968: 30, 1994: 92) state that the western Mari phonemes *a* and *ä* that correspond to eastern Mari *o* and *a* are the result of a secondary development. The problem has been discussed at length by several scholars, and I refer to Róna-Tas (1988: 769–772) for details. In my opinion, Róna-Tas (1988), Räsänen (1920) and Bereczki (1994), all give convincing evidence for the secondary nature of the vocalism in western Mari. The evidence includes cases in which a copy of a Chuvash word in MaMo contain the vowel *ä* in spite of the fact that this vowel did not exist in the Chuvash word. An example is the word MaMo *päläs* 'to know', MaMe *palas* 'id' that goes back to a Chuvash *pal-*, *pĕl-* 'to know'. In Kazan Tatar, the form is *bel-* 'to know' and in Mishar Tatar *bil-* 'id'. Bereczki (1994: 92) has shown that many words of Russian origin have undergone the same sound change in the western dialects of Mari, and it is probable that also many Tatar words have changed the same way, c.f. MaMo *jaltaš* 'fellow, MaMe *joltaš* 'id' (Róna-Tas 1988: 770).

This means that the vocalism in the western dialects of Mari is secondary and that the majority of the words of Chuvash origin were copied into Mari after the 13th century. It also means that the words belonging to Category I are of a later date than the words belonging to Category II. Róna-Tas (1988: 772) claims that the majority of the Chuvash words in Mari come from the Viryal dialect. It is very likely that this is the case. According to Bereczki (1994: 16) it is not possible to conclude that the Mari have been present in their areas of inhabitation prior to the 13th century (for a different opinion, see Bartens 1997: 330, 334). It is also a historical fact that the centre of the Volga Bulgar empire was transferred to the areas north of the river Kama after the arrival of the Golden Horde. However, the assumption that the western dialects better reflect an original Chuvash vocalism is still made occasionally. Adamovič (1985) bases his discussion of the origin of the Chuvash plural morpheme on this assumption.

3.2.1.2 Consonant phonemes

In the eastern literary language of Mari, there are 19 consonant phonemes whereas the western literary language has 23 (table 2). Dialectally, more consonant phonemes occur, especially palatalised.

The western Mari consonant phonemes *f*, *t́* and *χ* are comparatively late and less frequent phonemes. According to Alhoniemi (1985: 16–17) they occur mainly in words of Chuvash origin and in onomatopoetic words, c.f. *əfəläš* 'to blow', *pərχäš* 'to spray' and *pat́a* 'lamb'.

Of the phonemes mentioned, it is probably only *χ* that can be said to be a copy of a Chuvash consonant phoneme. The phoneme *f* is not an original consonant phoneme in Chuvash, it occurs mainly in words of Russian origin (Krueger 1961: 84). As for the palatalised *t́*, the picture is not entirely clear. In western Mari, it occurs in words of Chuvash origin, c.f. MaMo *äťä* 'father', *paťa* 'lamb' (Räsänen 1920: 19–20) but the character of the Chuvash phoneme is uncertain. According to Krueger (1961: 82), *ť* is an allophone of *t* or the result of metathesis. Neither Benzing (1959b: 708) nor Clark (1998: 435) seem to count *ť* as a separate phoneme in Chuvash. It is probable that the palatalisation of *t* in Mari and Chuvash is the result of influence from some other language, in all likelihood Russian (Róna-Tas 1988: 773).

Of the phonemes mentioned, it is thus only *χ* that with certainty can be described as a copy of a Chuvash model, since it occurs mainly in global copies of Chuvash words. The words in the western dialects in which the phoneme occur all belong to the first of the categories discussed in the previous section, 3.2.1.1.2, full vowels. The fact that these words all contain a secondary consonant phoneme indicates that they are all later copies, which have undergone less phonological restructuring as a result of an increased competence in Chuvash.

3.2.2 Stress

Bereczki (1994: 143–145) gives a detailed account of the stress patterns in Mari. At present, three different stress patterns exist in Mari, according to Bereczki: Stress on the last full vowel, stress on the penultimate syllable and stress on the last syllable.

3.2.2.1 Stress on the last full vowel

Stress on the last full vowel is, according to Bereczki (1994: 144), characteristic of the main part of the Mari language area, that is MaMe, the largest of the dialects in terms of number of speakers. Bereczki points to the fact that this is the predominant stress pattern in the Viryal dialect of Chuvash and in the Chuvash literary language. Bereczki is of the opinion that such similarities in the stress patterns between two languages, which for centuries have been in close contact with each other, can not be the result of chance. The fact that it is the northern dialect of Chuvash, where it is possible to count with Finno-Ugric substratum influence, in which this type of stress is the predominant one makes it possible to conclude that this is a Mari feature in ChuvV. In what follows, Bereczki tries to prove that it is the other way around and that Mari has copied a stress pattern of a Chuvash type. Bereczki bases the discussion on a couple of examples from the variety of MaE called the Vyatka subdialect—which according to him is archaic in many respects—and argues in favour of the possibility of seeing the traces of an original initial stress in Mari. In this way, Mari would once have been similar to other Finno-Ugric languages, such as Finnish and Hungarian. The type of stress characteristic of ChuvV can according to Bereczki be connected to sound changes in what he calls Middle Bulgar, in which reduced vowels occurred in a word final position, vowels that could not carry stress. Bereczki claims that the several hundred words of Chuvash origin in Mari and the qualified bilingualism among the Mari has facilitated the copying of a stress pattern of a Chuvash type. This process has been further facilitated by the fact that there are—according to Bereczki—only minor differences in the sound systems of Chuvash and Mari. Bereczki (1994: 145) also states that very little has been published on stress in Chuvash and that further studies can make a significant contribution in this respect.

Here, some remarks can be made. It is highly likely that the predominant stress pattern in Mari, stress on the last full vowel, can be linked to Chuvash influence if we see to the great number of global copies of Chuvash words in Mari and to the wide-spread bilingualism among the Mari. The social relations between the peoples have been of a kind that makes this even more probable. But the fact that it is the Viryal dialect of Chuvash in which this stress pattern is predominant could perhaps be explained in another way. Johanson (2000: 175–176) points to the fact that the reduced vowels in the first syllable in Chuvash are not the result of systematic sound changes as in other Turkic languages and that they possibly are linked to pronounciation habits of speakers of Finno-Ugric languages, carried over to the variety of Volga Bulgar they switched to speaking. Since the reduced vowels—albeit not reduced vowels of the first syllable—play an important role in the dominant stress pattern in Mari as well as in Chuvash, the possibility of Mari influence on Chuvash in this respect can not be excluded. Further studies of stress in Chuvash could, as Bereczki claims, perhaps help to clarify the picture. It could be mentioned that in Chuvash, as in Mari, the reduced vowels remain unaccented. If a word contains only reduced vowels, the stress falls on the first syllable both in Mari and Chuvash.

3.2.2.2 Stress on the penultimate syllable

According to Bereczki (1994: 143), stress on the penultimate syllable is a characteristic of the western dialects of Mari. In an earlier published paper, Bereczki (1988: 340) states that this is a "Verallgemeinerung des häufigstens Betonungsmunster'. I cannot judge the foundation on which this statement is based. MaMo and MaNw are frequently singled out for mention as examples of dialects under a strong Chuvash influence, but when it comes to the stress they differ dramatically both from MaMe and from ChuvV and have developed in their own way. The existing material on stress in the western dialects is scant and Bereczki (1994) does not discuss the problem in detail.

3.2.2.3 Stress on the last syllable

Stress on the last syllable in Mari is, according to Bereczki (1994: 143), the type of stress connected with the least problems. Bereczki refers to an article by E. Itkonen, in which stress on the last syllable in Udmurt is said to be the result of Tatar influence. According to E. Itkonen (1955: 10), the same applies to the eastern diaelcts of Mari, in which the last syllable is stressed. Stress on the last syllable can without any problem be said to be a selective copy of a Tatar model. In Tatar, stress generally falls on the last syllable, with the exception of certain unaccented suffixes such as the imperative forms of the 2nd person singular, some copula suffixes and the negative suffix *-mA*. Postpositions and enclitic particles are unaccented, and the same applies to the second member of compound words (Berta 1998b: 284). In Mari, this way of stressing is apparently not fully carried out, since the stress in some dialects—for instance in the so-called Ufa dialect—can fall on the penultimate syllable. In general, however, it is only the plural suffix *-βlak* that remains unaccented (Bereczki 1994: 143). The relevance of the stress patterns as a criterion for separating the Mari dialects can be questioned, since these stress patterns can vary within varieties of a single dialect, in this case MaE. The conclusion that stress on the last syllable is a copy of a Tatar model seems well founded, however, and in my opinion it is the best example of all of a phonological code-copy in Mari. It is a selective copy, since a phonological feature has been transferred to the basic code.

3.2.3 Vowel harmony

It seems as if it is a generally accepted opinion within Finno-Ugric linguistics that stress on the first syllable and vowel harmony are ancient features of the Uralic languages (Wickmann 1962: 671). Both stress on the first syllable and vowel harmony are features relevant for the discussion of the Turkic influence on Mari. According to Décsy (1990: 36), the term vowel harmony is comprehensive and can cover many disparate phenomena in different languages. According to Comrie (1988: 454–455), by vowel harmony is understood a rule according to which all vowels of a word "must belong to a number of partitions of the overall vowel system". In Uralic languages, the most common type of vowel harmony is the palatal-velar type, in which all vowels in a given word are either front or back. Labial vowel harmony, in which all vowels of a word are either rounded or unrounded plays a significantly smaller roll in Uralic languages (Comrie 1988: 455). According to Décsy (1990: 36), the labial vowel harmony occurring for instance in Hungarian and Mari, cannot be assumed to be an ancient feature of the Uralic languages since labial vowels did not occur in non-initial syllables in PU.

The palatal-velar vowel harmony can be said to be a salient structural feature of many Uralic languages, and occurs in most Baltic Finnic languages with the exception of Estonian and Livonian. Furthermore, it occurs also in Hungarian and certain dialects of Khanty (Comrie 1988: 455). Even in some dialects of Mari, vowel harmony is a characteristic feature, especially of the palatal-velar type, but in some cases also of the labial type.

In MaMe and in the eastern literary language, vowel harmony does not exist at all. Serebrennikov (1976: 35–40) has studied the disappearance of vowel harmony from Mari and the Permian languages. Serebrennikov arrives at the conclusion that the loss of vowel harmony has been a gradual process, mainly caused by an increasing frequency of reduced vowels in the first syllable, followed by an increase in the frequency of reduced vowels also in non-initial syllables.

In other varieties of Mari, two types of vowel harmony can be distinguished, labial and palatal-velar vowel harmony. Bereczki (1994: 137–152) gives a detailed account of the problem of vowel harmony in Mari. This account is characterised by a number of examples but comparatively few references. A characteristic feature of both types of vowel harmony in Mari is that they are not always fully carried out and that they do not always coincide with dialect borders. As a result of this, it might be questioned whether vowel harmony is a suitable criterion for the subdivision of Mari dialects. In some dialects, both types of vowel harmony occur, and in others, a palatal-velar vowel harmony occurs with some vowel phonemes but not with others (Bereczki 1994: 139).

3.2.3.1 Labial vowel harmony

According to Kuznetsova (1996: 235), the labial vowel harmony has developed under Tatar influence. Labial vowel harmony has, according to Bereczki (1994: 137–138), a limited distribution and seems concentrated to the eastern dialects. In some dialects, there is a labial vowel harmony in word final position after certain vowel phonemes: after *o*, *u* and *o* occurs and *ü* is followed by either *ö* or *ü*, c.f. *nuδo* 'Schwägerin', *šülö* 'Schoss' (Bereczki 1994: 137). In most dialects, these vowel phonemes remain unaccented, which is an indication of their secondary character. According to Bereczki (1994: 138), it is possible to find traces of a palatal-velar vowel harmony in these dialects, this, however, is not a characteristic feature according to Bereczki. The term "trace" is perhaps less well chosen since it implies the existence of a palatal-velar vowel harmony in older stages of Mari.

As for the labial vowel harmony, Bereczki (1994: 138) states that it is a recent development and that its distribution is restricted to an area immediately to the north of the Mari-Tatar linguistic boundary. However, Bereczki maintains that it is not possible to speak of a direct Tatar influence on Mari in this respect since analogous processes do not occur in Tatar. The labial vowel harmony in Mari originates in a labialisation of reduced vowels in a word final position, c.f. *nuδo* 'Schwägerin' < *nuδə̑* 'id'. In what follows, however, Bereczki (1994: 138) states that the Tatar labial vowel harmony, in which reduced vowels in non-initial syllables were labialised "machte aber ihre Wirkung bemerkbar". Since labial vowel harmony played a restricted role in the Uralic Protolanguage, and labial vowel harmony is a characteristic feature of many Turkic languages—but not Chuvash (Krueger 1961: 74)—this seems like a somewhat ambiguous statement. It suggests that labial vowel harmony in Mari is a result of both an inner development and Tatar influence. I find it impossible to say anything with certainty about the labial vowel harmony in Mari. It can be a selective copy of a Tatar phonological feature, but it can also be the result of an inner development in Mari. However, it is possible that the labial vowel harmony in Mari existed as a tendency, which increased in frequency as a result of intensified contacts with Tatar.

3.2.3.2 Palatal-velar vowel harmony

The second type of vowel harmony, the palatal-velar type, occurs in the western parts of the Mari language area, and in the easternmost dialects. Bereczki (1994: 138) points to the fact that western dialects without palatal-velar vowel harmony exist and that there are several types of palatal-velar vowel harmony in the eastern dialects. That there are several types of a palatal-velar vowel harmony in the eastern dialects is a seldom discussed and rarely clearly defined phenomenon in the literature on the palatal-velar vowel harmony in Mari. In what follows, I will only discuss the main characteristics of Bereczki's description of the situation.

The palatal-velar vowel harmony, according to Bereczki, is in all likelihood a result of both Tatar and Chuvash influence. The palatal-velar vowel harmony of MaMo has a direct counterpart in Chuvash (Bereczki 1994: 142). In a Chuvash word, the order of vowels is regulated by the rules of vowel harmony, as in other Turkic languages (Benzing 1959b: 703), and the vowels in a Chuvash word stem are consequently either front or back vowels. In derived words, the same principles apply, with the exception of a small set of suffixes. Among these are (in the literary language, but not in ChuvV) the plural suffix *-sem*. Other suffixes not following the rules of vowel harmony are the possessive suffix of the third person singular *-ĕ, -i,* the attributive suffix *-i* and certain adverb formants such as *-len* and *-seren*. A small set of words denoting kinship such as *atte* 'father', *anne* 'mother' (Clark 1998: 436) do not obey the rules of vowel harmony. In ChuvV, front and back allomorphs of some of these suffixes occur, c.f. the plural ending *-sem, -sam*, ChuvV *yalsam* 'villages', *annesem* 'mothers'.

The palatal-velar vowel harmony in the eastern dialects of Mari has developed under Tatar influence, and has also led to the emergence of a secondary vowel phoneme *ä* in certain positions, c.f. the plural marker *-βlak, -βläk* and the dative suffix *-lan, -län*. In Tatar, this type of vowel harmony is more systematic than in Chuvash: in a word stem only front or back vowels can occur, and the same applies to derived or inflected words to which derivational suffixes or case endings are added. The only type of words not fully obeying the rules of vowel harmony is compund words. As for words of foreign origin, the vowel or vowels in suffixes are dependent on the last vowel of the stem, c.f. *telefonnar* 'telephones' (Poppe 1963: 15–16).

Given the existence of a palatal-velar vowel harmony in the western and eastern dialects of Mari, and the absence of a systematic palatal-velar vowel harmony in MaMe (spoken in the central parts of the Mari language area), it seems possible to conclude that the palatal-velar vowel harmony in Mari is the result of both Tatar and Chuvash influence. But it is interesting to note that it is the northern dialect of Chuvash, ChuvV, which is characterised by the existence of front and back allomorphs of certain suffixes. In the southern dialect, ChuvA and the Chuvash literary language, only one form of some suffixes occurs. Even though Chuvash has exerted a considerable influence on Mari, we cannot totally exclude the possibility that the systematic palatal-velar vowel harmony in MaMo originates in a phonological feature preserved in this dialect and that the phonology of ChuvV has been influenced by MaMo in this respect. In this case, the principle of "lateral areas", areas in which older features of a language have been preserved, would be applicable (see Korhonen 1986). Another possibility is of course that the palatal-velar vowel harmony in ChuvV is the original one and that ChuvA has undergone change, although not to the same extent as MaMe.

The data given by Bereczki can be summarized in the following way: the dialects lacking a systematic vowel harmony (of both types), spoken by the majority of the population, can be considered the most unchanged in this respect. Labial vowel harmony is the result of an inner development, in spite of the fact that it is restricted to an area bordering on the Tatar language area and that labial vowel harmony exists in Tatar. The palatal-velar vowel harmony is, depending on dialect, the result of Tatar and Chuvash influence. I find it likely that it is only the palatal-velar vowel harmony in the eastern dialects that with certainty can be said to be a selective copy of a Tatar phonological feature. The palatal-velar vowel harmony in MaMo, on the other hand deserves a detailed study that makes comparisons with the palatal-velar vowel harmony in Chuvash.

4 Morphological code-copies

In their morphology, Mari and the Turkic languages are similar in many ways. Mari, Tatar and Chuvash all have an agglutinating morphology, and they all possess a large number of derivative endings, by use of which substantives, adjectives and verbs are formed. There are also similarities between the languages in the sense that they all make frequent use of enclitics and other particles.

4.1 Particles

The term particle is comprehensive and can cover several different types of morphemes. As will become evident, many scholars, especially in Mari linguistics do not define the term particle and frequently the term particle is used for any kind of uninflecting word, including adverbs, conjunctions and postpositions. I too will refrain from a proper definition of the term and just account for the different morphemes regarded as particles in a broad sense in Mari.

In Mari, a particular morpheme can be used as an emphasizing particle in some contexts, and in others it can be used as a disjunctive conjunction or a postposition. As was indicated above, one scholar in Mari linguistics may define a certain morpheme as a particle whereas another defines it as a postposition. Thus it may be hard to draw a line between the morphology and syntax of a language and Collinder's (1962: 247) statement that the lexicon, morphology and syntax of a language are closely connected to each other is worth emphasizing. The varied contexts in which the Mari morphemes occur, makes it hard to categorize them properly since they can acquire many different morphological and syntactic functions. An example of this is the morpheme *βara* 'later, then' which can function as an interrogative or emphasizing particle, but also as an adverb or a postposition. Many of the Mari morphemes falling into this rather vaguely defined class of particles are copies of Turkic morphemes which, as will become evident, in Tatar and Chuvash can function as particles in some contexts and as adverbs in other. In Tatar and Chuvash too, a morpheme filling the function of a particle or adverb can be used as a postposition, and they may be geminated to serve as disjunctive conjunctions. This means that many of the particles in Mari copied from the Turkic languages will be discussed also in Chapter 5, Syntactic code-copies.

In the Turkic languages, there are several morphemes labelled as particles. According to Thomsen (1959: 420) most of the Tatar particles are emphatic ("hervorhebende") and in some way emphasize the meaning of the word to which they are added. In what Thomsen refers to as "verstärkendem Sinne", these particles can become diminutive or comparative suffixes. The particles can be added to words in all word categories. Thomsen gives the following examples of particles in Tatar: *-γına/ -qına, ber genä* 'nur einer', *yazıp qına* 'er schrieb nur'; *-ta/ -da, mindä* 'eben ich'; *-dır/ -tır, kem* 'wer', *kemder* 'irgendwer', *ul kilgän* 'er ist gekommen', *ul kilgänder* 'er ist wahrscheinlich gekommen' (Thomsen 1959: 420).

Benzing (1959b: 749–750) lists the morphemes that in Chuvash are regarded as particles. According to Benzing (1959b: 749) the term particle is a vague term which comprises a number of uninflected "Hilfswörter", which when used have the character of enclitics. According to Benzing, neither the exact function nor the origin of the particle is clear in every case, but mostly these particles are what Benzing (1959b: 749) refers to as "hervorhebende, verallgemeinernde, einschränkende u.ä. Partikeln".

Many of the particles that will be discussed below are not restricted to Mari. Karpova (1995) has shown that many of them occur also in Udmurt and that they originate in the Turkic languages. The Mari particle *γə̑na* 'only, just' corresponds to the Udmurt particle *gine* 'id'; the Mari particle *δə̑r, tə̑r* corresponds to Udmurt *də̑r*, and Udm *olo* has a parallel in the Mari particle *ala, älä*. In both Mari and Udmurt, these particles have been copied from Tatar.

4.1.1 The particle MaE *-ak, -ok*, MaMe *-ak,* MaMo, MaNw *-ok*

According to Galkin (1964: 183), the particle *-ak, -ok* is an emphasizing particle that occurs in all dialects of Mari. Saarinen (1986: 37) claims that the particle is of Chuvash origin. A problem, according to Saarinen, is the differences in vocalism between MaMo and MaMe, to which no acceptable explanation has been given. Galkin (1964: 184) argues that the MaMo *-ok* could be of Tatar origin in MaMo, whereas the MaMe *-ak* could be ascribed to Chuvash influence. Saarinen (1986: 38) sees this as improbable from a chronological perspective, "denn es gibt kaum Wörter, die aus dem Tatarischen nur in das Westtscheremissische entlehnt worden wären". Both Galkin (1964: 184) and Saarinen (1986: 37) point to the fact that the form *-ok* occurs also in the eastern dialect of Mari. In MaMo, the particle can carry stress, which is surprising since stress generally does not fall on the last syllable in this dialect. In the eastern dialects, *-ak, -ok* is generally stressed. The Mari particle has no meaning of its own, it is used emphatically or to designate simultaneity or identity (Saarinen 1986: 39). It is clearly an enclitic particle since case and plural endings precede it. According to Saarinen (1986: 38), the particle is so well integrated into the language system that it must constitute a suffix of comparatively high age in Mari. Below, only examples from MaMo, in which the particle is most frequent, are given. The particle can be added to substantives and reflexive pronouns:

MaMo jara, kelesəš kornə̑št-ok, əńə məńəm pušteš əľə 'Wahrlich, sie hat's unterwegs gesagt, jetzt hätte sie mich erschlagen' (Beke 1951: 151).

MaMo *ti sapľə̑ məńən ške-ok ik minutə̑štə̑ šüδö təžəm eδeməm roen kerδeš* 'Dieses Schwert ist imstande, ganz allein, in einer Minute hunderttausend Menschen niederzumetzeln' (Beke 1951: 184)

The particle can also be added to gerunds and imperative forms of the verb:

MaMo *olʹicäštə kə̂δə̂žə̂ katajat, mə̂rə̂*[*m:* Ö. B.] *mə̂rat, βara mə̂rə̂ mə̂ren-ok keät tokə̂štə̂* 'Auf der Gasse treiben manche die Pferde auf und ab, sie singen und singend fahren sie nachhause' (Beke 1951: 80)

The particle can further be added to the conjunction *δon* and to adverbs:

MaMo *keδä ti γornə̂ δon-ok* 'Geht nur auf diesem Weg' (Beke 1951: 166)

MaMo *məń kəzət-ok tə γuγižäm lə̂pfšen goδem* 'Ich werde jenen König sofort niederschlagen' (Beke 1951: 198)

In Chuvash, there is a particle that has formal and functional resemblances with the Mari particle *-ak, -ok*. In Chuvash, the particle *-aχ, -eχ* is a very frequent "intensifying particle" (Krueger 1961: 171). In Chuvash, most particles are enclitic and do not carry stress, but *-aχ, -eχ*—used emphatically—can be stressed in some cases (Krueger 1961: 171). According to Krueger, the particle is not separated from the main word by use of a hyphen, and this is the case in the material that I have examined. The particle has combinatorial properties similar to that of the Mari particle *-ak, -ok* and occurs with words in nearly every word category. It is added to substantives and reflexive pronouns:

ChuvA *untan χăvărtraχ ăyri patne kaynăta utlansa alăkranaχ tuχsa tarnă* 'Dann begab er sich eilig zu seinem Hengst, stieg auf und ritt durch die Tür hinaus und floh' (Paasonen 1949: 130)

ChuvA *śapla kalasanaχ vitrisem χăysemeχ kile šusa kaynă* 'Sobald er diese Worte gesprochen hatte, gingen die Eimer ganz von selbst nach Hause' (Paasonen 1949: 108)

The particle can be added to gerunds and imperative forms of the verbs:

ChuvA *śapla kalasanaχ vitrisem χăysemeχ kile šusa kaynă* 'Sobald er diese Worte gesprochen hatte, gingen die Eimer ganz von selbst nach Hause' (Paasonen 1949: 108)

ChuvA *aχ, ăstarik, χăvărtraχ pusaχ, viletĕp* 'Ach, Mann, schlachte denn eiligst, ich sterbe [...]' (Paasonen 1949: 191)

The particle can further be added to the so-called "instrumental relational morpheme" (Krueger 1961: 108–110) with the endings *-pa, -pe*. This ending corresponds functionally to the Mari conjunction *δon*, expressing the instrument by use of which an action takes place, or the actual place of the action:

ChuvA *śapla valiśe χaχla pavuskipeχ külle yarsa vilernĕ* 'So schleppte der Hirt Valis mit dem Wagen in den See und tötete ihn' (Paasonen 1949: 137)

The particle can also be added to adverbs:

ChuvA *χĕr tuχnăta pĕččeneχ kaynă* 'Das Mädchen machte sich auf und ging allein' (Paasonen 1949: 148)

In my opinion, the Chuvash origin of this particle cannot be doubted. In Tatar, a particle *-uk, -ük* meaning 'exactly' (Poppe 1963: 85) does occur, but in the Tatar material that I have examined it has a very low frequency, which makes it even more probable that the Mari particle is copied from Chuvash. The Mari particle *-ak, -ok* is possible to classify as a global copy, but the varied contexts in which it occurs can be labelled as mixed copies, since also the combinatorial properties of this particle have been selectively copied (see also Saarinen 1997b: 393). It is also possible to classify the particle as a conventionalised copy since it occurs in texts published in both literary languages of Mari:

MaEL *ergə̂čə̂m erlak kuγə̂ža δeke pokten kolto* 'Send your son to the Tzar tomorrow' (Taygiljdin 1993: 53)

MaWL *toštə̂ semə̂ń-ok ə̂laš tüŋalə̂na!* 'Let's start living in the old way!' (Petukhov 1994: 71)

4.1.2 The particle MaMe, MaE *-at,* MaMo, MaNw *-at, -ät*

The particle MaMe, MaE *-at,* MaMo, MaNw *-at, -ät* has a meaning that corresponds to the Finnish particle *-kin* 'too' and conjunction *ja* 'and' (Alhoniemi 1985: 75). Galkin (1964: 184) emphasizes that it is a particle with a wide distribution, occurring in all dialects of Mari, and that it has an emphasizing function, occasionally also the function of a conjunction. Galkin claims that there are no direct equivalents of the particle, either in other Finno-Ugric languages or in Turkic languages. However, Galkin draws attention to a morpheme *t* in the Ugric languages Hungarian and Mansi. According to Galkin, this morpheme and the Mari particle could have a common origin, the Mari particle thus being a Finno-Ugric one. Gordeev (1979: 160) differs between the emphatically used particle *-at, -ät* and the one used as a conjunction, but is apparently of the opinion that both have an Indo-Iranian origin. This inclination of Gordeev to explain many of the particles in Mari as elements originating in the Indo-Iranian languages is problematic from a chronological point of view. Words from Indo-Iranian languages do occur in the Mari vocabulary, although direct evidence for the copying of particles does remain scant.

The question of the origin of the emphasizing particle MaMe, MaE *-at*, MaMo, MaNw *-at, -ät* is complicated for several reasons. It has an emphasizing function but can also be used as a conjunction and in this regard it has similarities with the Mari conjunction *δa, δä* 'and' which according to Galkin (1964: 177) is of Russian origin.

Moisio (1993) gives a detailed account of the morphemes *-at* and *δa* and similar morphemes in the Turkic languages and in Russian. Moisio (1993: 74) is of the opinion that the Russian *da* used as a conjunction is of what he refers to as 'a different kind' than the Mari *-at* and *δa* and the morpheme *da* in the Turkic languages. According to Moisio, the Mari particle *-at* and the morpheme *δa* in the Turkic languages have many common characteristics and Moisio arrives at the conclusion that Ma *-at* and *δa* are variants of one and the same morpheme which have become separated for different reasons. Moisio (1993: 76) states that the Mari morphemes *-at* and *δa* have the following characteristic features in common:

1) Both are originally particles: *-at* has the basic function of a particle, but also *δa* has originally had this function, a fact that according to Moisio is evident in older dialect texts. In the modern literary languages, *δa* is written as a separate word, but in older texts it is added to the main word by use of a hyphen. It is perhaps possible to see Russian influence on Mari in this respect since the Russian *da* is always written as a separate word. 2) The particles *-at* and *δa* are always stressed, no matter how long the word is to which they are added: Moisio makes the assumption that either the stressed particle *-at* has become separated from the main word and emerged as an element of its own, or it is the case that an older morpheme **tä* has been added to the stem and then acquired a new morphological shape for phonetic reasons. 3) Parallel forms occur, without any change in meaning, e.g. *manešta—manešat* 'said and…'. 4) The difference in vocalism between MaMo and MaMe is a Chuvash feature: MaMe *-at* and *δa* corresponds to MaMo *-at, -ät* and *δa, δä*. The original form in Mari can, according to Moisio have been **tä*, the vowel *ä* subsequently changing into *a* in MaMe. Here, I will refrain from a detailed discussion of whether an original *ä* has changed to *a* in MaMe (my opinion on this is presented in section 3.2.1.1.2) and instead focus on other interesting circumstances. As will become evident in several of the following sections, a characteristic feature of several of the particles in Mari that have been copied from the Turkic languages is that they can function not only as emphasizing particles but also as disjunctive conjunctions. It is therefore perhaps worthwile to make comparisons between the Mari morphemes *-at* and *δä* with their equivalents in the Turkic languages.

The particle MaMe, MaE *-at*, MaMo, MaNw *-at, -ät* is added to words in all word categories in Mari, for example to pronouns:

MaMo *tǝń-ät mǝńǝn erγǝm ǝlat* 'Auch du bist mein Sohn' (Beke 1951: 153)

MaNw *ik erγǝnä ül'ü, tüδ-ät jamǝ* 'Wir hatten [bloss; Ö. B.] einen Sohn, [und; Ö. B.] auch der ist umgekommen' (Beke 1957: 35)

MaMe *ej tǝ̂jat, ik sösnat ten čǝ̂la ješetǝ̂m puštǝ̂n pǝ̂taršǝ̂č* 'Wehe dir, wegen deinem einen Schwein hast du deine Ganze Familie umgebracht' (Alhoniemi & Saarinen 1983: 62)

MaE *tǝ̂je (tǝ̂ńe) puštun pǝ̂taret kǝ̂n, mǝ̂j-at oš kečǝ̂ške lektǝ̂na [ǝ̂]l'e tǝ̂j (tǝ̂ń) δenet* 'Wenn du ihn tötest, möchten auch wir mit dir an die Oberwelt gehen' (Beke 1961b: 414)

The particle *-at* is also added to substantives:

MaMo *näläš marə̑-βəlä-ät kəcken tolə̑t süän tomaškə̑* 'Auch die Leute spannen ein, die die Braut zu holen gekommen sind, und gehen ins Hochzeitshaus' (Beke 1951: 64)

MaNw *šužet tə̑k, urža kind-ät kalac liješ* 'Bist du hungrig, so mundet die Kornbrot wie das Weizenbrot' (Beke 1957: 22)

The particle is also added to verbs:

MaE *jeŋ lüδeš-at kuδaleš* 'Der Mann erschrickt und beginnt zu laufen' (Beke 1961b: 398)

If we leave the emphasizing, conjunctive particle *-at* and turn to the conjunction *δa*, this too is found in similar contexts. This conjunction MaMe, MaE *δa*, MaMo, MaNw *δa, δä* connects sentences and is frequently added to verbs:

MaMo *βara marə̑ kə̑rək βəlecən βala-δä keä ruš tokə̑ jaδaš, təδə kuzen ili uke kə̑rək βəlkə* 'Nun steigt er vom Berge herab, geht zum Russen, zu erfragen, ob er auf dem Berg gewesen, oder nicht?' (Beke 1951: 54)

MaNw *ik alašam kackes, kackes δä jäsläš puren βazeš—küzü* 'Mein Wallach frisst [und; Ö. B.] frisst und legt sich [dann; Ö. B.] in die Krippe—Das [Taschen; Ö. B.] Messer' (Beke 1957: 22)

MaMe *kuβa δen kuγza kelšat ta üδə̑ržə̑n šoβə̑čə̑m puat* 'Frau und Mann willigen ein und geben (dem Freier) ein Tuch des Mädchens' (Alhoniemi & Saarinen 1983: 30)

MaE *βuβer kuγuza šürüžüm pörök poδə̑lə̑n neleš ta lektə̑n kaja* 'Der βuβer-Alte verschlingt die Suppe auf einen Zug, geht hinaus und entfernt sich' (Beke 1961b: 408)

The conjunction *δa, δä* is frequently added to verbs in the second preterite tense, in Mari a tense used to express actions and events not witnessed by the speaker, it is thus mainly a narrative tense:

MaMo *iziš loen kaštə̑n-dä kolə̑m ńi-ma-t kə̑čen ker[t]te* 'Er fischt eine kurze Weile, kann aber keinen einzigen Fisch fangen' (Beke 1951: 48)

MaNw *ir γoδə̑m teδə paškuδo maret kəńələn dä iδəməškəžə lektə̑n* 'Morgens stand der Nachbar auf und ging auf die Tenne (hinaus)' (Beke 1957: 54)

MaMe *kunam βatə̑žə̑ pisman mariž δeč naln, luδə̑n ta βik šortə̑n koltə̑n* 'Als die Frau von ihrem Mann den Brief bekam, las sie ihn und brach direkt in Weinen aus' (Alhoniemi & Saarinen 1983: 96)

MaE *tuδum kolə̑n δa koŋg[a;* Ö. B.]*-ümbäč rüšt šokten müγürälten opśam komδə̑k βiš koδen lektə̑n kuržun* '[Die Frau; Ö. B.] hörte das und plumps, sprang sie schreiend vom Ofen herab, liess die Tür sperrangelweit offen und stürmte hinaus' (Beke 1961b: 176)

Occasionally, the conjunction *δa, δä* is added to the imperative form of the verbs:

MaMo *ir γoδə̂m taβarə̂m näl-δä kuzə̂ kə̂rə̂k βəlkə oksa zikəm βärəškə* 'Am Morgen nimm eine Axt, steig auf den Berg, an die Stelle, wo das Geld verborgen ist' (Beke 1951: 54)

MaMo *təńə kə̂δal mi-δä loγal γoltə̂!* 'Du lauf [nur; Ö. B.] und stoss ihn mit deinen Hörnern' (Beke 1951: 94)

The conjunction *δa, δä* is also added to substantives to connect sentences:

MaMo *päləm eδem-dä roalaš lüδən* 'Der Mann war ihm ein Bekannter und so traute er sich nicht, ihn zu erschlagen' (Beke 1951: 54)

MaNw *məń eše näləδəšəm kalacə̂m δa ma δa, cəlä oksam kucultum* 'Ich kaufte noch Weizenbrot [und; Ö. B.] dergleichen und gab mein ganzes Geld aus' (Beke 1957: 11)

In the Turkic languages, there are morphemes that formally and functionally have a close resemblance with the Mari particle *-at, -ät* and the conjunction *δa δä*. In Tatar, the particle *-dÄ, -tÄ* is a postpositional particle meaning 'and, as well as'. In Poppe (1963: 86) only one example is given:

TaT *bıel arıš ta boday da yaχšı uńdı* 'this year rye as well as wheat has grown well'

In the material that I have examined the particle occurs as an emphasizing particle which is added to pronouns:

TatM *miña ber närsä-dä kiräkmiy* 'Ich brauche nichts' (Kakuk 1996: 59)

The particle is also frequently added to substantives:

TatK *kuš-ta sayramiy, at-ta pičen ǯim ašemėy* 'Auch der Vogel singt nicht und auch das Pferd isst weder Heu noch Hafer' (Kakuk 1989: 14)

The particle *-dÄ, -tÄ* can adopt the function of a conjunction in Tatar (Poppe 1963: 128). This too is evident from the material that I have examined:

TatM *üze karzinkaga tükeräder-dä altïn alïp kiräder* 'Dieserund spie in den Korb und aus dem Auswurf wurde eine Goldmünze' (Kakuk 1996: 70)

In Tatar, the particle can also be added to the imperative form of verbs:

TatK *muna üzėñ yat-ta dürt batėr kėz sinėñ üstüñde küterėp tursunnar* 'Jetzt aber legt dich hin, vier starken Mädchen sollen mich über dich halten' (Kakuk 1989: 20)

Chuvash too is a language that provides much material for comparison when it comes to the Mari particle *-at, -ät* and the conjunction *δa, δä*. There are several morphemes in Chuvash functioning as conjunctions (Krueger 1961: 170). Adamovič (1985: 81–84) has discussed the Chuvash particle *ta, te* which according to him has three basic functions. It is used in the formation of indefinite pronouns, but it can also function as conjunction. According to Krueger (1961: 170) it is a connective conjunction. The particle *ta, te* can furthermore be geminated, e.g. *ta…ta…, te…te…* and then serve as a disjunctive conjunction with the meaning 'either…or…'. Adamovič claims that *ta, te* is rarely used as an emphasizing particle. In the material I have examined, however, the morpheme *ta, te* is very frequent in this context.

The particle *ta, te* can be added to personal pronouns:

ChuvA *epĕte kursa laram* 'Ich [auch] werde dasitzen und zusehen' (Paasonen 194: 228)

It is further added to the so-called coordinate converb with the ending *-sa, -se*:

ChuvA *śapla kalasa larnă śĕre kupsa ıvălin ilmeyurin aslamăšĕ pavuskapa pırsata kĕnĕ* 'Während er mit solchen Worten dasass, kam die Grossmutter des Kaufmanssohnes Ilmeyur in einem Fuhrwagen herangefahren und trat ein' (Paasonen 1949: 249)

Another characteristic occurrence of the particle in Chuvash is with the so-called perfect participle, ending in *-nă, -nĕ*. In the material I have examined, this is very frequent. According to Krueger (1961: 153) this participle is "a non-eyewitness form" and when used predicatively in a tense-like function, it often has a narrative meaning, especially in folktales. This participle thus corresponds functionally to the second preterite tense in Mari:

ChuvA *untan larnă śĕrteχ üsĕrĕlse kaynăta yurlasa yara panĕ* 'Während er so sass, wurde er betrunken und fing zu singen an' (Paasonen 1949: 153)

The particle *ta, te* can also occur with the imperative form of the verb:

ChuvA *esĕr ăna śitsen śavărsa iľirte tapranaymi tăviččen χĕnese urapi śine χursa yarăr, tenĕ* 'Packt ihn und, nachdem ihr ihn unbewegelich gemacht habt, prügelt ihn und lasst ihm in Wagen wegfahren' (Paasonen 1949: 140–141)

I find it likely that both the particle MaMe, MaE *-at*, MaMo, MaNw *-at, -ät* and the conjunction MaMo, MaNw *δa, δä,* MaMe, MaE *δa* are copied from a Turkic language. Given the large similarities in form and function of the conjunction *δa, δä* in Mari and its counterparts in the Turkic languages, it is not this morpheme that calls for an explanation but rather the emphasizing particle MaMe, MaE *-at*, MaMo, MaNw *-at, -ät*. Moisio's assumption that the particle goes back to an original form **tä* is principally correct but it may be argued that the original form was **ta* and not **tä* if it is the vocalism in MaMo that is secondary, and not the vocalism in MaMe (see section 3.2.1.1.2). Moisio further assumes that the form has emerged for phonetic reasons but the possibility that it is an earlier copy than *δa, δä* and therefore differs in shape cannot be excluded. The question of Russian influence on Mari in this respect is controversial. If Moisio is right in that there are more similarities between Mari and the Turkic languages in the use of the emphasizing and conjunctive morphemes *-at, -ät* and *δa, δä* it can be argued that the Russian influence is secondary, if it exists at all. In this particular case, the material representative of MaNw that I have examined has a lot to offer. In the MaNw material, collected from a prisoner of war named Nikolay Akhtulov from the village Ot'ə̂k-sala (Otyukovo) in the Jaransk area, included in the collections of Beke (1957: 6–63), I have found nine examples in which the conjunction *δa, δä* occurs. The emphasizing particle *-at, -ät* is not very frequent either, it occurs 15 times, often in connection with negative indefinite pronouns. Given the fact that this dialect has had the most extensive contacts with Russian of all the dialects of Mari, the number of occurrences of the conjunction *δa, δä* is surprisingly low, if it is copied from Russian. In the material representative of MaNw collected by Beke, the conjunction *i* 'and' is far more frequent, and this conjunction is undoubtedly copied from Russian. The material shows that this conjunction in MaNw seems to fill the same functions as *δa, δä* in the other dialects. In the material from MaNw, the conjunction *i* 'and' occurs no less than 88 times, that is almost 10 times as often as the conjunction *δa, δä*.

In the MaMe material that I have examined, both the conjunction *i* 'and', copied from Russian, and the conjunction *δa*, in all likelihood copied from the Turkic languages, occur:

MaMe *"jöra" maneš i kaja* 'Gut, sagt er und geht' (Alhoniemi &Saarinen 1983: 110)

MaMe *"jöra" maneš ta aδak kaja* 'Er sagt "gut" und geht weiter' (Alhoniemi & Saarinen 1983: 110)

The MaMe material also shows that the conjunctions *i* and *δa* can occur parallel to each other. Such parallel occurrences are frequent in the material and I will only give two examples:

MaMe *kuγza lačə̂m naleš ta i kaja* 'Der Alte nimmt den Ranzen und geht' (Alhoniemi & Saarinen 1983: 118)

MaMe *βara kuγu limek kuγža δek puren ulə̂t ta i oľat*: 'Als sie gross geworden wahren, gingen sie zum Zaren und sagen:' (Alhoniemi & Saarinen 1983: 124)

In the material representative of MaE, conjunctions are apparently less frequent, but it seems as if the conjunction *i* 'and' is more frequent than *δa, δä* in spite of the fact that this is the dialect of Mari which has been less exposed to Russian influence than the other dialects.

Nevertheless, I find it safe to conclude that the conjunction *δa, δä* and the emphasizing particle *-at, -ät* both have been copied from the Turkic languages and that the Russian influence later has led to the copying of a conjunction *i*. The contexts in which the conjunctions *δa, δä* and *i* occur parallel to each other are comparable to instances of copying of other conjunctions from Russian, e.g. the conjunction *jesli* 'if' which can occur parallel to the Mari conjunction *γə̂ń* 'if' (see section 1.2.1.3).

First, the emphasizing function of the particle has been copied and the copy has undergone morphological restructuring resulting in the form *-at*. This metathesis is irregular in Mari, but it should be remembered that copies can differ considerably from the original and the morphological restructuring may well include sound-changes not otherwise occurring in the language. Later on the conjunctive function of the particle has been copied, but one can assume that this has happened in stages of a more widespread bilingualism and that the copy for this reason has not undergone any morphological restructuring. In my opinion, the emphasizing particle *-at, -ät* and the conjunction *δa, δä* are globally copied from the Turkic languages and when they are added to native stems in Mari they form mixed copies, combining a globally copied morpheme with the selective copying of combinatorial properties of these morphemes. The copies are so well integrated in the Mari language that they can be classified as conventionalised copies, evidence of this being that they occur in both literary languages of Mari:

MaEL *Pajašat ala-kuze tuško mijen lektə̂n* 'Pajaš too went there in some way' (Izhboldin 1994: 15)

MaEL *pire, rə̂βə̂ž δa maska pə̂rľa sonarə̂š lektə̂nə̂t* 'The Wolf, the Fox and the Bear went hunting together' (Izhboldin 1994: 56)

MaWL *Jašpaj solaškat kə̂δal pə̂rə̂š* 'Jašpaj came running into the village' (Petukhov 1994: 60)

MaWL *sola χoza Käβri δä erγə̂žə̂ Matju* 'The village elder Käβri and his son Matju' (Petukhov 1994: 30)

Given the fact that the particle *-at, -ät* and the conjunction *δa, δä* has the highest frequency in MaMo and MaMe it is a reasonable assumption that it is Chuvash that has been the model code and that Tatar influence has played a more restricted role, although a similar morpheme exists in Tatar. Tatar influence can thus be secondary in this respect, unless we choose to see the particle *-at, -ät* as something copied from Chuvash and the conjunction *δa, δä* as an element copied from Tatar, which is a possibility that cannot be excluded. That a Russian *da* should have been copied into Mari is, in my opinion, unlikely. The conjunction *δa, δä* is not frequent in MaE, the dialect with the least extensive contacts with Russian, and the low frequence of the conjunction *δa, δä* in this dialect could in principle be interpreted as indicating that a copy of a Russian *δa* has not yet been habitualised and conventionalised. This explanation is not applicable to MaNw, though. In MaNw, the conjunction *i* 'and' is almost ten times as frequent as the conjunction *δa, δä*. This dialect is often said to be the dialect of Mari in which the number of Russian words is highest (Saarinen 1985: 197), MaNw thus exhibiting more copies from

Russian than the other dialects. Had the conjunction *δa, δä* in fact been copied from Russian, it would be logical to assume a higher frequency of the conjunction in this dialect. A far more plausible explanation of the lower frequency of the particle *-at, -ät* and the conjunction *δa, δä* in MaNw and MaE is that these dialects have lost contact with speakers of Chuvash earlier than the speakers of MaMo and MaMe, dialects which are characterised by the fact that their contacts with Chuvash have lasted up to the present day.

4.1.3 The particle MaE *laj, läj*

The particle *laj, läj* occurs rarely and is used mainly in songs, although not in all dialects (Galkin 1964: 185). It is not used in MaMo and according to Ivanov & Tuzharov (1970: 196), it does not occur in MaNw. Galkin maintains that the particle is not only used emphatically but that it has a diminutive function too. According to Ivanov & Moisio (1998: 37) the origin of the particle is uncertain, whereas Galkin (1964: 186) claims that it originates in an adjective *laj* meaning 'weak, mild'. It is correct that the particle does not occur in all dialects—it seems restricted to MaE—and that is is used mainly in songs. In the material I have examined, the particle is frequent in the songs from Bashkortostan collected by Paasonen (1939: 93–180), Wichmann (1931: 385–476) and Beke (1961b: 280–343):

MaE *βujeδə̑m-at šerat kə̑n, βiźə̑te it punal!*
Kə̑resə̑n lai üδür-ät tiń otə̑l
Kə̑resə̑n lai üδür-ät, ai, tiń otə̑l
Äpišär läi uδürleč kem otə̑l

'Wenn du dich (eig. deinen Kopf) kämst, flicht [das
Haar: Ö. B.] nicht in fünf Zöpfe,
Du bist kein Christenmädchen.
Hei, du bist kein Christenmädchen,
Du bist nich geringer als eine Offizierstochter' (Beke 1961b: 290)

In the songs from MaE, the particle occurs with pronouns:

MaE *ti-lai roδə̑lan šužə̑žə̑ uke* 'Doch gibt es keinen, der diesem Verwandten gliche' (Beke 1961a: 354)

MaE *nemnanlaj arka, jamle arka* 'Unser Berg, schöner Berg' (Paasonen 1939: 149)

The particle can also be added to adverbs and adjectives:

MaE *küšnö läi tə̑lə̑ze peš βolγə̑δo* 'Der Mond oben [scheint; Ö. B.] sehr hell' (Beke 1961b: 447)

MaE *kükšə̑laj kurə̑k bujə̑štə̑žo* 'Auf dem Gipfel des hohen Berges' (Paasonen 1939: 140).

It is furthermore added to substantives:

MaE *βatə̂laj δaŋem peš motor da jolašəžə̂ mučaštə̂* 'Meine (Frauen)geliebte ist sehr schön, aber ihre Unterhose ist im Badehaus' (Beke 1961a: 486).

MaE *pasulaj köryö užaryə̂n koješ* 'Der Acker ["das Innere des Ackers"; H. P.] sieht grün aus' (Paasonen 1939: 162)

Finally, the particle can occur with participles and gerunds:

MaE *čaj jüjšašlaj payə̂t šuə̂ldə̂n* 'Die Zeit des Teetrinkens ist gekommen' (Paasonen 1939: 176)

The particle occurs mainly in songs, but can be used also in speech:

MaE *tə̂ye lai βujžo košten kija, maneš* 'Dieser Mensch (eig. er) hat nur Kopfschmerzen' (Beke 1961b: 181)

In MaMo and MaNw, the particle is not in use at all, and the same seems to apply to MaMe. The fact that the particle is frequent in songs from Bashkortostan makes it probable that it is a copy of a Tatar particle. A more detailed study of the Tatar particles shows that the explanation given by Galkin is erroneous, and that the claim made by Ivanov & Moisio (1998: 37), that the origin of the particle is uncertain, is not correct either.

In Tatar, there are—among others—two suffixes that are used to form adverbs of manner from different types of stems. The suffix *-dÄy, -dEy*, forms adverbials of manner from substantives, adjectives and participials, e.g. *ayuday* 'in a bear-like manner': *ayu* 'bear'; *belerdey* 'as if he knows': *bel* 'to know' (Poppe 1963: 106). The suffix *-lÄy, -lEy* forms adverbials of manner when added to substantives, pronouns and adjectives, e.g. *orlıklay* 'in an embryonic stage': *orlık* 'embryo'; *bolay* 'so, in this manner': *bu* 'this'; *korılay* 'dryly': *korı* 'dry' (Poppe 1963: 106). This particle is not restricted to Tatar but occurs also in other Turkic languages, for example in Karaim (Pritsak 1959: 332) and Baskhir (Benzing 1959a: 429). In Tatar, as in Mari, the particle occurs in songs:

TatK *alay itseñ-de yarıy*
Bolay itseñ-de yarıy
Bzniñ elė yaš čayıbız
Ničik itsek-de yarıy

'Wenn du so tust, schickt es sich,
wenn du so tust, ziemt es sich;
in unserer jetzigen Jugend
schickt es sich, wie wir auch tun' (Kakuk 1980: 28)

The Mari particle *laj, läj* is in all likelihood a copy of the Tatar adverbial suffix *-lÄy, -lEy*. The fact that the Mari particle occurs in contexts similar to the ones the Tatar suffix occurs in, is an indication of this. It is also likely that the Tatar adverbial suffix *-dÄy, -dEy* has exerted a certain influence since the Mari particle seems to combine the combinatorial properties of both the Tatar suffixes. Since the particle is restricted to MaE and occurs mainly in songs, it is possible to classify it as a habitualised copy. The probability that the Mari particle *laj, läj* is a copy of a Tatar original is further strengthened by the fact that global copies of Tatar pronouns to which the suffix is added occur in the material I have examined, e.g. the Tatar determinative pronouns *bu* 'diese' and *sul* 'jene' (Kakuk 1996: 121, 171):

MaE *šulaj, bulaj, kapkaδəm počsa! kulaj, bulaj, nalaš leksa!* 'šulaj, bulaj, öffnet euer tor! kulaj, bulaj, kommt heraus [uns] zu empfangen! (Wichmann 1931: 277)

Like other copied suffixes, the Tatar suffix *-lÄy, -lEy* has been inserted into an equivalence position reserved for a suffix in the basic code. It seems as if this suffix is possible to identify: As was stated above, the suffix *laj, läj* does not occur in MaMo and MaNw and in songs from the western parts of the language area, the morpheme *γańe* apparently fills the same functions as the MaE *laj, läj*:

MaMo *Mükš-βəl'a γańə äťäm koδeš,*
Paštekem anžen šalγen koδeš;
Mükš-äβä γańe äβäm koδeš,
Paštekem anžen šalγen koδeš

"Wie ein Bienenstock bleibt mein Vater zurück,
hinter mir schauend bleibt er stehen;
wie eine Bienenkönigin bleibt meine Mutter zurück,
hinter mir schauend bleibt sie stehen' (Wichmann 1931: 171)

The particle *γańe* has the meaning 'as, like, just like' in MaMo (Gordeev 1983: 222) and it has several allomorphs in the different dialects of Mari, e.g. MaNw, MaMe and MaE *γaj* 'id'. Gordeev discusses the etymological explanations given for this morpheme, by Anduganov (1991: 109) classified as a postposition. One of the etymologies presented in Gordeev connects *γańe* to the Tatar postposition *güyä* 'as if' (c.f. Poppe 1963: 85) but Gordeev seems to assume an Indo-Iranian origin. Both explanations seem daring. Copies of Turkic postpositions exist in Mari, but had the Tatar postposition *güyä* 'as if' been copied, the Tatar vowel *ü* would have been represented by *ö* in Mari and not by *a*, c.f. the Tatar postposition *kürä* 'in view of, because of', MaE *köra* 'because of'. Considering the fact that there are no more than six words of Indo-Iranian origin in Mari in which the meaning is the same in Mari and in the Indo-Iranian languages, it is hardly likely that a morpheme with such widespread distribution as *γańe* would originate in the Indo-Iranian languages.

Galkin (1977) has shown that indigenous morphemes and morphemes of different origin can exist side by side in a language influenced by another in a language contact situation. Considering this, it is possible to assume that, if the Tatar adverbial suffix *-lÄy, -lEy* has been identified with a Mari *γańe, γaj*, examples in which both suffixes occur parallel to each other would exist. In my material, there are a few examples of this:

MaE *küšnö läi tə̂lə̂ze peš βolγə̂δo,*
Kečə̂-βal keče̮ γaje (γańe) lai βek oγə̂l

'Der Mond oben [scheint; Ö. B.] sehr hell,
Doch nicht so hell wie die Mittagssonne' (Beke 1961b; 447)

MaE *koltalalam, koltalam, salamem o šu,*
Mo-γańe lai umsuz-at postoβoj

'Ich sende und sende Grüsse (Sing.), doch sie kommen (Sing.) nich an,
Wie vergisslich ist [doch; Ö. B.] die Post! (Beke 1961b: 338)

MaMe *šište γańe sare laj imńe küleš* '[…] Braucht man einen Fuchs (eig. gelbes Pferd), so gelb wie Wachs' (Beke 1961b: 332)

I find it likely that the Mari particle *laj, läj* is a copy of the Tatar adverbial suffix *-lÄy, -lEy*. There is similarity in form, and the meaning and the combinatorial properties of the Mari particle are almost identical to those of the Tatar suffix. Furthermore, the fact that the morphemes can occur parallel to each other is also a strong indication for this, e.g. *Kečə̂-βal kečə̂ γaj (γańe) lai βek oγə̂l*. In the example *tə̂γaj tuγaj üδə̂ržə̂m šükalna δa koδə̂na* 'Ein Mädchen, das so ist, schieben wir ab und verlassen es' (Wichmann 1931: 276), the suffix *γaj* has been added to the demonstrative pronouns *te* 'this' and *tu* 'that' in the same way as in the Tatar *bolay* 'in this manner' and *šulay* 'in that manner'. In this respect, the Mari particle *laj, läj* is a striking parallel to the particle *γə̂na*, to be discussed below. There is a difference between the Mari particle *γańe* and the particle *laj, läj* in that the former as far as I have been able to tell is added exclusively to substantives. The particle *laj, läj* thus has more combinatorial properties than *γańe*. Since the particles occur in contexts with direct equivalents in Tatar, the major part of the forms in Mari can be classified as mixed copies; they combine the global copying of a Tatar adverbial suffix with the selective copying of the combinatorial properties of that suffix. The particle is used mainly in songs and almost exclusively in MaE and does not occur in either of the literary languages of Mari, and for this reason it can be said to be a habitualised copy.

4.1.4 The particle MaE *tə̂r, δə̂r*

The particle MaE *tə̂r, δə̂r* is briefly described by Galkin (1966: 191) and is said to occur in some varieties of MaMe and MaE. Galkin further seems to be of the opinion that the particle is of Turkic origin and gives examples from both Tatar and Chuvash, e.g. Tat *kilgänder* 'he has probably come'. Gordeev (1983: 277–278) does not give much space to the discussion of this particle either, but states that the examples given by Galkin only show the Turkic character of the particle and that it—since it does not occur in MaMo—in all likelihood is not of Chuvash origin. In Tatar, the particle *der, dır* is according to Poppe (1963: 86) an indefinite particle, the meaning of which corresponds to English 'ever' in sentences like 'whoever' and 'wherever'. Poppe gives the following examples: *kemder* 'somebody, *nindider* 'somekind of', *kaydadır* 'someplace, wherever', *ul kilgänder* 'he has probably come' (c.f. Thomsen 1959: 420; Galkin 1966: 191).

Gordeev is right in that the particle is not of Chuvash origin in Mari; the distribution of the particle is sufficient evidence of this. In the material that I have examined, the particle occurs several times in the texts from the area in which MaE is spoken. This concerns both the texts from Malmyzh and Birsk collected by Beke and the texts from Birsk collected by Paasonen:

MaE *tiń, maneš, peš-ak pojan ulat-tə̑r?* 'Bist du (sagt er) sehr reich? (Beke 1961b: 143)

MaE *uruksatə̑m puet-tə̑r* 'erlaubst du es (eig. gibst du die Erlaubnis)?' (Beke 1961b: 216)

MaE "*tuγań, tuγań sanat tene kə̑zə̑tat ojlen šińčattə̑r*", *manə̑n* ' "Bei dem und dem Senator sitzen sie vielleicht jetzt noch und sprechen darüber", sagte er' (Paasonen 1939: 24)

In the first two examples, the particle has the function of an interrogative particle and in the last example it expresses assumption, the same as in the Tatar example given by Poppe, *ul kilgänder* 'he has probably come'. The particle occurs also in the Tatar material that I have examined, but the instances are fewer than in Mari. In the following example, the particle functions as an interrogative particle:

TatM "*sin nindi bäγeran; sinəñ atañ anañ bardïr*" *digän* 'Was für ein B. bist du? Hast du ein Vater und ein Mutter?' (Paasonen 1953: 26)

The Mari particle *tə̑r, δə̑r* can be classified as a copy of a Tatar original. Furthermore, it is apparently a particle that is conventionalised since it is used also in the eastern literary language of Mari:

MaEL *te marij sokə̑r oγə̑l δə̑r?* 'Isn't this man blind?' (Izhboldin 1994: 45)

4.1.5 The particle MaE, MaMe *γə̑na* 'only, just'

The Mari particle MaE, MaMe *γə̑na* 'only, just' is of Turkic origin according to Galkin (1964: 186). It does not occur in MaMo and MaNw. It is more frequent in MaE than in MaMe which according to Galkin makes it possible to assume that it is a particle of Turkic origin. The particle *γə̑na* often occurs in songs from areas where MaE is spoken and in the songs from Bashkortostan collected by Beke (1961b) and Paasonen (1939) it occurs—like the particle *laj*—often in every other verse. This is the case for instance in Beke's collection of songs from the village Staro-Orjebaš (Beke 1961b: 280–343). Below, a few examples are given:

MaE *Orja γə̑nai βüδün śerže śümürlen, mańə̑č,*
mijal γə̑nai ončal'ə̑m: tap taza.
'mińə̑n-at lai čüčijem öpkelen', mańə̑č,
tolδal γə̑nai ončal'ə̑m, čon gańe

'Das Ufer des Orja-Flusses stürtzte ein, sagte man.
Ich ging [hin; Ö. B.] und schaute es an: es war vollkommen unversehrt.
Mein Onkel ist böse, sagte man.
Ich ging (eig. kam) [hin; Ö. B.] und schaute ihn an, [er war (Präs.) so gut; Ö. B.] wie die Seele' (Beke 1961b: 319)

MaE *izə̂rak kə̂na kapan tor alašam*
kajmə̂že γə̂na šuδe jortaleš.
tə̂ńə̂m γə̂na, roδem, peš jöratem.
kajmem γə̂na šuδe pörtə̂lam

'Mein dunkelbrauner Wallach, klein an Wuchs,
trabt, ohne dass der Wunsch zu gehen kam [=unlustig; H.P.].
Dich, mein Verwandter, liebe ich sehr,
ich kehre heim [begebe mich auf die Heimfahrt; H.P.], obgleich meine Lust nicht gekommen ist [obgleich nicht gern; H.P.]' (Paasonen 1939:130)

In other varieties of eastern Mari dialects, the particle *γə̂na* is not as common in songs, if it occurs at all. In eastern Mari songs from Malmyzh and Urzhum—both located outside of the republic of Mari-El—collected by Beke (1961a) I have only found a few verses in which the particle occurs. In the songs from the village of Saβə̂-jal (Beke 1961a: 346–381), consisting of 60 verses, I have only found four examples of the particle, in all four examples together with the adjective *izi* 'small'.

In Beke's and Paasonen's collections of songs from Baskortostan the particle is added to both nouns and adjectives:

MaE *marδež γə̂na pua βüt tolkə̂nžə̂m* 'Der Wind bläst Wellen auf' (Paasonen 1939: 147)

MaE *kükö γə̂näj muralme tə̂lə̂źə̂šte* 'In jenem Monat, da der Kuckuck ruft' (Beke 1961b: 307)

The particle is also added to verbs in the inifinite mode and to gerunds:

MaE *lüjaš kə̂na o lij, čoŋə̂šta* 'schiessen kann man nicht, sie fliegen' (Paasonen 1939: 145)

MaE *mijal γə̂nai ončalʹə̂m: tap taza* 'Ich ging [hin; Ö. B.] und schaute es an: es war vollkommen unversehrt' (Beke 1961b: 319)

The particle *γə̂na* can also occur with other forms, among them possessive and reflexive pronouns:

MaE *nemnan γə̂nai pasu laj tajə̂l pase* 'Unser Feld ist ein abschüssiges Feld' (Beke 1961b: 312)

MaE *ške γə̂nai čeβer, ške motor* 'Er ist schön, er ist munter' (Paasonen 1939: 100).

The particle also occurs with imperative forms of verbs:

MaE *"mural γə̂na", manarkə̂n, mə̂j muralam* 'Wenn du sagst "Singe", dann singe ich' (Paasonen 1939: 149)

The particle *γə̂na* also occurs in other types of texts apart from songs songs, for instance folk-tales and proverbs from areas where eastern Mari is spoken:

MaE *iźə̂ γə̂na jə̂rγə̂ške, kitkə̂č kiδə̂š košteš—okśa* 'Er ist zwar klein [und; Ö. B.] rund, geht aber: Ö. B. von Hand zu Hand—Das Geld' (Beke 1961b: 153)

The Mari particle *γə̂na* is undoubtedly of Tatar origin. In Tatar, the particle *gEnÄ, kEnÄ,* has the meaning 'only' (Poppe 1963: 185). It can be added to adjectives and nouns:

tatK *patša tėnėč- γėna yatkanda* 'Der Padischah blieb ruhig' Kakuk 1989: 62)

tatK *Br niče künler-gine ütken idė* 'Es verging nur einige Tage' (Kakuk 1989: 82)

The particle can also be added to converbs and pronouns:

tatK *Patša karttan bu išlernė iplep-gine suraša bašliy* 'Der Padischah begann den Alten gründlich nach diesen Dingen zu Fragen' (Kakuk 1989: 56)

tatK *lakin mini-gine χarab ittėñ* 'doch hast du mich zugrunde gerichtet' (Kakuk 1989: 168)

In Ignác Kúnos' collection of Kazan Tatar texts published by Kakuk (1989), the particle is relatively frequent:

tatK *kapkanė-γėna čıkkanlar idė* 'Sie traten aus dem Tor hinaus' (Kakuk 1989: 14)

tatK *bürė-de yulda-γėna kütėp tura iken* 'Am Weg aber wartete der Wolf' (Kakuk 1989: 10)

The particle also occurs in Kazan Tatar folk-songs:

tatK *Al-japkıčıñ kiñ-gine*
billeriñe tiñ-gine
bütenlerde jok aǯetim
aǯetlerim sin-gine

'Deine Schürze ist ein wenig weit,
passt gut an die Taille;
Ich brauche niemand anders,
ich brauche nur dich' (Kakuk 1980: 33)

In Chuvash there is a particle *kăna* 'nur, bloß' which according to Benzing (1959b: 749) is of Tatar origin. In Chuvash, the particle is often added to adjectives to express what Benzing (1959b: 749) refers to as "Abschwächung der Bedeutung":

Chuv *lutra kăna χurăn* 'ein ganz niedrige Birke' (Benzing 1959b: 749)

The particle also occurs with converbs:

Chuv *χărani-pe čĕtĕr-se kăna tă-tămăr* 'vor Angst standen wir ganz zitternd da' (Benzing 1959b: 749)

The geographical distribution of the Mari particle *γə̂na* 'only, just' makes it probable that it is a copy of a Tatar, rather than Chuvash, particle and the Chuvash particle *kăna* too is probably a copy of the Tatar particle *gEnÄ, kEnÄ*. Judging from the geographical distribution of the particle and the fact that it occurs in contexts with clear parallels in Tatar, it would be possible to classify the particle as a habitualised global copy. This is due to the fact that it occurs mainly in areas where the contacts between Mari and Tatar have been intensive but since the particle is present also in the Eastern literature language of Mari, it is more likely that it can be classified as a conventionalised copy. The particle does not only occur in songs, proverbs and folktales but also in texts published during the 20th century:

MaEL *tuγe šol...—šonalten-šonalten γə̂na mutə̂m uša Pajaš* 'Well naturally, Pajaš added thoughtfully' (Izhboldin 1994: 80)

The Mari particle *γə̂na* seems to differ from its Tatar counterpart in the way that it is more frequent in songs than what is the case in Tatar. However, it is probable that it is not possible to draw this conclusion on the basis of the material I have used. But, since songs, proverbs and fairy-tales of the Turkic and Finno-Ugric peoples of the Volga area share common motifs or are identical to each other, I find it possible to conclude that these common songs and proverbs have played an important part as far as the copying of the particle is concerned.

It is also likely that the particle *γə̂na* has been inserted into an equivalence position that originally was reserved for a native morpheme. The particle *γə̂na* does indeed have a counterpart in the Mari particle *βele* 'only', which according to Gordeev (1983: 84) occurs in all dialects of Mari. Galkin (1964: 186) states that the particle is of uncertain origin but that it possibly can be connected with Finnish *vielä* 'yet another, again'. The particle *βele* occurs in all types of texts, including songs and proverbs.

Galkin (1977) has shown that native morphemes can exist parallel to morphemes of foreign origin in language contact situations. Therefore, it would be reasonable to assume parallel occurrences of *γə̂na* and *βele*, if *γə̂na* has been inserted into an equivalence position reserved for *βele*. In my material, there are examples of this:

MaE *iźi γə̂na βelə̂, kaskam tarβata—ti* 'Es ist nur klein [und doch; Ö. B.] bewegt es Baumstämme. (Sing.)—Die Laus' (Beke 1961a: 385)

The particles *γə̂na* and *βele*, their geographical distribution and combinatorial properties are in this respect a striking parallel to the distribution and properties of the particles *laj* and *γańe, γaj*. The particles *γə̂na* and *laj* are frequent in dialects with the most extensive contacts with Tatar, whereas *γańe* and *βele* mainly occur in the western parts of the Mari language area.

4.1.6 The particle MaMo *βärä*, MaNw, MaMe *βara*, MaE *βara*, *βärä*

Galkin (1964: 188) calls the particle *βara, βärä* an interrogative particle and according to Moisio (1994: 21) it is an emphasizing particle in questions. Galkin links the particle to the adverb *βara*, meaning 'then, later' and there does indeed seem to be a close connection between the two. Bereczki (1971: 80) claims that it is a word of Chuvash origin in Mari. Gordeev (1983: 42) states that the adverb *βara* is present in all dialects of Mari and discusses the etymological explanations given for the origin of the adverb. Among these is the assumption that it has a Finno-Ugric origin. Gordeev connects it with the Vepsian *varha* 'in reserve' and the Finnish *vara* 'store, fortune'. The semantic differences between the Mari adverb and the proposed Finno-Ugric equivalents make them unlikely as the source for the Mari word. Gordeev (1983: 42–43) furthermore makes a distinction between the adverb *βara* and the particle *βara* that according to him is an emphasizing particle occurring in MaMe and MaE. Gordeev (1983: 43) claims that the emphasizing particle is of Ossetic origin, thus arguing for an Indo-Iranian origin which seems hard or almost impossible to prove.

In Mari, the adverb *βara* has a narrative function and is often used in the beginning of a new sentence:

MaMo *βara süän-buj pua kapka-orollan oksam. βara kapka-orolə̂ pačeš kapkam. βara pə̂ra süän* 'Dann gibt das "Haupt der Hochzeit" Geld dem Torhüter. Dann öffnet der Torhüter das Tor, dann gehen die Hochzeitsleute hinein' (Beke 1951: 66)

MaMe *βara jumo ončə̂č šüγatlaš šumeške. βara nužδa jə̂ŋə̂n kolšə̂m purtat čerkə̂ške, [βara tuδə̂m pop kurə̂m-kurə̂mlan kajnat βes svetə̂ške] βara pop luδə̂n šaβa* 'Das Heiligenbild wird dann bis zum Friedhof vorne getragen (eig. geht vorne). Dann trägt man die Leiche des armen Mannes in die Kirche. [Alsdann (spricht) der Priester zu ihm: "[Nun also; Ö. B.] gingest auf ewig ins jenseits"; Ö.B.] Sodann bestreut ihn, betend der Priester' (Beke 1995: 284)

It is not impossible that an adverb with the meaning 'then' can have started to function as an interrogative particle in Mari. In English, the adverb 'then' can be added to question words, e.g. *what then*?, c.f. Swedish *än sen?* 'what then?' and Finnish sitten in *entäs sitten* 'what then?'. The development from an adverb to an interrogative particle in Mari is not unique in this respect. In the material I have examined, the adverb *βara* occurs as an interrogative marker in all dialects apart from MaNw:

MaMo *papajet jaδən: "tirən ulat βara?"* 'Das Mutterchen fragte: "Bist du wohl mit einem Schlitten?" '(Beke 1951: 160)

MaMe *iza maneš: "molan malen otəl βara?"* 'Mein älterer Bruder spricht: "Warum übernachtest du nicht [irgendwo; Ö. B.]" ' (Beke 1995: 224)

MaE *"təδəm kö əšta βara?"* 'Wer macht dieses denn, sagte er' (Paasonen 1939: 223)

βara can further be used as an interrogative particle in texts published in the literary languages of Mari:

MaWL *kəcerak βara? əlet-šület?* 'Well, how is it now? Are you healthy (lit. Are you living and breathing?)' (Petukhov 1994: 24)

MaWL *Gennadij čəčəmok at əl βara?* 'Aren't you uncle Gennadij?' (Petukhov 1994: 279)

MaEL *nu, kuzerak βara, Sanepa?* 'Well, how is it now, Sanepa?'

In Chuvash, an adverb *vara* with similar form and functions exists. It has the meaning 'then, later' and one etymology, according to which the Chuvash adverb is of Mari origin is given by Gordeev (1983: 42). In Chuvash too, this adverb can have a narrative function and is often used to begin a new sentence. In comparison with Mari, the Chuvash adverb *vara* is not quite as frequent in this context but examples can be found in the material that I have examined:

ChuvA *vara ikĕšĕ: "vut χuras" tenĕ. Vara kačakka taki ută kapană śinččen măyraki śine părtakă ută χursa pınată* [...] 'Dann meinten sie beide: "Es soll ein Feuer angezündet werden". Dann holte der Ziegenbock auf seinen Hörnern aus einem Heuscheuber ein wenig Heu [...]' (Paasonen 1949: 210–211)

It is probable that the interrogative particle *βara* in Mari can be connected to Turkic influence. In Chuvash, the adverb *vara* can function as an emphasizing particle in questions:

ChuvA *kam valli vara? śĕnĕ kupsa Ilmejur valli* 'Für wen denn? Für den neuen Kaufman Ilmejur, sagte sie' (Paasonen 1949: 247)

ChuvA *esĕ mĕšĕn ăšănmastăn vara, tenĕ* 'Warum wärmst du dich denn nicht [sagte er; H.P.]' (Paasonen 1949: 211)

The assumption that the Chuvash adverb *vara* is of Mari origin seems less convincing. Given the fact that several interrogative particles in Mari are copied from the Turkic languages, the possibility that one particle could have been copied in the opposite direction is less likely. According to Galkin (1964: 188) the particle *-i* is used as an interrogative particle in the Zvenigovo region in Mari-El, bordering on the Chuvash republic (see map 3). This particle is copied from Chuvash and is used parallel to the interrogative particle *mo*—to be discussed in Chapter 5—

which displays functions which are due to the selective copying of functions of the Tatar interrogative suffix *-mV*.

The Mari adverb *βara* is of Chuvash origin in Mari, according to Bereczki (1971: 80) and Räsänen (1920: 119) seems to be of the same opinion. Räsänen, connects it, cautiously, with a Tatar postposition *ary* 'jenseitig, nach, hinter. However, there is another morpheme in Tatar that could have been the model for both the Chuvash and the Mari adverb. In Tatar, the converb *bara* 'going' apparently occurs in contexts which are not unlike the adverbial use of Chuv *vara* and Ma *βara*:

TatM *ulusu bara bara ber šähärgä barïp ǯitte* 'Der Grössere, als er lange seines Weges gezogen war, kam zu einer Stadt' (Kakuk 1996: 69)

TatK *bara bara bular br seherge barėp jiteler* 'Sie gingen gemächlich weiter und kamen in eine Stadt' (Kakuk 1989: 10)

TatK *uzak bara turγač, br patšanėñ šehrine barėp jiteler* 'Nachdem sie [schon] lange gegangen sind, erreichten sie die Stadt eines Padischas' (Kakuk 1989: 10)

Kakuk (1996: 117) states that TatM *bara-tura* means 'gehend-wandernd' but it apparently also has a temporal meaning, 'später, mit der Zeit'. It is possible that the Chuvash *vara* is a copy of this Tatar converb *bara* 'going' which has acquired a more explicit adverbial function in Chuvash and later on has developed into an interrogative particle. Mari has copied both functions from Chuvash.

The morpheme *βara* is also part of what may be labelled a double postposition in Mari. This postposition will be discussed below in section 5.2.6 and has a close resemblance to a double postposition in Chuvash, formed with the morpheme *vara*. This makes it even more probable that the Mari *βara* is copied from Chuvash since the Mari *βara* can fill all the functions of its Chuvash counterpart.

4.1.7 The particle MaMe, MaE *aδak*, MaNw *äδäk* 'again, besides'

The particle MaMe, MaE *aδak,* MaNw *äδäk* has the meaning of 'again, besides' and according to Galkin (1964: 187), its origin is not quite clear but one can assume that it originates in a compounding of the particles *-at* and *-ak*. According to Gordeev (1979: 50), the particle occurs in MaMe and MaE but not in MaMo and MaNw. Ivanov & Tuzharov (1970), however, include it in their list of particles in MaNw. Bereczki (1971: 65) claims that the particle is of Chuvash origin and that it originates in a form *tataχ* 'again, besides'. The Chuvash *tataχ* has the same meaning and occurs in the same contexts as the Mari *aδak, äδäk*, which makes it highly likely that the Mari particle is a copy of a Chuvash. It is however not mentioned by Räsänen and the loss of the initial *t* in the Mari form is irregular. An initial *t* in words of Chuvash origin in Mari is generally kept unchanged (Räsänen 1920: 11). Galkin's etymological explanation is probably correct though, since the Chuvash *tataχ* is made up of an emphatic particle *-aχ* and a gemination of the particle *ta*. In Chuvash, the parallel form *tata* means 'again, and, also' and according to Paasonen (1974: 158) the form originates in a double occurrence of the particle *ta, te* 'noch'. Below, examples of both forms in Chuvash are given:

ChuvA *věsem tata malalla kaynă* 'Sie gingen dann weiter' (Paasonen 1949: 256)

ChuvA *amĕšĕ tataχ, "tămana ukśi ăśta", tese ıytnă* 'Seine Mutter fragte wieder: "Wo ist das Geld der Eule?"' (Paasonen 1949: 222)

In my opinion, Bereczki's explanation to the origin of the Mari particle is the correct one. Along with the particle *vara*, the particle *tataχ* is very frequent in Chuvash and the same applies to the Mari equivalents. That the particle does not occur in MaMo is probably due to the fact that it has been replaced by the particle MaMo *eše, eče* which is a copy of the Russian *ešče* 'again', a particle that occurs parallel to the particle *äδäk* 'again' in MaNw (Ivanov & Tuzharov 1970: 197). In Mari, *aδak* seems to be a conventionalised global copy of a Chuvash particle, occurring in all dialects apart from MaMo and also in the eastern literary language:

MaNw *äβämet məlänem äδäk äťämlec šolə̂p kolə̂ teŋe oksam puš* 'Meine Mutter gab mir noch im geheimen, ohne Wissen meines Vaters, 20 Rubel' (Beke 1957: 8)

MaMe *βara tuδə̂ ok čə̂tə̂, aδak škak Ajδuš tek kaja* 'Dann kann er nicht (mehr länger warten), er geht wieder selbst zu Ajdusch' (Alhoniemi & Saarinen 1983: 164)

MaE *aδak βuβer kuγuza nöltälən šoγalta Temə̂r βatə̂rə̂m* 'Nun packt wieder der βuβer-Alte Held Temə̂r' (Beke 1961b: 417)

MaEL *e-ej, aδak taγam šüškə̂laš monδenam* 'oh-oh! Besides, I forgot to slaughter the goat!' (Izhboldin 1994: 44)

4.1.8 The particle MaMe *ala*, MaE *ala, älä,* MaNw *älä*

According to Gordeev (1979: 78) the particle *ala, älä* occurs in maNw, MaMe and MaE. Gordeev also claims that it is of Tatar origin. Galkin (1964: 189) states that the particle does not occur in MaMo but is also of the opinion that it is of Turkic origin. Moisio (1994: 7) describes it as a particle that expresses possibility, e.g. *ala muraltem* 'I might start to sing', or improbability, e.g. *tuδo toleš mo?—ala* 'Is he coming?—hardly'. The meaning of the particle is thus 'perhaps' and 'probably not'. In Mari, the particle *ala* can function as an interrogative particle with a meaning that corresponds to the English 'or what?'. All functions of the Mari particle have parallels in the Turkic languages, especially in Tatar but also in Chuvash, and for this reason the Turkic origin of the particle seems evident enough. The particle also occurs in the formation of indefinite pronouns (see section 4.2.1.1) and when geminated *ala...ala...* it is a disjunctive conjunction with the essential meaning of 'either...or...' (see section 5.1.1.1).

In Mari, the particle *ala, älä* can express assumption or probability. In this function, it is especially common in the eastern dialects:

MaMe "*ala ik kumə̑ržə̑m puet?*" 'Gibst du (mir) wohl eine Kopeke?' (Alhoniemi & Saarinen 1983: 192)

MaMe *ala mə̑j jöröm?* 'Tauge ich denn nicht?' (Alhoniemi & Saarinen 1983: 64)

MaE "*molan müškürem kuγemeš? älä aza šotneže?*" *maneš* 'Warum wird mein bauch [immer: Ö. B.] grösser? Vielleicht bekomme ich ein Kind (eig. will ein Kind geboren werden)", sagt er' (Beke 1961b: 438)

MaE *älä, maneš, jumo ške tolə̑n əl'e, maneš, šə̑m šinče* 'Vielleicht kam der liebe Gott selbst zu mir (sagt sie), ich erfuhr es nicht (sagt sie)' (Beke 1961b: 433)

The particle *älä* can also be used to express assumption in MaNw. Ivanov & Tuzharov (1970: 198) give the following example:

MaNw *älä teš toleš* 'he may come here'

In the eastern literary language, *ala* can function as an interrogative particle in questions:

MaEL *Mom šonen luktə̑n, ala?* 'Well, what has he found out then?' (Izhboldin 1994: 126)

In Tatar, the morpheme *ällä* has the meaning 'perhaps, some, ever' (Poppe 1963: 265). It occurs in the formation of indefinite pronouns and geminated, *ällä... ällä...,* it functions as a disjunct conjunction with the meaning 'either...or...'. The particle *ällä* can also function as a interrogative particle:

TatK *bu urmanda üstė-mė elle* 'ist sie vielleicht im Walde aufgewachsen' (Kakuk 1980: 100)

The Mari particle *ala, älä* closely resembles the Tatar particle *ällä,* both in form and function. These morphemes are not just interrogative particles; they can also function as disjunctive conjunctions and as elements in the formation of indefinite pronouns. It seems safe to conclude that the particle *ala, älä* is a copy of a Tatar original and that it furthermore is a fairly conventionalised global copy since it occurs in most dialects and in one of the two literary languages.

4.2 Indefinite pronouns and adverbs

The original Finno-Ugric pronominal system has remained largely intact in Mari, a fact that is easily observed in the forms of the personal pronouns, all originating in stems common to Mari and other Finno-Ugric languages. It is mainly in the category of indefinite pronouns that Mari has undergone fundamental change as a result of language contacts.

The indefinite pronouns, and adverbs, in Mari form a mixed group and can be made up of single morphemes or of more complex morpheme sequences. The latter can be labelled compound indefinite pronouns or adverbs, and are usually formed with prefixes that can occur also as particles, e.g. *ala*. The category of indefinite pronouns was weakly developed in the Finno-Ugric languages (Bereczki 1983: 217) and in Mari, there are several examples of both single and compound indefinite pronouns that have been copied from other languages. Among the morphemes functioning as indefinite pronouns are for instance MaMe *kažnə̑j*, MaMo *kažδə̑j* 'every', which has been copied from Russian, and the originally Tatar indefinite pronoun Ma *pütə̂ń* 'all' < Tat *böten* 'whole, entirely, all' (Poppe 1963: 208). These morphemes are global copies of Russian and Tatar originals, but in the category of indefinite pronouns in Mari mixed copies too occur.

4.2.1 Indefinite pronouns and adverbs formed with the morpheme *ala, älä*

In Mari, indefinite pronouns and adverbs can be formed with the morpheme *ala, älä*, copied from Tatar. This morpheme has a generalising function and is placed immediately before the pronominal stem, e.g. Ma *ala-kuδo* 'someone' ← *kuδo* 'who'; *ala-molan* 'for some reason' ← *molan* 'why'; *ala-kunam* 'sometime' ← *kunam* 'when'. In Mari, the morpheme *ala* has the basic meaning of 'perhaps, hardly' (Moisio 1994: 7) and can function as a particle (see above, section 4.1.8). The morpheme can be doubled and then fills the function of a disjunctive conjunction. In the material I have examined, this way of forming indefinite pronouns and adverbs is characteristic of MaNw, MaMe and MaE, all dialects in which the particle *ala* and the disjunct conjunction *ala...ala...* 'either...or...' also occur.

MaNw *pužə̂m ruen kerδən aγə̂l. Älä-ma lin tolə̂n* 'Er konnte keine Bäume (Sing.) fällen. Es fehlte ihm etwas (eig. ist ihm etwas zugestossen)' (Beke 1957: 34)

MaMe *kuβa, kutan ala-mo lin* 'Frau, dem Hinterteil ist bestimmt was passiert' (Alhoniemi & Saarinen 1983: 66)

MaE *kajmə̂ γoδə̂m jolet ruδalt kaja γə̂n, tińə̂n kuβaδə̂m älä-kö kuješ* 'Wenn deine Bastschuhe (Sing.) unterwegs aufgehen, schläft jemand mit deiner Frau' (Beke 1961b: 349)

The Tatar model for the Mari morpheme has the form *ällä* and the meaning 'perhaps, some, ever' (Poppe 1963: 265). As in Mari, the Tatar morpheme can be used as an interrogative particle. Indefinite pronouns and adverbs in Tatar can be formed with this particle *ällä*, placed immediately before the pronoun in question, e.g. *ällä ni* 'something, anything', *ällä nindi* 'some, any' (Poppe 1963: 265). Interestingly, this way of forming indefinite pronouns in Tatar seems restricted in use and only few examples occur in the material that I have examined:

TatM *satlarïndaχï almanï ällä nästä aši ikän* 'Irgendjemand ass von den Äpfeln des Gartens' (Paasonen 1953: 12)

TatM *"minda ällä nästä ise bar" diyep ezlägännär* ' "Was ist denn hier für ein Geruch?" sagten sie und suchten' (Paasonen 1953: 43)

Here, two interpretations are possible. Either Mari reflects an older way of forming indefinite pronouns and adverbs no longer in extensive use in Tatar or it is the case that this way of forming indefinite pronouns and adverbs for some reason has become more frequent in Mari than in Tatar. Code-copying can be assumed to include a change in the frequential pattern so that the copied form and its functions become more frequent in the code they are inserted into. The indefinite pronouns and adverbs in Mari formed with the morpheme *ala, älä* can be classified as mixed copies since they combine the global copying of a Tatar morpheme with the selective copying of the combinatorial properties of the morpheme. Because of the fact that this way of forming indefinite pronouns and adverbs occurs also in texts published in the eastern literary language, the copies can be regarded as conventionalised copies:

MaEL *aδak ala-kön kartuz koδən* 'Besides, someone's cap was left behind' (Oδar 1993: 34)

4.2.2 Indefinite pronouns and adverbs formed with the morpheme *ta, tä*

The morpheme *ala, älä*, copied from Tatar is used in the formation of indefinite pronouns and adverbs in MaNw, MaMe and MaE but it does not occur in MaMo. In this dialect, indefinite pronouns and adverbs are formed with the morpheme *ta, tä*, placed immediately before the pronoun or adverb in question:

MaMo *tokə̂žə tolə̂n-dä äťäžlän kelesen: "ta-maχań imńi tašken"* 'Er kam nachhause und erzählte seinem Vater: "Irgend ein Pferd hat [den Weizen; Ö. B.] niedergetreten' (Beke 1951: 201–202)

MaMo *äβäžə kelesen: "äťät ta-γə̂nam kejen Siβirəškə, kərtńi cepš-ät təγänen pətä ənδə* 'Seine Mutter antwortete: "Dein Vater ging einst nach Sibirien, auch seine Eisenketten müssen schon abgewetzt sein"' (Beke 1951: 141)

Adamovič (1985: 81–84) gives a detailed account of the formation of indefinite pronouns and adverbs in Chuvash. According to Adamovič, the Chuvash particle *ta, te* has three functions: it is a free particle and it is also used in the formation of indefinite pronouns and adverbs. The morpheme is placed immediately before the pronoun or adverb, e.g. Chuv *ta-kam* 'someone' (Krueger 1961: 138). Furthermore, the particle can be doubled and then functions as a disjunctive conjunction. No instances of the particle used in the formation of indefinite pronouns and adverbs occur in the material I have examined, but Krueger (1961: 138) gives several examples of this. Still, I find it very likely that the indefinite pronouns and adverbs formed with the morpheme *ta, tä* can be analysed as code-copies. These copies, like the ones formed with the morpheme *ala, älä*, can be classified as mixed copies, combining the global copying of a Chuvash morpheme *ta, te* with the combinatorial properties of this morpheme. It is also possible to classify it as a conventionalised copy since it occurs in texts published in the western literary language:

MaWL *βara təδə̂ uγəc tamaχań pumaγaβläm kiδə̂š näl'ə̂* 'then he again took some kind of papers in his hand' (Petukhov 1994: 237)

4.2.3 Indefinite pronouns and adverbs formed with the morpheme *kerek*

In some dialects of Mari, the morpheme *kerek* is used in the formation of indefinite pronouns and adverbs meaning for example 'anything, anyone'. The morpheme functions as a prefix and is placed before the pronoun or adverb in question, e.g. Ma *kerek-kö* 'whoever, someone'. Anduganov (1991: 156) states that *kerek* is of either Tatar or Chuvash origin in Mari. Galkin (1964: 190) on the other hand claims that it most likely is of Chuvash origin. The morpheme occurs in the formation of indefinite pronouns and adverbs in most dialects, but there are no examples in the material from MaNw that I have examined. It is not included in the list of morphemes filling this function given by Ivanov & Tuzharov (1970). Furthermore, there are no examples in the material from MaMo that I have examined, but it is included in the glossary of Ramstedt (1902: 45), which makes it possible to conclude that this way of forming indefinite pronouns and adverbs does exist in MaMo.

MaE *te tiδə̂ kazam kerek-kuškə̂ čikə̂źa, to naŋgajza möŋgeš šoŋgə̂ kuγə̂źa δekə̂!* 'Bringt (eig. steckt) diesen Ziegenbock, wohin ihr wollt, bringt ihn meinetwegen dem Alten zurück!' (Beke 1961a: 339)

The Turkic origin of the morpheme is stressed both by Anduganov and Galkin. In Chuvash, indefinite pronouns and adverbs can be formed with the morpheme *ta, te* but also with the morpheme *kirek* (Krueger 1961: 138). In the Chuvash material I have examined only a few examples occur:

ChuvA *kayas, atte, esĕ kirek ăśta yarsanta kayĕp* 'Ich werde gehen, Vater, wohin auch immer du mich senden willst, werde ich gehen' (Paasonen 1949: 176)

I have found no examples of a similar morpheme with the same function in Tatar and at first glance it seems as if Mari and Chuvash are closely connected when it comes to the formation of indefinite pronouns and adverbs with the morphemes *kerek* and *kirek* respectively. As was stated above in the discussion of the particles *ta, tä* and *ala, älä*, these morphemes can be doubled and they fill the functions of disjunctive conjunctions with the meaning 'either…or…'. Although a morpheme *kiräk* apparently does not occur in the formation of indefinite pronouns and adverbs or as a free particle in Tatar, the morpheme can be geminated and fill the function of a disjunctive conjunction 'either…or'. In VTD II (1960: 1355), the following example is given:

TatK *kiräk suvaš, kiräk čırmıš, kiräk Ar, kiräk nidı kiši bulsun barasıda Allanıñ mändäläri ikän!* 'mögen es Tschuwaschen, Tscheremissen, Wotjaken, oder irgendwelche andere Leute sein, alle sind die Sklaven Gottes!'

This morpheme has a widespread distribution in the Turkic languages and a disjunctive conjunction *käräk...käräk...* also exists in Uyghur and other Turkic languages. In Turkish, the disjunctive conjunction *gerek...gerek...* means 'either...or...', e.g. *gerek büyük gerek küçük* 'either big or small' (COTD 1959: 112)

I find it likely that the morpheme *kerek* in Mari is copied from Tatar rather than Chuvash for the following reason: in Tatar, the form is *kiräk* and in Chuvash *kirek*. A Tatar *i* in the first syllable goes back to an original *e* (Räsänen 1923: 16) which in Chuvash normally corresponds to *a* in the first syllable in words of common Turkic origin, e.g. Tat *bir-* 'to give', Chuv *par-* 'id' < CT **ber* 'to give' (Krueger 1961: 61). The form of the Chuvash morpheme thus indicates a later origin. Both the Chuvash *kirek* and the Mari *kerek* have surely been copied from Tatar and it can be assumed that Mari and Chuvash have preserved an older way of forming indefinite pronouns, no longer productive in Tatar.

The indefinite pronouns and adverbs formed with the morpheme *kerek* in Mari can be classified as mixed copies since they combine the global copying of a Tatar morpheme with the combinatorial properties of the morpheme. The morpheme *kerek* is not frequent in the material I have examined and could possibly be an example of a habitualised copy, but since it occurs in texts published in both the literary languages, it is evidently a conventionalised copy of a Tatar original:

MaEL *kerek-moγaj pašaštat βet en ončə̑č βuj küleš, βuj...* 'In a job of any kind, first of all you need a boss, a boss...' (Izhboldin 1994: 93)

MaWL *kerek-ma δä obstjinə̑n nurβläm χresańβlälan šənδə̑ktə̑mə̑la* 'They made the peasants work on some kind of common fields' (Petukhov 1994: 24)

4.2.4 Negative indefinite pronouns and adverbs

The formation of negative indefinite pronouns and adverbs, and the possible Turkic origin of this, has not attracted much attention in Finno-Ugric linguistics as far as I have been able to ascertain. Nevertheless, there is a close resemblance between Mari and Chuvash in this respect. In Mari, negative indefinite pronouns and adverbs are formed in the following way: a morpheme *ńi* is placed immediately before the stem, to which also the particle *at, ät* is added. The morpheme *ńi* is of Russian origin. In the material that I have examined, this way of forming indefinite pronouns and adverbs occurs in all dialects of Mari:

MaMo *mare βaštə̑l kolta: "məńən βätə ńi-γə̑nam-at ak šəδəškə"* 'Der Mann lacht: "Meine Frau ist nie böse auf mich"' (Beke 1951: 150)

MaNw *amsažə̑m pacə̑n ńü-γüm-ät užə̑n aγə̑l* 'Sie öffnete die Tür, sah [aber; Ö. B.] niemandem' (Beke 1957: 32)

MaMe *nəmomat lüem ketən oγət ul* 'Es gelang ihnen nicht, irgendetwas zu erlegen' (Alhoniemi & Saarinen 1983: 84)

MaE *korak korak šińčam nə-γunam-at o čüŋgäl* 'Eine (eig. die) Krähe hackt der anderen nie die Augen aus (eig. h. das Auge der anderen n. a.)' (Beke 1961b: 159)

If we compare the Mari way of forming negative indefinite pronouns with the formation of the corresponding forms in Chuvash, it becomes evident that Chuvash has been the model code in this particular case. In Chuvash, negative indefinite pronouns and adverbs are formed with the morpheme *ni*, placed before the pronoun or adverb in question. To this, the particle *ta, te* is added (Krueger 1961: 138). In the Chuvash material I have examined, there are numerous examples of this:

ChuvA *χĕrĕ χăranipe nimĕnte śavărsa kalayman* 'Das Mädchen konnte vor Furcht garnichts erzählen' (Paasonen 1949: 150)

ChuvA "*esĕ tata un śinčči tumtirne yıšănatni? nikamta śaramas śüremeśt*" 'Eignest du dir auch die Kleider an, die er trägt? Es kann doch niemand nackend gehen' (Paasonen 1949: 209)

There can hardly be any doubt that the formation of negative indefinite pronouns in Mari is a copy of a Chuvash model. In Tatar, the corresponding pronouns and adverbs are formed with the prefigated morpheme *hič*, e.g. *hičkem* 'nobody', *hičnärsä* 'nothing' (Poppe 1963: 81). The particle *at, ät* (see section 4.1.2) in Mari is thus systematically inserted into positions in which Chuvash makes use of the particle *ta, te*. The fact that the particle occurs in the formation of negative indefinite pronouns and adverbs in Mari makes it even more likely that it is copied from Chuvash and just adds another example to the list of equivalents. The prefigated morpheme *ńi* in Mari, however, is of Russian origin and is probably a copy of a copy in Mari. The negative indefinite pronouns and adverbs in Mari can be classified as mixed copies since they combine the global copying of morphemes with the selective copying of combinatory patterns typical of them. Since they occur in all dialects and in both literary languages of Mari, they constitute a conventionalised copy of a Chuvash original:

MaEL [...] *no tuδəžo nimomat ok pelešte* '[...] but he says nothing' (Taygiljdin 1993: 60)

MaWL [...] *a gosudar'-imperator tiδe gišan nimat ak pälə* '[...] but the Emperor of the State knows nothing of this' (Petukhov 1994: 40)

4.3 Adjectives

The distinction between the word categories adjectives and substantives is not very clear in Mari, and this is the case also in other Finno-Ugric languages (Alhoniemi 1985: 42). In the Proto-Uralic language, it seems as if adjectives and substantives were not morphologically distinct word categories (Abondolo 1998: 18). In this respect, there is a close typological affinity between Finno-Ugric and Turkic languages. With the exception of the comparison of adjectives, substantives and adjectives in Mari can be declined in principle in the same way in Mari. In Mari, there are several stems functioning either as adjectives or substantives depending on context. Alhoniemi (1985: 42) gives the following examples: *kelγe* 'deep; depth', *šeme* 'black, blackness'. Even derived stems containing an adjectival derivational ending can be used as substantives, e.g. *tamle δeč tamlə̑m kočkat, čaple δeč čaplə̑m čijet* 'You eat the tastiest of the tasty, you dress in the fanciest of the fancy' (Alhoniemi 1985: 42).

4.3.1 Comparison of adjectives

4.3.1.1 The formation of comparative forms

Mari adjectives can take the positive, comparative and superlative forms. The comparative can be expressed morphologically by use of the suffix MaMe, MaE *-rak*, MaMo, MaNw *-rak, -räk* which is added to the adjectival stem, e.g. *sajrak* 'better' ← *saj* 'good'; *kuγə̑rak* 'bigger' ← *kuγu* 'big'. According to Bereczki (1988: 315) there is no Mari equivalent to the Mordvin comparative suffix MoE *-ška*, MoM *-škă*, etymologically related to the Finnish adjectival suffix *-hka, -hkä*. Bereczki (1971: 33) states that the Mari suffix *-rak, -räk* is of Turkic origin and Saarinen (1997b: 391) is of the opinion that it is of both Tatar and Chuvash origin. The suffix *-rak, -räk* is used to express the comparative morphologically in all dialects of Mari:

MaMo *koγorak eδeməm piš žäläjät* 'Der alternde Mann tut ihnen sehr leid' (Beke 1951: 162)

MaNw *kuγurak üδüržüm kecəlän marlan puen ulut, iźiräk üδüržüm ätänlän marlan puen ulut* 'Die ältere Tochter gaben sie der Sonne, die jüngere Tochter einem Hahn zum Weibe' (Beke 1957: 48)

MaMe "*purə̑ kuγža, mlanna aδak-at iziš kuγurak küleš, βes kirə̑m ə̑štəktə̑*" 'Guter Zar, wir brauchen ein noch etwas grösseres Gewich, lass ein anderes anfertigen!' (Alhoniemi & Saarinen 1983: 126)

MaE *ške Temə̑r βatə̑r tarla kok paša-jeŋə̑m, kok paša-jeŋlan pua kuγurak üδürβəläkə̑m, ške naleš izə̑rak üδüržüm* 'Temə̑r dingt zwei Knechte (Sing.) [und; Ö. B.] gibt die älteren Mädchen den zwei Knechten (Sing.) [zur Frau; Ö. B], er selbst nimmt das jüngste (eig. jüngere) Mädchen [zur Frau; Ö. B.]' (Beke 1961b: 430)

The comparative suffix *-rak, -räk* is also in use in both literary languages:

MaEL *tače šaγal kučaltə̑n γə̑n, erla utlarak kučə̑na* 'If we have caught little today, we will catch more tomorrow' (Oδar 1993: 12)

MaWL *Jašpaj Akcora bəkə̑ turanrak anzal'ə̑* 'Jashpay gave Akcora a stern look' (Petukhov 1994: 17)

The comparative suffix can also be added to words in other word categories in Mari, for example to adverbs such as *βaške* 'fast, quickly':

MaMe *βara üδə̑r tiδə̑ jə̑ŋə̑m βaškerak šə̑lten izi pülemə̑š* 'Da versteckte das Mädchen den Mann rasch in einem kleinen Zimmer' (Alhoniemi & Saarinen 1983: 112)

Also adverbs of place, formed from demonstrative pronouns declined in cases, e.g. *tušto* 'here' ← *tu* 'this, that' can occasionally take the comparative suffix *-rak, -räk*, e.g. *tuštə̑rak* 'exactly here, more in this direction'. Interrogative pronouns like *kušto* 'where', *moγaj* 'of what kind' and *kuze* 'how' can also occur with the comparative suffix *-rak, -räk*:

MaE *Ajδa, kornə̑m ončə̑kto, kuštə̑rak!* 'Wohlan, zeige mir den Weg, wo ist er? (sagt er)' (Beke 1961b: 30)

MaEL *Nu, kuzerak βara, Sanepa?* 'Well, Sanepa, how is it? (Izhboldin 1994: 10)

MaEL *βara, moγajrak kojo?* 'Well, how does it look?' (Izhboldin 1994: 79)

Also substantives and postpositions with case endings can be compared in Mari:

MaMo *toma χoza-βəläštə manə̑t: "šu liδä, šəctä-ok anzə̑kə̑rak!* 'Der Hausvater [und seine Familie; Ö. B.] sagt: "Seid gesund! Setzt euch da obenan!"' (Beke 1951: 57)

The close resemblance in form between the Mari comparative ending and the Chuvash and Tatar counterparts makes the assumption that the Mari suffix originates in the Turkic languages probable. In Tatar, the comparative ending is *-rÄk* and the form expresses, according to Poppe (1963: 92) "a quality stronger than that of another object". Berta (1998b: 286) states that the form of the suffix in Tatar and Bashkir is *-rAK*. The Chuvash comparative suffix has the allomorphs *-raχ, -reχ, -taraχ, -tereχ* (Krueger 1961: 126). In the Turkic languages, these suffixes can be added also to other stems besides the adjective stems. In Chuvash, for instance, the suffix *-raχ, -reχ* (Krueger 1961: 126–127) can be added to adverbs and to postpositions:

Chuv *kunta* 'here', *kuntaraχ* 'closer this way'

Chuv *patne* 'towards', *pürt patnereχ* 'a bit more towards the house'

The suffix can also be added to substantives declined in cases:

Chuv *kilelle* 'towards the house', *kilellereχ* 'a bit more towards the house'

The Tatar suffix can occur in similar contexts, e.g. *birerek kil* 'come nearer!' < *bire* 'hither, in this direction' (Poppe 1963: 108)

The Mari comparative suffix *-rak, -räk*, is thus possible to classify as a copy of a Turkic suffix, mainly used to express comparativity morphologically. However, this suffix can also acquire an emphasizing function and occur with other stems than the pure adjectival stems. The comparative suffix *-rak, -räk* has penetrated the Mari language system to the extent that it is present in all dialects, and it is the suffix used in both literary languages. The suffix is thus possible to classify as a conventionalised copy of a Turkic original. The suffixe itself is a global copy in Mari, but many of the words in which it occurs can be classified as mixed copies, combining global copying of a morpheme with the selective copying of for example combinatorial properties of the morpheme. In Mari, the suffix seems to have acquired all the combinatorial properties of the Turkic original and is added not only to adjectives but also to adverbs, postpositions and nouns with case endings.

The suffix *-rak, -räk* can be a global copy of a Tatar or a Chuvash model (Bereczki 1983: 217). It is however, not possible to identify a single source language. Variants of the suffix occur both in Tatar and Chuvash, and both languages can have been, and probably are, the source language in this respect. Saarinen (1997b: 391) assumes that it is of both Tatar and Chuvash origin, an assumption that seems well-founded. Since the suffixes in Tatar and Chuvash share a common origin, both languages have probably served as model codes when the suffix was copied into Mari.

4.3.1.1.2 The formation of superlatives

In the formation of superlatives, there is a difference between MaMo and the other dialects of Mari. In MaMo, superlatives are formed with the prefigated morpheme *samoj*. This morpheme has been copied from Russian. In MaMe and MaE, superlatives are formed by use of the morpheme *en* < Tat *iñ*, which precedes the adjective in question:

MaMe *Tantuš en čaplə̑ üδə̑rə̑m ojren naleš ta terə̑š šə̑nten kuδaleš, a kolšə̑ aβažə̑m uremeš šuen koδa* 'Tantusch wählt die schönste Tochter, setzt sie in den Schlitten und fährt (fort), seine tote Mutter aber wirft er auf die Strasse' (Alhoniemi & Saarinen 1983: 148)

MaE [...] *oksaštə̑m nalə̑n, kerδə̑m nalə̑n, en peš poro šäple imńeštə̑m örńerten kuškužunδa kuδalə̑n* '[...] nahm ihr Geld, nahm einen Säbel, ihr sehr, sehr gutes starkes Pferd, sattelte sie und sass auf und ritt fort. (Paasonen 1939: 229)

In MaNw, both *samoj* and *en* are possible to use in the formation of superlatives, and besides them, a number of other morphemes are used in this context in the dialect, for example *zansek, sek* and *či* (see Ivanov & Tuzharov 1970: 130 for a detailed account). MaNw shows influence not only from Russian and Tatar in this case, but also from Chuvash, in which a morpheme *či* occurs in the formation of superlatives. According to Krueger (1961: 127) *či* is the most frequent superlative formant in Chuvash. In Mari, the use of the morpheme *en* is not restricted to adjectives, it can also be added to adverbs to form superlatives of them as well:

MaMe *en počeš tuδə̑ starik tek pura izi šol'ə̑žə̑ i ol'a*: 'Zu allerletzt geht der jüngste Bruder zu diesem Alten und sagt:' (Alhoniemi & Saarinen 1983: 86)

MaE *ške marjə̑štlan murmöŋgö kuɣo βeŋə̑lan murat, tümbürźülän, šüβürźülän, śäjüślän, en βara śüjän tarβatə̑šə̑lan* 'Als sie für ihre eigenen Gatten gesungen haben, singen sie für den "Grossen Schwiegersohn", für den Trommler, den Dudelsackpfeifer, den śäjüś [und; Ö. B.] zuletzt für den Hochzeiteröffner' (Beke 1961b: 210)

Superlatives of the adjectives formed with the morpheme *en* can be labelled as mixed copies in Mari since they combine global copying of a morpheme with selective copying of combinatorial properties of this morpheme. This way of forming superlatives can further be classified as a conventionalised copy since it occurs in texts published in the eastern literary language:

MaEL *en kuɣu pojanlə̑k* 'the greatest richness' (Izhboldin 1994: 65)

4.4 Derivational suffixes

Mari is in a unique position among the Finno-Ugric languages when it comes to the number of copies of derivational endings originating in the Turkic languages, endings which have become more or less integrated parts of the Mari language system. The derivational endings can be grouped together with respect to which derivatives they produce. There are endings that derive substantives from different types of stems, endings that derive both substantives and adjectives, endings that derive adjectives and finally verb forming derivative endings. In the literature, many of these endings are assigned a certain degree of productivity. As will become evident in the discussion of these endings, the notion of productivity is highly questionable since most of the endings in question occur only in global copies of derived Tatar or Chuvash stems. To some extent, the endings also occur in what may be labelled mixed copies, in which a global copy of a Turkic derivative ending is attached to a Mari stem, which in turn is a selective copy of semantic properties in the Turkic languages.

4.4.1 Substantive forming derivational suffixes

4.4.1.1 MaMe, MaE *-če, -čo, -čö*

According to Alhoniemi (1985: 154) the suffix MaMe, MaE *-če, -čo, -čö* is an improductive suffix used to derive substantives from substantives. It denotes the doer of an action, e.g. *bajanče* 'accordionist' ← *bajan* 'accordion', *kaβakče* 'inn-keeper' ← *kaβak* 'inn'. Galkin (1966: 27) states that the suffix occurs in MaMe and MaE, whereas in MaMo and MaNw the suffix *-zə̑, -zə* is used (see section 4.4.1.2). Galkin further claims that the suffix is of Tatar origin in Mari, an opinion shared by Bereczki (1971: 60).

The Tatar origin of this suffix is evident enough. In Tatar, a morpheme *-čE* with similar form and function exists (Poppe 1963: 88). This suffix forms what Poppe refers to as "professional names", e.g. *balıkčı* 'fisherman' ← *balık* 'fish'. The Mari suffix has a high frequency in global copies of Tatar words, e.g. *satučo* 'salesman, merchant' and particularly in the eastern dialects. It is interesting to note that this Turkic suffix, usually called "nomen agentis" according to Johanson (1992: 230) exists in several non-Turkic languages exposed to Turkic influence.

4.4.1.2 MaMe, MaE *-ze, -zo, -zö*, MaMo, MaNw *-zə̂, -zə*

Alhoniemi (1985: 155) describes the suffix MaMe, MaE *-ze, -zo, -zö*, MaMo, MaNw *-zə̂, -zə* as a slightly productive suffix that derives substantives from substantives and verbs, e.g. MaMe, MaE *tümə̂rzö*, MaMo, MaNw *təmərzə* 'drummer' ← *tümör, təmər* 'drum'. Galkin (1966: 51) claims that the suffix, which derives substantives from nouns and verbs, is improductive in Mari. Galkin further states that the suffix is of Chuvash origin, an opinion that is expressed also by Bereczki (1971: 60). It may be assumed that the suffix occurs mainly in global copies of Chuvash words, e.g. *jomakze* 'story-teller' ← *jomak* 'story, fairy-tale' (Galkin 1966: 51; see also Räsänen 1920: 135 on the Chuvash origin of the word). In rare cases, the suffix is added also to indigenous Mari stems, e.g. MaE *kolə̂zo* 'fisherman' ← *kol* 'fish' (Galkin 1966: 51). In my opinion, these words are examples of mixed copies, combining the global copying of an originally Chuvash morpheme MaMe, MaE *-ze, -zo, -zö*, MaMo, MaNw *-zə̂, -zə* with the selective copying of semantic content, since close parallels occur in Chuvash. In this language, the suffix *-śă, -śĕ* denotes "the occupation of the person, or the person logically associated with some object and its function" (Krueger 1961: 177), e.g. *pulăśă* 'fisherman ← *pula* 'fish'. From the point of view of Turkic historic linguistics, this suffix is the same as the Tatar suffix *-čE* discussed above and copied into Mari in the form MaMe, MaE *-če, -čo, -čö* (see also Galkin 1966: 28). Mari has thus copied two variants of one and the same Turkic suffix from two different languages. One possible explanation for this is that the ending for the present participle in Mari, MaMe, MaE *-še, -šo, -šö*, MaMo, MaNw *-šə̂, -šə* is used to denote the doer of an action, e.g. MaMe, MaE *tunə̂ktə̂šo* 'teacher' ← *tunə̂ktam* 'to teach'. The formal and semantic resemblance between the Mari present participle and the Tatar and Chuvash suffixes has made the copying of the Turkic derivative endings easier.

4.4.1.3 MaMe, MaE *-čə̂k*, MaMo, MaNw *-zə̂k, zək*

Alhoniemi (1985: 156) states that the suffix MaMe, MaE *-čə̂k*, MaMo, MaNw *-zə̂k, zək* is an unproductive suffix in Mari, originally deriving substantives from verbs, e.g. *ondalčə̂k* 'imposter' ← *ondalem* 'to cheat'. Alhoniemi furthermore states that the derived words have a direct origin in what he calls "Turco-Tatar". According to Galkin (1966: 42), the suffix derives substantives from verbs and is added to stems ending in *l, n* or *r*. Galkin also stresses that the suffix is not productive in all dialects, and that it is of Turkic origin but not productive in any other

Turkic language than Chuvash. From this, Galkin (1966: 43) arrives at the conclusion that the suffix is of Chuvash origin in Mari. I find it very probable that this suffix is not—and never was—productive in any sense in Mari and that it occurs mainly as part of global copies of Chuvash words in Mari. The example *ondalčək* 'imposter', given by both Galkin (1966: 42) and Alhoniemi is in all likelihood copied from Chuvash since the Chuvash verb *ultala* has the meaning 'betrügen' (Paasonen 1974: 192).

4.4.2 Substantive and adjective forming suffixes

4.4.2.1 MaMe, MaE, MaMo, MaNw *-lək*

In Mari, the suffix *-lək* is regarded as a productive suffix that derives substantives and adjectives from all types of stems. Lazar (1975: 220–224) gives a detailed account of the use of this suffix in his monograph on the formation of abstract nouns in the Uralic languages. Galkin (1966: 30) stresses that the suffix *-lək* is very productive and that it occurs in all dialects of Mari. Galkin (1966: 31) further states that the suffix is of Chuvash origin. Lazar (1975: 220) too claims that the suffix is of Chuvash origin and "the most widely used abstract formant in Cheremis [Mari], and it is affixed to the entry form of the derivational base". According to Lazar, the bases include adjectives, denominal and deverbal caritive adjectives, substantives, verbal nouns, verbs and numerals. The account that Lazar gives of the formation of abstract nouns in Mari can serve as a starting point for the discussion of what kind of copies the derivatives with the suffix *-lək* constitute, and I will make extensive use of his examples and discussion in what follows. Lazar (1975: 220) gives the following examples of abstract substantives in *-lək* derived from adjectives:

čaŋga 'stingy' → *čaŋgalək* 'stinginess'
kukšo 'dry, arid' → *kukšələk* 'dryness, aridity'

The suffix is also affixed to denominal and deverbal caritive adjectives, adjectives expressing the lack of a certain quality or describing a state. Lazar gives, among others, the following examples:

čonδəmələk 'lifelessness, insensitiveness' ← *čonδəmo* 'lifeless' ← *čon* 'soul, living being'
jočaδəmolək 'childlessness' ← *jočaδəme* 'childless' ← *joča* 'child'
jönδəmələk 'discomfort, inconvenience' ← *jönδəmö* 'uncomfortable' ← *jön* 'method, way'

The suffix *-lək* is affixed also to substantives. Lazar exemplifies this with the following examples:

joča 'child' → *jočalək* 'childishness'
kul 'slave, thrall' → *kullək* 'slavery, thraldom'

Lazar also states that the derivatives in *-lə̂k* often acquire a concrete meaning:

aβa 'mother' → *aβalə̂k* 'uterus'
keče 'sun, day' → *kečə̂lə̂k* '(provisions etc.) sufficient for a day'
korno 'way, journey' → *kornə̂lə̂k* 'provisions/money for the journey'

Lazar (1975: 222) assumes that the denominal derivatives with a concrete meaning in all likelihood have come from Turkic models and states that many of these derivatives often are translational loans or direct borrowings. Lazar exemplifies this with Ma *sińča* 'eye' → *šińčalə̂k* 'eye-glasses' and compares this with Tat *küz* 'eye' → *küzlek* 'eye-glasses'

The suffix *-lə̂k* is also affixed to verbal nouns in Mari. Lazar (1975: 222) only gives a few examples of this:

kelšə̂mašlə̂k 'conciliation, compromise' ← *kelšə̂maš* 'friendship, reconciliation' ← *kelšaš* 'to like, to make friends, to be reconciled'

Lazar (1975: 223) further claims that the suffix is affixed to verbs:

küleš 'it is necessary' → *külešlə̂k* 'necessity, need(fulness), importance'
uke 'there/it is not → *ukə̂lə̂k* 'absence, lack'
ulo 'there/it is' → *ulə̂lə̂k* 'comfort, abundance, income, good circumstances'

According to Lazar, these types of derivatives are common in compounds of the following kind:

kuγu külešlə̂k 'great importance, significance'
artam ukə̂lə̂k 'incapacity, inability, incapability'

The suffix *-lə̂k* is added also to numerals. Lazar (1975: 223) gives the following examples:

kumə̂t 'three' → *kumə̂tlə̂k* '(sg) sufficient/enough for three persons'

The suffix is also added to adverbs:

joŋgə̂lə̂š 'erroneously, error' → *joŋgə̂lə̂šlə̂k* 'faultiness, incorrectness'
ońčə̂ko 'to before' → *ońčə̂kə̂lə̂k* 'future'
tora 'far away/off' → *toralə̂k* 'remoteness, distance'

Lazar further states that the suffix is added to what he calls loan-words:

kultura 'culture' → *kulturalə̂k* '(standard of) culture'

Lazar (1975: 224) is of the opinion that the incorporation of a great number of words of Turkic origin in Mari includes the borrowing of both adjectives and their derivatives in *-lə̂k*. Because of this it is sometimes difficult to determine whether we are dealing with a genuine Mari abstract form or a loan word. The combinatorial properties of the suffix *-lə̂k* in Mari have parallels in the Turkic languages where a similar suffix is not restricted to the formation of abstract nouns from adjectives. As was mentioned above, there are examples of what can be classified as mixed copies in Mari and several of them have been formed with the suffix *-lə̂k*.

In the Turkic languages the suffix *-lVk* has an extensive distribution and it existed already in the earliest stages of the Turkic languages and has remained productive ever since (Erdal 1991: 121). The suffix derives abstract and concrete substantives from adjectives, substantives and verbs, e.g. Tat *maturlık* 'beauty' ← *matur* 'beautiful' (Poppe 1963: 89). In Chuvash, as in Tatar, the suffix obeys the rules of vowel harmony and has the allomorphs *-lăχ, -lĕχ*. In Turkish, the suffix can be used to derive adjectives and substantives from numerical expressions, e.g. *binlik* 'a thousand-lira note' ← *bin* 'thousand' and can also express the purpose of something, or the characteristic features of something, e.g. Tu *kitaplik* 'library, book-case' ← *kitap* 'book' (Lewis 1989: 68–69). Lazar's assumption that the derivatives with a concrete meaning in Mari have come from models in the Turkic languages is basically correct. The example given by Lazar, *kornə̂lə̂k* 'provisions/money for the journey' has direct counterparts in the Turkic languages, e.g. Tu *yolluk* 'provisions for a journey, journey-money', Tat *yullık* 'für den Weg (Geld, Proviant) ← *yul* 'Weg'. In Turkic languages, the suffix is affixed also to verb stems, e.g. Tat *barlık* 'Dasein; Existenz; Bestehen; Vorhandensein' ← tat *bar* 'ist; es gibt; es existiert; vorhanden', Tu *varlık* 'existence, possessions, wealth' ← *var* 'existent; present; at hand; available'. This is a good model for the Mari derivative *ulə̂lə̂k* 'comfort, abundance, good circumstances'. Kangasmaa-Minn (1998: 244–245) mentions the suffix *-lə̂k* that according to her is of Chuvash origin and points to the fact that the suffix can be affixed even to finite verb forms, e.g. "*küleš=lə̂k* 'necessity' (*küleš* 'it is necessary', a third person singular present tense form)". Also in this case there is a parallel in Tatar. The Tatar *kirek* 'necessary, suitable' can take the suffix *-lə̂k* and the form *kireklik* has the meaning 'necessity' (Poppe 1963: 223). Apparently, *kirek* is a verb form; in Turkish the verb *gerekmek* means 'to be necessary' (Lewis 1959: 116). In Mari, the abstract word *küleslə̂k* can thus be classified as a mixed copy of a Tatar original.

The obvious conclusion is that most, if not all derivatives in *-lə̂k* in Mari in which the suffix is affixed to a Mari stem can be classified as mixed copies. They combine a globally copied derivational suffix with the selective copying of semantic properties. The productive use of the suffix, stressed by many scholars in Finno-Ugric linguistics is thus restricted to cases with strong parallels in the Turkic languages.

Denominal and deverbal caritive adjectives formed with the suffix *-lə̂k* are no exceptions in this respect since they too have parallels in the Turkic languages. Caritive adjectives and substantives in the Turkic languages are formed with the suffix *-sVz*, e.g. Tat *akılsız* 'Dummheit; Unvernunft' ← *akıl* 'Verstand; Vernunft'. In Chuvash, the suffix has the ending *-săr, -sĕr*. In Mari, the suffix MaMe, MaE *-δə̂me, -δə̂mo, -δə̂mö, -tə̂me, -tə̂mo, -tə̂mö*, MaMo, MaNw *-δə̂mə̂, -δəmə, -tə̂mə̂, -təmə* fills the same function and is added also to words of Turkic origin, e.g. *akə̂lδə̂me* 'mad' ← *akə̂l* 'reason'. With respect to this, there is nothing surprising in the fact that the suffix *-lə̂k* can be affixed to these forms in Mari since the derived form has a direct counterpart in the Turkic languages, e.g. Tat *akılsızlık* 'Dummheit; Unvernunft'. In many cases the Mari ending *-δəmo* etc is affixed to a global copy of a Turkic stem, e.g. *akəlδəme* 'mad' which in this way is inserted into the base code. To this form, the copied suffix *-lə̂k* can be added, e.g. *akə̂lδə̂mə̂lə̂k* 'madness'. Copies of this type are highly creative formations and hard to classify. In the form *akə̂lδəmə̂lə̂k* 'madness' we are dealing with two globally copied morphemes and these copies can perhaps be classified as double copies.

Lazar (1975: 220) claims that the suffix *-lə̂k* is of Turkic origin, "more Chuvash than anything else" as he puts it. This can be questioned since Chuvash, like Mari, has been exposed to long-term Tatar influence, and the Chuvash suffix *-lăχ, -lĕχ* too may well be of Tatar origin, since a word final *k* in Chuvash often is lost in words of common origin in Tatar and Chuvash (Krueger 1961: 62). Forms like Chuv *pulă* 'fish', Tat *balık* 'id' make it reasonable to assume a Chuvash suffix with the allomorphs *-lă, -lĕ* instead of *-lăχ, -lĕχ* (Benzing 1993: 79).

The originally Tatar suffix *-lə̂k* used in the formation of abstract nouns in Mari occurs also in other Finno-Ugric languages influenced by Tatar. One example, mentioned by Lazar (1975: 237) is the Ugric language Mansi. Far more interesting are the derivatives in *-lyk* in Udmurt, derivatives with strong similarities to the derivatives in *-lə̂k* in Mari. In Lazar (1975: 195–199) it is evident that the Udmurt suffix is affixed to adjectives, denominal and deverbal caritive adjectives, to substantives and to verbs, but evidently not to adverbs or numerals, as these are not included in the examples given by him.

The Udmurt suffix too is of Tatar rather than Chuvash origin. In both Mari and Udmurt it seems to have been copied extensively because of its great combinatorial properties. This means that the suffix *-lə̂k* in Mari may well have taken over functions originally filled by other suffixes and structures in Mari. It can be assumed that such suffixes have existed or still exist in the formation of abstract nouns in Mari and that they once occupied the equivalence position into which the Tatar suffix has been inserted. Lazar (1975: 224) gives an account of the use of the suffix *-t* which in Mari is a continuation of a Uralic suffix used in abstracts of measure:

kelγe 'deep' → *kelγə̂t* 'depth'
nele 'heavy, difficult' → *nelə̂t* 'weight (of load)'

Assuming that the suffix *-lə̂k*, originating in Tatar, has come to fill the equivalence position filled by the suffix *-t*, and considering the fact that foreign suffix and other items often exist parallel to their native counterparts, it would be possible to expect such parallel occurrences. Judging from Lazar's examples, it is evident that this is the case. Beside forms like *kelγə̂t* 'depth' and *nelə̂t* 'weight (of load)' also forms like *kelγə̂lə̂k* 'depth' and *nelə̂lə̂k* 'weight' occur.

Lazar (1975: 215–219) is of the opinion that Mari often "resorts to verbal nouns and paraphrased word-groups to render abstract concepts" and the basic assumption is apparently that this is a more primitive—and this notion of a division between more and less primitive Finno-Ugric languages seems dubious in my opinion—way to render these abstract concepts than in certain other Finno-Ugric languages. In many cases, these paraphrased word-groups have a meaning close to one of the abstract substantives formed with the suffix *-lə̑k* affixed to caritive adjectives, e.g. *joča uke lijmaš* 'childlessness' (lit. "child-there-is not being") (Lazar 1975: 219), *jočaδə̑mə̑lə̑k* 'childlessness'. The suffixed *-lə̑k*, copied from Tatar, has apparently been copied since it has facilitated the formation of abstract nouns because of its greater combinatorial properties and it has gradually come to fill the function of both the suffix *-t* and the paraphrased word-groups and verbal nouns used to render abstract concepts.

4.4.3 Adjective forming derivational suffixes

4.4.3.1 MaMe, MaE, *-le, -lo, -lö*, MaMo, MaNw *-lə̑, -lə*

The suffix MaMe, MaE, *-le, -lo, -lö*, MaMo, MaNw *-lə̑, -lə* is according to Alhoniemi (1985: 159) a slightly productive suffix that derives adjectives from nouns. Alhoniemi gives the following examples: MaE *kuatle*, MaMo *kuatlə̑* 'strong' ← MaE, MaMo *kuat* 'strength, ability', MaMo *ləmlə* 'famous, known' ← MaMo *ləm* 'name'. Galkin (1966: 72) emphasizes that this suffix occurs in all dialects of Mari and that it has a tendency to be increasingly spread, which makes it a productive ending in Mari. Galkin is of the opinion that the suffix is of Chuvash origin in Mari and Kangasmaa-Minn (1998: 244) supports this view. In the material I have examined, the suffix occurs in all dialects apart from MaNw:

MaMo "*βara pumə̑ pajet piš totlə. maγań pajə̑m pušə̑c?*" 'Das zuletzt gegebene Stück Fleisch [war; Ö. B.] besonders schmackhaft. Was für Fleisch gabst du mir?' (Beke 1951: 170)

MaMe *Tantuš en čaplə̑ üδə̑rə̑m ojren naleš ta terə̑š šə̑nten kuδaleš, a kolšə̑ aβažə̑m uremeš šuen koδa* 'Tantusch wählt die schönste Tochter, setzt sie in den Schlitten und fährt (fort), seine Tote Mutter aber wirft er auf die Strasse' (Alhoniemi & Saarinen 1983: 148)

MaE *poro küδürätle kuγo jumo, amiń* 'Gütiger, unendlich grosser Gott, Amen!' (Beke 1961b: 206)

The suffix also occurs in both literary languages of Mari:

MaEL *jorlo δen pojan izak-šol'ak* 'the poor and the rich brother' (Taygiljdin 1993: 62)

MaWL *marjaβlä dorc ertə̑mə̑ γoδə̑m totlə̑ pə̑š šärla* 'A pleasant smell spread as the women went past' (Petukhov 1994: 28)

It is evident that many of the scholars who have discussed this suffix are of the opinion that it is of Chuvash origin. In Chuvash there is an adjective forming suffix with the allomorphs *-lă, -lĕ* after consonant stems, *-llă, -llĕ* after vowel stems. The meaning is "mit...versehen, ...habend" (Benzing 1959b: 717). Krueger (1961: 130) states that the suffix is very frequent in Chuvash and according to Krueger has the meaning 'having, possessing, having the nature of'. Krueger includes the following examples:

ChuvA *čaplă* 'famous, having fame' ← *čap* 'fame', *yatlă* 'named (so-and-so), having the name...' ← *yat* 'name'

In the Chuvash material I have examined, the suffix is frequent:

ChuvA *untan vărman χušipe pırsan pĕr aslă ĕšnene tuχnă* 'Nachdem sie dann mitten in dem Walde gegangen war, kam sie auf einen grossen Rasenplatz' (Paasonen 1949: 148)

ChuvA *ikkĕ amanăn pilĕkšĕr ača, purte pĕr yatlă—ura-čĕrnisem* 'Zwei Mutter haben je fünf Kinder, alle sind gleichnamig.—Die Nägel an den Zehen' (Paasonen 1949: 94)

The Mari suffix MaMe, MaE, *-le, -lo, -lö*, MaMo, MaNw *-lə̂, -lə* and the Chuvash *-lă, -lĕ, -llă, -llĕ* have a formal and functional counterpart in the Tatar suffix *-lE* (Poppe 1963: 91) and for this reason it is possible to reckon not only with Chuvash but also with Tatar influence on Mari in this case. Poppe includes the following examples:

Tat *akıllı* 'clever, intelligent' ← *akıl* 'intellect', *kerle* 'filthy ← *ker* 'filth

The suffix occurs in the Tatar material I have examined:

TatM *Äwäl zamanda käcä kumanda sayïskan sutnik, baka pulutnik bulgan bik yarlï-gïna br kiši aniñ bulgan üc ulï* 'In alter Zeit, als die Ziege Oberst, die Elster Hauptmann und die Kröte Zimmerman war, lebte ein sehr armer Mann, der hatte drei Söhne' (Kakuk 1996: 93)

TatK *sul uakėtta biyėk buylė, zur sakallė, kalėn kursaklė br bay* 'Da ging ein grossgewachsener Herr mit einem langen Bart und einem grossen Bauch rufend auf und ab' (Kakuk 1989: 172)

The Mari suffix MaMe, MaE, *-le, -lo, -lö*, MaMo, MaNw *-lə̂, -lə* is undoubtedly copied from the Turkic languages but it is hardly probable that Chuvash alone has been the model code. In Saarinen's (1997b: 391) view the suffix is of both Chuvash and Tatar origin and it is impossible to distinguish between the sources. Kangasmaa-Minn (1998: 234, 244) argues that the word *tamle* 'sweet' is of Chuvash origin in Mari. This, however, is not correct. Both the stem *tam* 'taste' and the derived adjective *tamle* are of Tatar origin (Räsänen 1923: 66). In Mari, the occurrence of the suffix is generally restricted to global copies of Tatar and Chuvash words, e.g. Ma *jorlo* 'poor', Chuv *yurlă*, 'arm' (Paasonen 1974: 32) Tat *yarlı* 'id'; Ma *tamle* 'sweet' Tat *tämle* 'schmackhaft, lecker'; Ma *čerle* 'ill, sick', Tat *čirle* 'krank'. The ways in which Tatar and Chuvash vowel phonemes are rendered in Mari can be used to identify the model code, and in the example *jorlo* given above it is evident from the sound correspondences that the word originates in Chuvash, whereas *tamle* and *čerle* are of Tatar origin. The suffix MaMe, MaE *-le, -lo, -lö*, MaMo, MaNw *-lə̂, -lə* apparently has a native Mari equivalent in the suffix *-an, -än*. This suffix derives adjectives from all types of stems (Alhoniemi 1985: 158); for a detailed account for the origin of this suffix, see Galkin (1966: 64–66). One can assume that this is the suffix with which the copied suffix MaMe, MaE, *-le, -lo, -lö*, MaMo, MaNw *-lə̂, -lə* has been identified and that it has been inserted into an equivalence position once reserved for *-an, -än*. There are instances in which a stem, be it copied or not, occurs with both suffixes:

čeran 'ill, sick', *čerle* 'id' ← *čer* 'disease'
lüman 'called, named', *lümlö* 'famous, known' ← *lüm* 'name'
taman 'tasting, tasty', *tamle* 'sweet, tasty, delicious' ← *tam* 'taste'
kuatan 'strong', *kuatle* 'id' ← *kuat* 'strength, ability'

tam, čer and *kuat* are all copied from Tatar and the words have originally taken the Mari derivational ending *-an, -än*. The suffix MaMe, MaE, *-le, -lo, -lö*, MaMo, MaNw *-lə̂, -lə* has not entirely replaced its native equivalent *-an, än* which according to Alhoniemi (1985: 158) still is used productively. There is a difference between the suffixes in the sense that *-an, -än* derives adjectives from all types of stems, whereas MaMe, MaE, *-le, -lo, -lö*, MaMo, MaNw *-lə̂, -lə* seems restricted to substantives. This may well mean that the Tatar and Chuvash suffixes, etymologically related to each other, have fewer combinatorial properties and that this has had a restricting influence on the copying of the suffix. For a discussion of the differences between the suffixes, see Galkin (1966: 72).

It is a frequently expressed opinion that the suffix MaMe, MaE *-le, -lo, -lö,* MaMo, MaNw *-lə̂, -lə* is productive in Mari. The word *lümlö* 'famous, known' is often (Kangasmaa-Minn 1998: 234, 244; Saarinen 1997b: 391) given as an example of this productive use of the suffix but apart from a couple of other examples given by Galkin (1966: 72), the word *lümlö* stands out in isolation. I am of the opinion that most of the words including the suffix can be classified as global copies and that it is possible to classify a word like *lümlö* as a mixed copy combining a globally copied suffix with selective copying of a semantic property. In Chuvash, the word *yatlă* does not only mean 'having the name of', apparently it can also mean 'famous, known':

ChuvA *ku šăllămăr aččene čirtse ıră yatlă pulat* 'Dieser unser jüngerer Bruder wird unserem Vater heilen und sich einen guten Namen verschaffen [lit. will have a good name]' (Paasonen 1949: 132)

The suffix MaMe, MaE *-le, -lo, -lö*, MaMo, MaNw *-lə̂, -lə* occurs in all dialects and in both literary languages. It occurs mainly in words of Tatar and Chuvash origin and is only occasionally affixed to native Mari stems, e.g. *lümlö* 'famous'. Saarinen (1997b: 391) claims that the suffix can also be affixed to words of Russian origin. I find it likely though that these words have been globally copied from Tatar or Chuvash in which they result in the insertion of global copies of Russian words into the basic morphology of either Tatar or Chuvash and that they are not examples of genuine Mari derivations. This puts them on the same level as *gerojlik* 'Heldentum' (Wintschalek 1992: 454) ← Tat *geroj* 'hero' (Poppe 1963: 210) < Ru *geroj* 'hero'.

4.4.3.2 MaMe, MaE *-sə̂r*, MaMo, MaNw *-sə̂r, -sər*

The suffix MaMe, MaE *-sə̂r*, MaMo, MaNw *-sə̂r, -sər* is an unproductive suffix in Mari, mainly occurring in words of Chuvash origin (Alhoniemi 1985: 159). Galkin (1996: 72) also claims that the suffix is of Chuvash origin. The suffix MaMe, MaE *-sə̂r*, MaMo, MaNw *-sə̂r, -sər* derives caritive adjectives from all types of stems and denotes the lack of a certain property or ability. Alhoniemi gives the examples MaMe, MaE *törsə̂r*, MaMo, MaNw *törsər* 'uneven' ← *tör* 'even', MaE *jönə̂sə̂r* 'unpleasant' ← *jön* 'way, method', MaE *čonə̂sə̂r* 'hysterical, senseless' ← *čon* 'spirit, soul'. The suffix is undoubtedly of Chuvash origin in Mari and occurs mainly in global copies of Chuvash words. In Chuvash, the corresponding suffix is *-săr, -sĕr*. According to Krueger (1961: 110) some Chuvash grammarians consider it a case, the so-called "privative case".

As was the case with the suffix *-le, -lo, -lö, -lə̂, -lə* discussed above in section 4.4.3.1, it is possible to connect the suffix MaMe, MaE *-sə̂r*, MaMo, MaNw *-sə̂r, -sər* copied from Chuvash with a native suffix in Mari: more precisely with the suffix *-δə̂mo, -δə̂me, -δə̂mö* etc. (Galkin 1966: 72), a suffix that derives adjectives from substantives. Here too, the same stem can occur with both suffixes, sometimes with a difference in meaning:

MaEL *čonδə̂mo* 'lifeless, dead' *čonə̂sə̂r* 'hysterical' (Moisio 1994: 357)

MaEL *jönδə̂mö* 'unpleasant, awkward' *jönə̂sə̂r* 'unpleasant(ness)' (Moisio 1994: 78)

The suffix *-δə̂mo*, etc. is used productively as a derivational ending in Mari. However, the suffix has other functions as well in the language and when affixed to verbal stems it forms negative participles of the verbs, e.g. MaE *tolδə̂mo* 'one who has not come, not coming' (Alhoniemi 1985: 140). The fact that the Mari suffix has wider functions has probably contributed to the suffix MaMe, MaE *-sə̂r*, MaMo, MaNw *-sə̂r, -sər* occuring mainly in global copies of Chuvash words and it is safe to assume the wider functions of the Mari suffix have exerted a restrictive influence on the copying of the suffix MaMe, MaE *-sə̂r*, MaMo, MaNw *-sə̂r, -sər*.

The copies can be classified as conventionalised copies of Chuvash words since they often occur in all dialects of Mari and in the literary languages. In the material I have examined, there are no instances in which the suffix is affixed to a native Mari stem; thus the suffix does not occur in what could be classified as mixed copies.

4.4.3.3 MaE *-sə̂z*

The suffix MaE *-sə̂z* is not mentioned by Alhoniemi (1985) but according to Anduganov (1991: 134) it is a suffix occurring in the eastern dialects of Mari. Galkin (1966: 73) states that it is restricted to MaE. This suffix is a copy of a Tatar suffix *-sEz* by use of which caritive adjectives are formed (Poppe 1963: 91) In an etymological sense, the suffix is the same as the Chuvash suffix *-săr, -sĕr*. Anduganov gives the following examples:

MaE *jönsə̂z ajδeme* 'a senseless person' (Anduganov 1991: 134)

MaE *jönsə̂z korno* 'an unpleasant road' (Anduganov 1991: 134)

In the material that I have examined, there are hardly any examples of this suffix. One exception is the example already given in section 4.1.3 and which is taken from Beke's collection of texts from Bashkortostan:

MaE *koltalalam, koltalam, salamem o šu*
Mo-γańe umsuz-at postoβoj

'Ich sende und sende Grüsse (Sing.), doch sie kommen (Sing.) nicht an,
Wie vergesslich ist [doch; Ö. B.] die Post! (Beke 1961b: 338)

In any case, judging from the material, this suffix appears to be no more than a sporadically occurring momentary copy. Further studies of the situation in MaE can help to clarify the picture.

4.4.4 Verb forming derivational suffixes

4.4.4.1 MaMe, MaE *-tar, -δar*, MaMo, MaNw *-tar, -tär, -δar, -δär*

The suffix MaMe, MaE *-tar, -δar*, MaMo, MaNw *-tar, -tär, -δar, -δär* is according to Alhoniemi (1985: 165) a slightly productive suffix that derives verb from verbs, occasionally also from nouns. The derived verbs are conjugated in the *em*-conjugation and have a causative meaning. Alhoniemi gives, among others, the following examples: MaMe, MaE *βožəltaraš,* MaMo, MaNw *βažəltaraš* 'to make someone feel ashamed' ← MaMe, MaE *βožəlaš,* MaMo, MaNw *βažəlaš* 'to be ashamed'; MaMe, MaE *uβertaraš,* MaMo, MaNw *uβertäräš* 'to make known' ← *uβer* 'news'. Alhoniemi states that this suffix, which he refers to as a Turco-Tatar suffix, mainly occurs in words of foreign origin. According to Galkin (1966: 135) the suffix is slighty productive in Mari and he further states (Galkin 1966: 137) that it is of Chuvash origin. If this suffix occurs mainly in verbs of foreign origin in Mari, these verbs can be classified as global copies. The productivity that Alhoniemi refers to but never defines, should probably be interpreted so that the suffix is added freely to Mari stems. Considering the way the derivational ending *-lək* is added to Mari stems, it is highly likely that the verbs formed when the suffix is added to a verbal stem will be possible to classify as mixed copies, combining global copying of a morpheme with the selective copying of semantic content, e.g. MaMe, MaE *βožə̂ltaraš* 'to make someone feel ashamed', Chuv *namə̂slantăr* 'beschämen' (Paasonen 1974: 90). The suffix MaMe, MaE *-tar, -δar*, MaMo, MaNw *-tar, -tär, -δar, -δär* has a formal resemblance with the causative derivational ending MaMe, MaE -ar, MaMo, MaNw *-ar, -är*, to be discussed in section 4.4.4.5.

4.4.4.2 MaMe, MaE *-tat*

The suffix MaMe, MaE *-tat* is according to Alhoniemi (1985: 163) an unproductive derivational ending, forming onomatopoetic words from verbs. Alhoniemi gives the example *kočə̂rtataš* 'to creak'. The derived verbs are conjugated in the *em*-conjugation and Alhoniemi states that they in general have Chuvash counterparts (see Paasonen 1974: 62 for the Chuvash equivalent of *kočə̂rtataš*). Galkin (1966: 84) is apparently of the opinion that the suffix is slightly productive in Mari and also states that the derived verbs are conjugated in the *em*-conjugation. Galkin (1966: 85) claims that the verb is of Chuvash origin in Mari. The fact that this suffix is improductive and often has formal counterparts in Chuvash, makes it possible to conclude that the derivations in which the suffix occurs rather are examples of globally copied Chuvash derived verbs than genuine derivations in Mari. Thus, the suffix is not and has never been productive in Mari.

4.4.4.3 MaMe, MaE *-lan*, MaMo, MaNw *-lan, -län*

In Mari, the suffix MaMe, MaE *-lan*, MaMo, MaNw *-lan, -län* is slightly productive according to Alhoniemi (1985: 162) and derives verbs from all types of stems. The derived verbs acquire a meaning that describes states or processes in the direction towards a certain state. All derived verbs are conjugated in the *em*-conjugation, e.g. MaMe, MaE *koktelanem* 'to hesitate'. Bereczki (1971: 62) claims that the suffix is of Turkic origin. In Chuvash, a passive-reflexive suffix *-lan, -len* exists, e.g. *tumlan* 'to undress oneself' (Krueger 1961:181) and this suffix is probably a combination of the denominal suffix *-la, -le* and a passive-reflexive suffix *-n*. This means of forming passive and reflexive verbforms is characteristic also of Tatar: *bašla* 'to begin → *bašlan* 'to be begun' (Poppe 1963: 97; see also Benzing 1959b: 718). In Tatar, the suffix *-lÄ* is used to derive verbs from adjectives and nouns (Poppe 1963: 96), verbs which then can be made passive by use of the suffix *-n* (Poppe 1963: 97).

The suffix MaMe, MaE *-lan*, MaMo, MaNw *-lan, -län* is with certainty copied from the Turkic languages, since it mainly occurs with adjective and substantive stems of Turkic origin, e.g. *sajlanem* 'to become better' ← *saj* 'good'; *čeβerlanem* 'to become beautiful' ← *čeβer* 'beautiful', *čerlanem* 'to become ill' ← *čer* 'disease'; *namə̂slanem* 'to be ashamed' ← *namə̂s* 'shame'. However, the suffix MaMe, MaE *-lan*, MaMo, MaNw *-lan, -län* can also occur with Mari stems, e.g. *koktelanem* 'to hesitate' ← MaMe, MaE *kokə̂te*, MaMo, MaNw *kokte* 'to split, two make into two'.

In my opinion, it is possible that the copied suffix MaMe, MaE *-lan*, MaMo,

MaNw *-lan, -län* has been identified with what Alhoniemi (1985: 162) considers the unproductive suffix MaMe, MaE *-γ, -k*. This suffix has derived verbs from all types of stems and the suffix MaMe, MaE *-lan*, MaMo, MaNw *-lan, -län* has probably been inserted into the equivalence position once occupied by this suffix. A couple of circumstances speak in favour of this assumption. As is the case with the suffix MaMe, MaE *-lan*, MaMo, MaNw *-lan, -län*, the derived verbs are conjugated in the *em*-conjugation. There are also parallel forms without any difference in meaning: Alhoniemi gives the example *čeβerγaš* 'to become beautiful' and *čeβerlanem* has the same meaning (Moisio 1994: 352).

4.4.4.4 MaMe, MaE *-γal, -kal*, MaMo, MaNw *-γal, -kal, -γäl, -käl*

The suffix MaMe, MaE *-γal, -kal*, MaMo, MaNw *-γal, -kal, -γäl, -käl* is a slightly productive suffix that derives verbs from verbs (Alhoniemi 1985: 161). The derived verbs have a frequentative meaning. The suffix is discussed by Galkin (1966: 104–106) who states that the slightly productive suffix is always added to verbs conjugated in the *em*-conjugation and the verbs acquire a frequentative meaning. According to Galkin (1966: 105) there are two explanations for the origin of the suffix. Lehtisalo (1936: 383) connects it—or rather proposes a connection—with a Proto-Uralic suffix **kk*. Galkin (1966: 106) points to the fact that a similar suffix does not occur in other Finno-Ugric languages with the exception of Hungarian, in which the suffix *-gál, -gél* is used to form frequentative verbs. Because of this, Galkin (1966: 106) claims that Lehtisalo's proposal hardly stands the test and that the suffix rather is of Turkic, above all Chuvash, origin in Mari. In the material I have examined there are several examples:

MaMe *tə̑štə̑ kuβa tiδə̑m Iβan Nańkinlak šotlen i čə̑la kalaskalen i joδə̑štə̑n kuze kuγžan üδə̑rə̑m utarkalen* 'Hier hielt die Alte ihn für Iwan Nańkin und erzählte alles und fragte wie er die Töchter (eigtl. Sing.) des Zaren gerettet hatte' (Alhoniemi & Saarinen 1983: 136)

MaE *üδə̑r jamδə̑lkala čə̑la oβeδə̑m üštə̑βake* 'Das Mädchen berietet (stellt) alle[rhand; Ö. B.] Speisen (Sg.) auf den Tisch' (Beke 1995: 140)

The suffix MaMe, MaE *-γal, -kal*, MaMo, MaNw *-γal, -kal, -γäl, -käl* is without doubt of Turkic origin since comparable suffixes occur in the Turkic languages. In Chuvash, the suffix *-kala, -kele* is an iterative suffix that denotes "repeated or strengthened actions" (Krueger 1961: 181). Examples occur in the material I have examined:

ChuvA *esir puśtarkalasa pırăr, tenĕ* 'Sammelt ihr (das Getreide) zusammen' (Paasonen 1949: 144)

Kangasmaa-Minn (1998: 245) stresses that the suffix is an iterative suffix "originally occurring in Chuvash borrowings, e.g. jamdə̑l=kalə̑ 'prepares repeatedly', but available now for (F)U roots as well: lüj=kalə̑ 'shoots repeatedly' from lüjə̑ 'shoots' ". Apparently, the suffix shows similarities with the derivational ending *-lə̂k* in this respect, an ending characterised by the combinatorial properties being regulated by conditions in the Turkic languages to some extent. It is not necessary to assume that Chuvash alone has served as the model code, although most verbal stems with which the suffix occurs are originally Chuvash. In Tatar, frequentative verbs denoting periodically repeated actions are formed with the suffix *-gAlA*. Berta (1998b: 291) gives the example *yazγala* 'write now and then' ← *yaz* 'to write'. In Mari there are examples of the suffix *-kala* entirely comparable with the suffix *-lə̂k*, and it is possible to form frequentative or iterative verbs of stems with direct equivalents in the Turkic languages, e.g. MaEL *βozγalem* 'to write often' (Moisio 1994: 32) ← *βozem* 'to write', Tat *yazγala* 'write now and then', Chuv *śırkala* 'to write a bit'.

The globally copied stems in which the suffix MaMe, MaE *-γal, -kal*, MaMo, MaNw *-γal, -kal, -γäl, -käl* occurs serve as inputs for further copying and can result in mixed copies of the type *βozγalem*. The Tatar verb *yaz* 'to write' and/or the Chuvash *śır* 'id' is identified with the Mari verb *βozem* 'to write' and after this the globally copied derivational ending *-kala* is added to the Mari stem. The suffix MaMe, MaE *-γal, -kal,* MaMo, MaNw *-γal, -kal, -γäl, -käl* is in this respect a perfectly analogous example of the suffix *-lə̂k.*

4.4.4.5 MaMe, MaE *-ar*, MaMo, MaNw *-ar, -är*

According to Alhoniemi (1985: 160), the suffix MaMe, MaE *-ar*, MaMo, MaNw *-ar, -är* is a slightly productive causative derivational ending in Mari that is added to verbs in the *em*-conjugation. Alhoniemi further states that this ending is of Chuvash origin and that it is always added to *t*, that is verbal stems ending in *t*, e.g. MaMe, MaE *ertaraš* 'to make pass', MaMo, MaNw *ertäräš* 'id' ← MaMe, MaE *ertas*, MaMo, MaNw *ertäs* 'to pass' (Alhoniemi 1985: 160). This derivational ending MaMe, MaE *-ar*, MaMo, MaNw *-ar, -är* has a close resemblance with the causative ending MaMe, MaE *-tar, -δar*, MaMo, MaNw *-tar, -tär, -δar, -δär* discussed above in section 4.4.4.1, which is also of Turkic origin. This according to Alhoniemi slightly productive suffix forms causative verbs from stems in the *em*-conjugation, but can apparently also be added to substantives, although this use of the suffix seems restricted (Alhoniemi 1985: 165). Galkin (1966: 134–135) discusses the suffix MaMe, MaE *-ar*, MaMo, MaNw *-ar, -är* which according to him is slightly productive and arrives at the conclusion that it is of Chuvash origin in Mari. Many of the examples given by Galkin are global copies of Chuvash verbs, e.g. MaMe *utarem* 'to save', MaMe, MaE *ertaraš* 'to make pass', MaMo, MaNw *ertäräš* 'id' (as to the Chuvash origin of these verbs, see Räsänen 1920: 237, 126). Saarinen (1997b: 392) claims that the suffix is productive in Mari but not at all in present-day Chuvash. She does not, however, present this more in detail.

It can be assumed, as was indicated above, that the suffix MaMe, MaE *-ar*, MaMo, MaNw *-ar, -är* is closely connected to the suffix 4.4.4.1 MaMe, MaE *-tar, -δar,* MaMo, MaNw *-tar, -tär, -δar, -δär*. The example given by both Alhoniemi and Galkin, MaMe, MaE *ertaraš* 'to make pass', MaMo, MaNw *ertäräš* 'id' is a verb of Chuvash origin in Mari. In Chuvash, it has the form *irt-* 'vorübergehen, vorbeiziehen; vergehen (v. der zeit)' (Paasonen 1974: 17). In Chuvash, causative forms of the verbs are formed by use of the suffix *-tar, -ter, -ttar, -tter* (Krueger 1961: 179), e.g. *irtter* (Paasonen 1974: 17), the causative form of the verb *irt-*. Since geminated consonants do not occur in Mari, it is is not unlikely that the geminated consonant *tt* in the causative verbs of Chuvash origin in Mari is given as *t* and that this *t* is perceived as something belonging to the stem and not to the causative ending, that is the ending is percieved as *-ar, -är* in Mari. An analogous example is the Chuvash *ll*, in Chuvash a rarely occurring geminated consonant, which, according to Räsänen (1920: 49) "aus verschiedenen konsonantenverbindungen herrührt". In Mari, the Chuvash *ll* is generally given as *l* according to Räsänen.

4.5 The plural category in Mari

4.5.1 Plural suffixes in Mari

A characteristic feature of Mari is that an original Uralic plural suffix **t* has disappeared from nominal declension and has been replaced by secondary plural suffixes of a more analytic character (Luutonen 1999: 73). In the verb declension and in the possessive suffix of the third person plural, however, the suffix **t* has been preserved. The loss of an original plural suffix **t* is characteristic also of the Permian languages. In these languages, the plural suffixes Ko *-jas* and Udm *-jos*/*-os* are used instead of the Uralic suffix **t*. Also Chuvash displays a (in comparison with other Turkic languages) different plural suffix, ChuvV *-sam*/*-sem*, ChuvA *-sem*.

The group of secondary plural suffixes is comparatively heterogenous in Mari and includes both originally Mari suffixes and morphemes that possibly could be labelled as code-copies. Among the suffixes used as plural endings are MaMo *-βlä*, MaE *-βlak* and MaMe *-šamə̑č*. These suffixes are used as the general plural suffixes in the dialects in question, and also in the literary languages. The distribution of the suffixes is illustrated in map 2. They are added to all types of substantives and are inflected in all cases. Apart from these more general suffixes, there are a number of other plural endings which are not added to all types of substantives and not inflected in all cases. In this group, the suffixes MaMe *-mə̑t, -la, -št*, MaMo *-βolkə̑* and MaNw *-polə̑k* can be singled out for mention. As regards the Mari-Turkic linguistic contacts, the three suffixes that have been ascribed a Turkic origin are of particular interest, and these are the suffixes MaMo, MaNw *-βlä*, MaE *-βlak* and MaMe *-šamə̑č*. The suffixes all have a significant word-like character and are further characterised by a process of grammaticalization varying in extent. The analytic character of the suffixes and the processes of grammaticalization have been described in detail by Luutonen (1997; 1999). Several different explanations have been given for the origin of these suffixes, for a detailed account of this, see Honti (1997: 65–70). However, there are some frequently proposed etymologies and in what follows, these will be discussed more in detail, and by the use of additional material evaluated in terms of what can be seen as probable.

4.5.2 MaMo *-βlä*

The plural suffix *-βlä* occurs as the plural suffix of the western dialects and the western literary language. The vowel is always a front vowel and the suffix has few allomorphs apart from *-lä*. In the literary language, it is always added to the main word without a hyphen.

4.5.3 MaE *-βlak*

The plural suffix *-βlak* occurs in the eastern dialect of Mari, both in the varieties spoken in the republic of Mari-El and in the ones spoken in adjacent areas and in Bashkortostan. The border that separates this plural suffix from the plural suffix *-samə̂č* runs through the Mari republic. This suffix has several allomorphs, e.g. *-βläk, -plak, -lak* and *-läk*. In the eastern literary language, the suffix is always added to the main word by use of a hyphen, e.g. *ija-βlak* 'devils'.

4.5.4 MaMe *-šamə̂č*

The suffix *-šamə̂č* is used as a plural suffix in the central parts of the Mari language area, in particular in MaMe, but it is used also in MaNw. It has several allomorphs, e.g. *-šämə̂č, -šaməc, -šač, -šäč, -šac* and *-šäc*. This suffix is occasionally used as a plural suffix in the eastern literary language and is added to the main word by use of a hyphen.

4.6 The origin of the Mari plural suffixes

4.6.1 MaMo *-βlä*, MaE *-βlak*

It is a common opinion that the suffixes MaMo *-βlä* and MaE *-βlak* are etymologically related to each other (Luutonen 1997: 57; Bereczki 1988: 341; Beke 1911: 171) and it is also assumed that they are of Turkic origin (Luutonen 1997: 57). Ramstedt (1952: 59) discusses the Chuvash plural suffix *-sam, -sem* and makes the assumption that Chuvash once had a plural suffix **böläk > wläk*. The argument for this is apparently that this suffix, according to Ramstedt, has been preserved in the Mari dialects. Ramstedt claims that the (not recorded) Chuvash suffix originates in a Turkic word **bölük*, which according to the author can be linked with Osm *bölük* 'Kompanie', Mong *böleg, bölüg* 'Gruppe, Schar, Horde, Abteilung, Kapitel (im Buche)'. According to Honti (1997: 67), most scholars who have addressed the question have accepted this etymology. In Finno-Ugric linguistics, the alleged Turkic origin of the suffix is frequently discussed in an almost mechanical way (see for instance Alvre 1996: 153).

In my opinion, it is very hard to understand how this etymology has become accepted by so many Finno-Ugrists, because the evidence presented is weak, to say the least. Ramstedt identifies a Chuvash suffix which has not been recorded with a Turkic word **böläk* and bases this on the existence of the Mari plural suffixes MaMo *-βlä* and MaE *-βlak*. First, it is hardly an acceptable method to identify an unrecorded Chuvash suffix with a word in the Turkic languages and in Mongolian. A suffix that has not been recorded is not possible to identify successfully with anything. Second, it is not possible to automatically conclude that the Mari suffixes MaMo *-βlä* and MaE *-βlak* are etymologically related to the unrecorded Chuvash suffix and the Turkic word this is said to originate from.

The proposal is furthermore open to other objections. The first recorded form of the plural suffix MaE *-βlak* does not support the Turkic origin of the suffix. Gordeev (1983: 14) states that the first occurrance of the word is in the form *jeŋbeľak* 'people'. This form, with a palatalised *ľ*, corresponds well to a morpheme *beľak*, occurring in place-names (Gordeev 1979: 213). This morpheme is part of many place-names in different areas where Mari is spoken, both within the borders of the republic of Mari-El and in adjacent areas, c.f. *Paražbeľak, Aržbeľak* (Gordeev 1979: 23), *Ivanbeľak, Toktaybeľak* (Gordeev 1979: 213). In a shortened form *-plak* it occurs in place-names such as *Esmekplak* and *Jadəkplak* (Bereczki 1994: 150, 152). Several Mari scholars have discussed the connection between the plural suffix *-βlak* and the place-name formant *beľak*. According to Luutonen (1999: 97, note 19) this connection has been refuted with the argument that the phoneme *l* in the plural suffix in the phonetically exact material collected in the end of the 19th and the beginning of the 20th century always is unpalatalised. This argument, however, is not tenable: in the first recorded form of the plural suffix, the phoneme is palatalised, just as the *ľ* in the place-name formant. That the plural suffix later contains only an unpalatalised *l* does not exclude a connection between these two forms. An unpalatalised *l* can occur also in place-names formed with *beľak*, c.f. *Kuγu Śüβəlak marin imńəže* 'Das Pferd des Mannes von Gross-Śüβəlak' (Beke 1961a: 265). *Kuγu Śüβəlak* is without doubt a place-name. According to Gordeev, the Mari place-name formant can be connected to a Mordvin *beľak*, a term that seems to designate villages. Kappeler (1982: 213) has shown that this and other terms were used as administrative terms in Mordvin territories, and that many of them date back to pre-Russian conditions. There is also an ending *beľ* in Mari that occurs in place-names, c.f. *Nurbeľ* (Gordeev 1979: 213)

The material to which we have access is thus of two different kinds. First, there is an element *beľak* occurring in place-names throughout the Mari language area, and that formally coincides with the first recorded form of the plural suffix *-βlak*. The element can—like the plural suffix *-βlak*—also be unpalatalised in place-names and in certain place-names, c.f. *Jadəkplak*, there is a close resemblance between the place-name element and the allomorph *-plak* of the plural suffix. The Russian form of the place-name *Jadəkplak*, by the way, is *Jadykbiljak* (c.f. Bereczki 1994: 152). Second, there is an alleged Chuvash plural suffix that has not been recorded but nevertheless identified with a Turkic word **böläk*. These Turkic forms have with little critizism been identified with the Mari plural suffixes MaMo *-βlä* and MaE *-βlak*. In my opinion, the fact that there are so many connections between the plural suffix *-βlak* and the place-name element *beľak* deserves a more detailed study. The same applies to possible connections between the place-name formant *beľ* and the plural suffix MaMo *-βlä*.

Kappeler (1982: 213) stresses that the administrative terms used in the Middle Volga region partly date back to pre-Russian conditions, but does not go into details in the discussion. Rorlich (1986: 30) states that the khanate of Kazan was characterised among other things by that the economic structure had preserved "the principal features of the Bulgar state". The cultivable soil was dominated by the large land-owners, among them the khan, the nobility and religious congregations. On these lands, the so-called three-field technique was in extensive use. It is worth noting that this technique was in use in areas inhabited by Mari as late as in the beginning of the 19th century. In Stipa (1977), a detailed description of an account of a journey undertaken by a certain August von Haxthausen, who in 1843 travelled in areas inhabited by speakers of the Mountain dialect, is given. I have not had access to the account by von Haxthausen and the summary below is based on the material to be found in Stipa. According to Stipa (1977: 31), the account by von Haxthausen from the Mountain Mari area begins with a description of the villages that he visited on his way from Kozmodemyansk to Kazan. A difference between the Mari villages and the Russian villages he had visited earlier was that the Mari villages were divided into smaller units, consisting of 10–30 houses, and these units constituted smaller village communities. August von Haxthausen remarks that "Die Bildung einiger derartigen Gemeinde scheint auf uralten Volkseinteilungen, die selbst mit religiösen Ideen zusammenhängen, zu beruhen" (Stipa 1997: 31). In these village communities, the cultivable soil belonged to the village community and the production mode in use was the three-field technique (Stipa 1977: 32). Each peasant, or household, was given one or a couple of shares in the three fields the soil was divided into. An almost identical divison of a Mari village is described in Paasonen (1939: 209). According to Paasonen, the village of Churaeva, situated to the north of Birsk in Bashkortostan, was divided into territorial units, each consisting of 10–15 houses, and the name of such a unit was *koγəľo-pökla*. The reasons for this divison seem to have been both economical and religious and were important in the celebration of religious feasts since the money and food neeeded in the celebrations were collected within each unit (Paasonen 1939: 209, note 2). Sebeok & Ingemann (1961: 103) state that the word *pökla* means 'group' and that *koγəľo pökla* means 'group that prays together at Easter'. It seems as if this traditional way of dividing villages into smaller units was in use also at the end of the 19th century. Heikel (1988: 69, note 1) points to the existence of so-called "Dorfsviertel" in Mountain Mari villages. According to Heikel, each such "Dorfsviertel" was made up of 10–15 houses and each of them had its own name. Stipa (1977: 31) refers to an Alexandra Fuks, who during a visit among the Meadow Mari noted the existence of a similar system and who apparently was of the opinion that it had its foundation in extended families. In this respect, there are interesting parallels in other Finno-Ugric languages. In Udmurt, *böľak, beľak* means 'Nachbar' (Munkácsi 1896: 629). Borisov (1991: 31) states that *böľak* means 'relatives, relative' whereas according to Wichmann (1987: 20) *böľak* means 'Verwandter, der getrennt von der Familie wohnt, Geschlecht'. Wichmann further indicates that the word is of Tatar origin. It is however not necessary to assume Tatar influence on Mari and Udmurt in this case, since there are words with similar forms and meanings also in Komi, c.f. *pe̜l* 'Geschlecht' (Fokos-Fuchs 1959), *pe̜ľ* 'Grossvater' (Fokos-Fuchs 1959) and even *pe̜ľa* 'Feld' (Fokos-Fuchs 1959). I argue that the Mari plural suffix *-βlak* originates in an administrative term, based on kinship and the distribution of cultivable lands, a term that has parallels in other Finno-Ugric languages in the Middle Volga region. It was probably initially used as collective suffix, gradually acquiring the function of a general plural ending. The Turkic influence can in this respect be restricted to an indirect influence in the form of a system for the distribution of land, but given the fact that the Volga Bulgars originally were cattle-keeping nomads, this does not seem very probable.

4.6.2 MaMe *-samə̂č*

Most scholars who have discussed the plural suffix MaMe *-šamə̂č* connect it to the Chuvash plural suffix *-sam, -sem*. This plural suffix is identical to the Volga Bulgar plural suffix *-sem*, recorded for the first time in a Volga Bulgar inscription from 1308 in the form *ulama-semne* 'Die Theologen' (Ackusativ) (Doerfer 1996: 37). The Volga Bulgar and the Chuvash suffix has no certain etymology and for this reason, the Turcologist Adamovič has tried to prove that it is a suffix of Finno-ugric origin in Chuvash. Adamovič argues that the explanations proposed for this suffix in Turcology are constructed and erroneous (Adamovič 1983b: 25). In Finno-Ugric linguistics, it seems as if the opinion that the Chuvash suffix is the base for the Mari plural suffix is the most accepted, but there are different explanations as to why the Mari suffix is longer than its Chuvash counterpart and also to what exactly the last element *-ə̂č* is. Bereczki (1988: 341) claims that it is either an original plural suffix **t* or a pronominal suffix *t*. Luutonen (1997: 61) suggests that it can be the possessive suffix of the second person singular. It also seems to be a generally accepted opinion that, given the geographical distribution of the plural suffixes in Mari, the plural suffixes MaMo *-βlä* and MaE *-βlak* have been replaced by the plural suffix MaMe *-samə̂č* in the central parts of the Mari language area.

Luutonen (1999: 92) stresses the fact that the suffix *-šamə̂č* does not occur in the dialects of Mari spoken in areas bordering on the Chuvash republic, that is MaMo. However, according to Luutonen, there are so many corresponding features between the Mari and the Chuvash suffixes that it is very likely that the Mari suffix is of Chuvash origin. As was mentioned above, Adamovič tries to prove that the Chuvash suffix *-sam, -sem* is of Finno-Ugric origin, but his own explanation seems at least as constructed as the ones he is arguing against. The explanation given by Adamovič includes metathetic processes in Mordvin, a couple of sound changes in Mari, of which at least one (*ä* > *a*) in all likelihood is erroneous (see section 2.3.1.1.2) and the loss of the vowel in final position in Chuvash. Since the difference in the vowel systems of MaMo and MaMe with respect to the vowels *a* and *ä* is dependent on a secondary development of *a* into *ä*, it is not possible to assume, as Adamovič (1983b: 25) does, the existence of an earlier plural suffix **sämeč* in Mari. It is furthermore not possible to conclude that this would have developed into *-sam, -sem* in Chuvash. Apparently, Adamovič also reckons with the existence of an earlier plural suffix *-lar* in Chuvash, as in other Turkic languages, and that this has been replaced by *-sam, -sem*.

Apart from this, Adamovič claims that the use of the Chuvash plural suffix *-sam, -sem* to designate all members of a family cannot be explained in any other way than as the result of influence from the Finno-ugric languages, since the Turkic plural suffix *-lar, -ler* is not used in the same way. This, however, is not correct. The Turkic plural suffix is indeed possible to use in a similar way, c.f. tu *Ahmetler* 'Ahmed und seine Familie' (Erdal 1993: 88, note 146). In this respect, Chuvash does not differ from other Turkic languages. Another characteristic of Chuvash is that the plural suffix *-sam, -sem*, contrary to what is generally the case in other Turkic languages, does not precede possessive suffixes, e.g. Chuvash *χĕrĕrsem* 'your girls' (Krueger 1961: 60), c.f. Tu *kızlarınız* 'id. However, the reverse pattern exists also in other Turkic languages, e.g. Tu *teyzemler* 'Meine Tanten' (Erdal 1993: 88, note 146).

That Chuvash possesses a secondary plural suffix—in spite of the problems connected with its etymology—is not surprising. In older stages of Turkic, the category of plural was not well developed and its use was limited (Doerfer 1996: 36). As a consequence of this, it is not strange that Chuvash—and Volga Bulgar—has a plural suffix with another form. The Chuvash plural suffix is of Chuvash rather than Finno-Ugric origin and is also part of the MaMe plural suffix *-samə̂č*. I find it highly likely, that the Mari suffix is a combination of two different suffixes with the same functions, the Chuvash suffix *-sam, -sem* and the Mari suffix *-mə̂t*. The distribution of the suffix *-mə̂t*, which generally follows the distribution of the suffix *-šamə̂č* (Luutonen 1997: 62), supports this theory. In Chuvash, the suffix *-sam, -sem* is used as a general plural marker and it can also be added to a place name and then refer to all the persons living in that place, e.g. *Jamaš-šam* 'inhabitant(s) of Jamaš' (Luutonen 1997: 60, 61). It can also be added to family names, and thus refer to all members of a particular family, e.g. *Ivanovsem* 'the Ivanoff's, members of the Ivanoff family' (Krueger 1961: 94). In Mari, the suffix *-mə̂t* fills the same function. Added to family names, it refers to all members of the family, e.g. *Čapaevmə̂t* 'The Chapaev family'. A word-final *t* in Mari can change into *č* in certain cases, as is the case with the possessive suffix of the second person singular, but this change occurs also in a mediate position. In any case, it can serve as an explanation to why the last element in the form *-šamə̂č* contains the phoneme *č*.

Copies of more complex units can be treated as simple, unanalysed units. Copies including affixes can function as primary stems, e.g. Osm *fuqara* 'Armer', which is a copy of an Arabic plural form (Johanson 1992: 178); compare this also to the Swedish *puttisar*, the plural form of the Italian *putto*, to which first an English plural marker *-s* is added, followed by the Swedish plural ending *-ar*. The Chuvash example given above, *ulama-semne* 'Die Theologen' (Ackusativ) is of the same kind, since the form *ulama* is a plural form of the word *alim* 'teacher', to which a Volga Bulgar plural suffix has been added. This suffix is perhaps not posssible to analyse as a proper plural suffix, since it might have been a collective suffix (Lars Johanson, personal communication). The Mari plural suffix MaMe *-šamə̑č* is a perfectly analogous example. Luutonen (1997: 60) gives the example Chuv *ku śın pirĕn jal-sam* 'dieser Mann ist aus unserem Dorfe (*jal* 'Dorf')'. This can be compared to MaMe *βara jal-šamə̑č tolə̑t u βat(e) ońčaš* 'Dann kommen die Dorfbewohner, die neue Frau anschauen [sic]' (Beke 1995: 122). The Mari word *jal* 'village'is a copy of the Chuvash word *yal* with the same meaning.

4.6.3 Reasons for the emergence of new plural suffixes

In my opinion, the plural suffixes MaMo *-βlä* and MaE *-βlak* can be explained as suffixes that in some way are connected to the place-name elements *beľak* and *beľ*, rather than originating in a Turkic word **böläk*, as assumed by Ramstedt. In this case, the material is evident enough. It is possible, thus, that the suffixes MaMo *-βlä* and MaE *-βlak* are etymologically related to each other. The Mordvin word *beľak* seems to refer to villages (Gordeev 1979: 213) and a place-name element *beľ* exists in Mari (and has a lexical meaning of 'surrounding, district, region') and it cannot be excluded that the plural suffix MaMo *-βlä* in some way is connected to the Mordvin *veľä*, an etymological explanation which according to Honti (1997: 67) was also proposed by Budenz. This work of Budenz has not been at my disposal. It is possible that we are dealing with two variants of a Mari word, originally used in administrative terms to designate members of smaller communities within villages and that this collective suffix subsequently has developed into a general plural marker.

A certain influence from the Turkic languages can however be traced in the use of the plural suffixes MaMO *-βlä* and MaE *-βlak*. Luutonen (1999: 96, note 14) claims that the plural morphemes in Mari are of Kipchak Turkic origin but that they do not show any influence from the Turkic languages in the sense that they can be used as diminutive endings or to express politeness. Luutonen puts it in the following way: "The fact that the central Mari plural morphemes are of Turkic origin [...] but that not all semantic properties of the Turkic plural category can be found in Mari indicates that the loaned Turkic elements have been used as substitutes for the Mari suffixes, the semantics of the original Finno-Ugrian plural ending thus remaining largely intact". It is entirely possible though that some functions of the plural endings in the Turkic languages have been subject to selective copying. The Mari plural suffixes MaMo *-βlä* and MaE *-βlak* are secondary, but they are not copies of a Turkic word **böläk*. There is however at least one example in which the plural suffix MaE *-βlak* is used to express politeness in the same way as in the Turkic langauges. Beke (1961b: 440) gives the example *sai ulδa surtanbəlak* 'Befindet ihr euch gut hier, Haus(wirt)'. In a note, Beke claims that the form is a "Begrüssungsform". This is the only example of the use of the plural suffix to express politeness in the material that I have examined, and it is probably a momentary rather than a habitualised copy.

Luutonen (1999) has discussed the secondary plural suffixes in Mari in an article dealing with secondary plural suffixes in several languages in the Middle Volga region. Using a very large amount of material and a parallel development in what he refers to as the Indo-Aryan languages, Luutonen arrives at the conclusion that secondary plural suffixes can originate both in language-internal phonological processes and in language contact situations (Luutonen 1999: 93). Luutonen (1999: 94) points out that the validity of his analysis rests on what is possible to reconstruct by use of the linguistic material available. The problem can be discussed in more detail, however. Beside the suffixes MaMo *-βlä*, MaE *-βlak* and MaMe *-samə̑č* there are also other suffixes in Mari, suffixes that are used in more limited contexts, e.g. the suffix *-mə̑t*, occurring mainly in connection with personal names and terms of kinship. Furthermore there is the suffix MaMo *-la, -lä* and MaMe *-la* which is used to form collectives of nature terms and the possessive suffix of the third person plural *-št* can express a generic, non-personal plural (Kangasmaa-Minn 1998: 227). The question of whether there originally existed several plural suffixes in Mari with different functions is thus an open one.

The copying of a plural suffix may also include the copying of frequential and combinatory patterns, thus transferred from one language to another. In Chuvash, the plural suffix *-sam, -sem* is added to all types of nouns. If the Mari plural suffix originates in global copies of the type *jal-sam* 'inhabitants of a village', one can not exclude the possibility that the combinatory and frequential properties of the Chuvash suffix too have been copied so that the new MaMe plural suffix *-samə̑č* has acquired an increased frequency and gradually has become a general plural suffix.

In language contact situations, the use of plural forms can increase. According to Johanson (1992: 182), this is the case in the variety of Turkish spoken in Germany, in which plural forms are more common than in Turkish spoken in Turkey. A similar tendency can be observed in the use of the plural suffix MaMe *-šamə̑č*; this suffix can be added also to personal pronouns in the third person plural, e.g. *nunə̑-šamə̑č kalasat: "tuδə̑n üδə̑r ulo"—man oľat* 'Jene antworten: "Er hat eine Tochter"—sagen sie' (Beke 1995: 20) and to adjectives, e.g. *pi-šamə̑č peš čaplə̑-šamə̑č* 'Die Hunde sind sehr schön' (Beke 1995: 60). The suffix *-βlak* too can also be added to the personal pronoun of the third person singular, *tuδo* 'he, she, it', e.g. *tutlak lišten ilen-lət pojan izaš(t) δene* 'Sie lebten und arbeiteten bei ihres Vaters reichem älterem Bruder' (Beke 1961b: 136) and occasionally occur also in phrases like *kok urβeźilak* 'zwei Burschen' (Beke 1961b: 136) in which the word *kok* 'two' normally would make the use of a plural suffix unnecessary. It is possible that forms such as *tutlak* 'they' in which the suffix is added to the personal pronoun of the third person singular are inspired by the use of the plural suffixes in the Turkic languages. In Chuvash, the form of the personal pronoun in the third person plural is *vĕsem* which originates in a combination of the personal pronoun in the third person singular *văl* 'he, she' and the plural suffix *-sem*. The same is the case in Turkish, e.g. *o* 'he, she, it', *onlar* 'they' (Lewis 1989: 26–27). However, plural forms of this type exist in other Finno-Ugric languages as well (see Honti 1996: 206).

5 Syntactic code-copies

There are comparatively few comprehensive studies of the syntactic influence the Turkic languages have exerted on Mari. One of the first attempts to present as detailed a picture as possible was made by Beke (1914) and although it is a general overview of the syntactic influence of the Turkic languages on the Finno-Ugric, several examples are taken from Mari. A more recent work, concentrated on syntactic resemblances between Finno-Ugric and Turkic languages in the Middle Volga region, is Wintschalek's *Die Areallinguistik am Beispiel syntaktischer Übereinstimmungen im Wolga-Kama-Areal*. Wintschalek (1993) works within the branch of linguistics called areal linguistics and aims at showing that there is a multitude of syntactic resemblances between the languages in the Middle Volga region but that these common features can not be said to originate in any of the languages in question. Wintschalek refers to such common features of uncertain origin as "areale Erscheinungen". In many cases, however, these "areale Erscheinungen" do have an attestable origin in the Turkic languages. Wintschalek deals explicitly with many of the structural features that are to be discussed below, and therefore it is a suitable reference work. Other scholars have discussed the subject of Turkic influence on Mari on the field of syntactics more in passing, so to speak, and often restrict themselves to a particular field. In Barten's *Mordvan, tšeremissin ja votjakin konjugaation infiniitisten muotojen syntaksi* (1979), much material on the Turkic influence on the system of infinite verb forms in Mari is to be found.

Saarinen (1997b: 388) expresses the opinion that it is difficult to trace the influence of the Turkic languages on the Finno-Ugric ones in the Middle Volga region, because the Turkic and Finno-Ugric languages are so close to each other typologically. Saarinen emphasizes the fact that both groups of languages have a basic word order of the type subject-object-verb (SOV) and that both Turkic and Finno-Ugric languages make frequent use of infinite verb forms instead of subordinate sentences. In my opinion, the structural resemblances between Finno-Ugric and Turkic languages are actually the prerequisite for large-scale copying of syntactic features and the typological affinity of the languages in question can actually be of assistance in determining the exact nature of the syntactic copying. There are many syntactic features in Mari that without difficulty can be ascribed a Turkic origin, i.a. the use of an interrogative particle *mo* (see section 5.8) and the use of several disjunctive conjunctions copied from the Turkic languages. The most obvious case of syntactic copying are the so-called auxiliary verbs, used to express the actionality of the verb and occurring in several Turkic languages in both distant and adjacent areas, but in no other Finno-Ugric languages than Mari and (less extensively used) Udmurt. The structural resemblances between Mari and the Turkic languages and frequent copying from Turkic languages into Mari will lead and has lead to the emergence of equivalence positions, facilitating further copying. As far as the formation and use of infinite verb forms in Mari is concerned, it is possible to point to features common to Mari, Chuvash and Tatar but originating in the Turkic languages.

In many cases, the syntactic code-copies in Mari are connected to the lexical and morphological copies. This is not surprising since the lexicon, morphology and syntax of a language are closely connected to each other (Collinder 1960: 247). In Mari, the dative case has apparently acquired extended functions as a result of the copying of Turkic verbs that require an object in the dative case. The same applies to the use of the dative case with a small number of postpositions in Mari. In Mari, copies of Turkic particles exist and in the Turkic languages these particles have wide functions in the sense that they can function as elements also in postpositional constructions and in disjunctive conjunctions. This means that a lexical or morphological copy also can acquire syntactic functions in Mari, following patterns existing in the Turkic languages.

In certain cases however, it can be hard to trace a possible Turkic influence in the Mari syntax, as pointed out by Saarinen, since the resemblances may well originate in the typological affinity of the languages. The possibility of a certain syntactic feature existing as a theoretical option in Mari but increasing in frequency as a result of Turkic impact can not be excluded. An example of this is perhaps the gemination of the affirmative instructive gerund *-en, -n*, which has parallels in the Turkic languages but also may originate in language-specific conditions.

5.1 Conjunctions

Conjunctions are unusual in older stages of both Finno-Ugric and Turkic languages. In the Uralic proto-language, there were no conjunctions according to Décsy (1990:82). In Mari, the conjunctions have a fairly limited scope and sentences are generally linked together by use of infinite verb forms (Kangasmaa-Minn 1998: 242; Bereczki 1971: 53). Of the conjunctions existing in Mari, several can be analysed as copied from Russian or the Turkic languages. In the Turkic languages many of the conjunctions are in turn copied from Persian, Arabic and Russian (Johanson 1998b: 48). Many of the conjunctions in Mari have formal and functional correspondencies in the Turkic languages, e.g. the disjunctive conjunctions *ala...ala..., älä...älä...* 'either...or...', *ja...ja...* 'either...or...' and *ta...ta..., tä...tä...* 'either...or...'

5.1.1 Disjunctive conjunctions

5.1.1.1 The disjunctive conjunction *ala...ala..., älä...älä...* 'either...or...'

The disjunctive conjunction *ala...ala..., älä...älä...* 'either...or...' is closely connected with the particle *ala* discussed in section 4.1.8. The conjunction occurs in all dialects of Mari apart from MaMo where the disjunctive conjunction *ta...ta..., tä...tä...* 'either...or...' is used. Galkin (1964: 177–178) emphasizes the fact that neither the particle *ala* nor the disjunctive conjunction occur in other Finno-Ugric languages with the exception of Udmurt. Galkin concludes that the disjunctive conjunction is of Turkic origin, in all likelihood Tatar. Wintschalek (1993: 77–78) too deals with the subject of disjunctive conjunctions and touches briefly upon the Mari *ala...ala..., älä...älä...* 'entweder...oder...' and its Udmurt counterpart *olo...olo...* 'entweder...oder...'. According to Wintschalek, both the Mari and the Udmurt disjunctive conjunctions are of Tatar origin.

As was stated above, this conjunction occurs in all dialects of Mari except MaMo. Galkin (1964: 18) claims that it does not occur in MaNw either, but this is not correct. In the material I have examined, the conjunction is frequent in the material representative for MaE, but it occurs also in texts from areas were MaNw and MaMe is spoken:

MaNw *kəźət älä kuδə̂škem kejen kerδə̂m älä aγə̂m, jumo βelə̂ šə̂nzä* 'Nun lässt man mich vielleicht nachhause fahren, vielleicht aber [doch; Ö. B.] nicht, Gott allein weiss es' (Beke 1957: 14)

MaMe *čə̂la uremžə̂m om šińče, ala saj, ala osal* 'Ich kenne nicht ihre alle Gassen [ich weiss nicht: Ö. B.], [sind: Ö. B.] sie schön oder hässlich (eig. schlecht)' (Beke 1995: 66)

MaE *älä šuko, älä šaγal kajmə̂žə̂ möŋgö, mijen šuo peš äjβät olma pakča δeke* 'Nach einiger Zeit [eig. nach entweder langer oder kurzer Zeit] kam er zu einem sehr guten Apfelgarten' (Paasonen 1939: 241)

The disjunctive conjunction *ala...ala..., älä...älä...* 'either...or...' is surely of Tatar origin in Mari. Poppe (1963) does not give explicit examples of the use of the disjunctive conjunction *ällä...ällä...* in his manual, but it is included in the word list of the same manual and the meaning is given as 'either...or...'. In the Tatar material I have examined, several examples occur:

TatK *elle urlė almiysėñ, elle satėp kaytarsėñ dip anė urušurγa tutėndė* 'entweder du kannst nicht stehlen oder du verkaufst sie' (Kakuk 1989: 164)

The disjunctive conjunction *ala...ala..., älä...älä...* 'either...or...' can be classified as a mixed copy since it combines the global copying of a morpheme with the selective copying of combinatorial properties. The copy can also be classified as conventionalised since it occurs in all dialects apart from MaMo. It is also characteristic of the eastern literary language:

MaEL *ala numal kajen, ala šəlten pəšten—šəmak mu* 'someone has either hidden or stolen [them]—I can not find them' (Oδar 1993: 34)

5.1.1.2 The disjunctive conjunction *ja...ja...* 'either...or...'

The disjunctive conjunction *ja...ja...* 'either...or...' seems to have a limited distribution in Mari and to be restricted to MaE. In the material consisting of dialect texts I have not been able to find one single occurrence of this conjunction, but it is included in Moisio's Mari-Finnish dictionary, e.g. *ja təj ja tuδo* 'either you or he' (Moisio 1994: 420) and occurs also in texts published in the eastern literary language:

MaEL *žapše uke: ja sonarəš, ja kol kučaš kaja* 'He has no time: he either goes hunting or he goes fishing' (Izhboljdin 1994: 65)

Galkin (1964: 178) states that the conjunction *ja* can be geminated and have the function of a disjunctive conjunction. Galkin further claims that this disjunctive conjunction occurs in no other Finno-Ugric languages besides Mari and Udmurt, and that it does not occur in MaMo. Galkin is of the opinion that the disjunctive conjunction is of Tatar and Bashkir origin in Mari.

This becomes evident by the fact that *ja...ja...* 'either...or...' has a formal and functional counterpart in the Tatar disjunctive conjunction *yä...yä...*, e.g. *yä min, yä sin* 'either I or thou' (Poppe 1963: 85). In the Tatar material I have examined, the conjunction occurs several times:

TatK *ye min, ye sin dip almas kılıčne alėp karčıknė čapkan idė, karčiknėñ bašė üzülėp jirge tüštė* 'Entweder ich oder du [bleibst am Leben], sagte er, zog sein Diamantschwert und hieb das alte Weib nieder, der Kopf des alten Weibes riss ab und fiel zu Boden' (Kakuk 1989: 8)

TatK *ya yeširtėn baram, ya moynėmnė čabėp bašėmnė üzem* 'Entweder ich werde ihn heimlich heiraten oder ich schneide mir den Hals durch, schlage mir den Kopf ein' (Kakuk 1989: 62)

TatK *uñγa kitken uñar, urtaγa kitken ye uñar ye uñmas* 'Wer nach rechts geht, wird Erfolg haben, wer in der Mitte geht, wird entweder Erfolg haben oder auch nicht' (Kakuk 1989: 8)

TatK *ye kaytırbız ye kaytmabız* 'entweder kehren wir zurück oder nicht' (Kakuk 1980: 60)

The Tatar disjunctive conjunction *yä...yä...* 'either...or...' is not an original element of the language. It has been copied from another language, possibly Persian (VTD III: 1) or Arabic. Thus, the Mari conjunction is a copy of a copy.

In Tatar, the morpheme *yä* has the meaning 'or' and can function as a conjunction. This is possible also in Mari in which *ja* means 'or' and is used as a conjunction, e.g. *avγust mučaš, ja sentjabr' tüŋaltəš* 'at the end of August or in the beginning of September' (Moisio 1994: 420)

Wintschalek (1993: 77) gives examples of the Tatar disjunctive conjunction *yä...yä...* 'entweder...oder...' but no examples of the Mari equivalent. However, he points to the existence of a disjunctive conjunction *ye...ye...* 'entweder...oder...' in Chuvash (see also Krueger 1961: 170; Galkin 1964: 178). As in Tatar and Mari, the single morpheme *ye* can function as a conjunction:

ChuvA *"śüle kayari ye śĕre kayari?" tenĕ* 'Werden wir hinauf reiten oder reiten wir in die Erde hinein?' (Paasonen 1949: 177)

The Mari morpheme *ja* can function as a conjunction but also as a particle in the same way as the particle *ala*. Moisio (1994: 420) states that the Mari *ja* has two meanings. It can function as a conjunction meaning 'or' but also as an interjection or a particle with a meaning similar to that of the English 'then', e.g. *ja, kalaskale!* 'Well, tell [me] then!' (Moisio 1994: 420). The particle also has the allomorph *jan*, e.g. *pu-jan* 'Give [then]!'. According to Poppe (1963: 261) the Tatar *yä* has two functions. It is used as a conjunction with the meaning 'or' but also as a conjunction with the meaning 'ah! then! indeed!'. In other Turkic languages the particle *ya* can function as an emphasizing particle, e.g. Tu *söyledi ya* 'he did say!' (COTD 1959: 358). For this reason, it is more than probable that the Mari particle *ja*, the disjunctive conjunction *ja...ja...* and the conjunction *ja* are copied from Tatar. Galkin (1964: 190) however assumes that the particle *ja* is of Finno-Ugric origin which to me seems rather unlikely. The formal and functional corresponding features are simply too many to be ignored.

The existence of a disjunctive conjunction *ye...ye...* in Chuvash is also to be explained as a result of code-copying. Chuvash too has undergone a large-scale Tatar influence and is a prime example of a language that has changed from being socially dominant to being socially dominated and can be used to illustrate the varying dominance relations in language contact situations.

5.1.1.3 The disjunctive conjunction *ta...ta..., tä...tä...* 'either...or...'

The disjunctive conjunction *ta...ta..., tä...tä...* 'either...or...' is restricted to MaMo and does not occur in other dialects of Mari. Galkin (1964: 179) is of the opinion that it is of Chuvash origin. Surprisingly, it does not occur in the dialect text material from MaMo that I have examined. There are however examples to be found in texts published in the western literary language:

MaWL *tä əlet, tä aγət, pälašəšat ak liš* 'You will either live or you will not, this will not be known' (Petukhov 1994: 280)

The question of the origin of this disjunctive conjunction is closely connected to the question of the functions of the particle *-at, -ät* and the conjunction *δa, δä* discussed above in 4.1.2. I have tried to show that these morphemes are copied from a Turkic language, most likely from Chuvash. The same applies to the disjunctive conjunction *ta...ta..., tä...tä...* 'either...or...'. Adamovič (1985: 81–84) has discussed the Chuvash particle *ta, te* and points to the fact that it occurs in the formation of indefinite pronouns and adverbs in Chuvash and also as a disjunctive conjunction. Adamovič states that a particle similar in form and function exists in Mari and although he does not explicitly say so, it seems as if Adamovič suggests a Mari origin of the Chuvash particle, he claims inter alia that the Chuvash particle can not be of Turkic origin. Adamovič is of the opinion that the existence of a particle and a disjunctive conjunction with similar forms and functions in two neighbouring languages must be considered as important and this is essentially right. But it is not possible to conclude from this that the Chuvash particle and conjunction are of Mari origin. The reason for this is that there are few Finno-Ugric languages, apart from Mordvin, in which a similar particle and conjunction occur and that there are better parallels in other Turkic languages, where both a particle *ta* and a disjunctive conjunction *ta...ta...* 'entweder...oder...' exist (VTD III: 763).

5.1.2 Copulative conjunctions

5.1.2.1 The copulative conjunction MaMe, MaE, MaNw *δen*, MaMo *δon*

In Mari, the morpheme *δe* serves as the morphological base for a number of postpositions (Gordeev 1983: 257–258). To this morpheme, according to Gordeev originating in an older form *δer*, different case suffixes are affixed, e.g. the illative suffix *-ke*: *δeke* 'to', the locative suffix *-ne (-no, -nö): δene* 'at, with', the lative suffix *-an*: *δeran* 'at, by' and the ablative suffix *-č, -c*: *δeč* 'from'. These postpositions, displaying considerable allomorphy in the dialects, occur in MaMe, MaE and MaNw. In MaMo, the base form is *δor* and this morpheme serves as the morphological base for postpositions with the same meanings as in the other dialects, e.g. MaMo *δono* 'at, with' (Gordeev 1983: 268).

In MaMo, a shortened form *δon* of the postposition *δono* 'at, with' can function as a copulative conjunction with the meaning 'and' (Gordeev 1983: 268) and in the other dialects the shortened form *δen* fills this function (Gordeev 1983: 260):

MaMo *äťäž-δon äβäžə manə̑t nälšäš* 'Seine Eltern sagen [ihm; Ö. B]: heirate (eig. [ein Mädchen; Ö. B.] ist zu nehmen)!' (Beke 1951: 56)

MaMe *ilen ulə̑t kuβa δen kuγza—šoŋkemə̑n ult* 'Es lebten ein Mann und eine Frau. Sie wurden alt' (Alhoniemi & Saarinen 1983: 72)

MaE *βara ačaž δen aβažlan tuβurum čikta, šoβə̑čə̑m pua* 'Dann hilft sie den Eltern (eig. dem Vater und der Mutter [des Bräutigams; Ö. B.]), die Hemden anziehen [und; Ö. B] überreicht die Tücher (Sing.)' (Beke 1961b: 230)

In MaNw, the longer form *δönü* can be used as a copulative conjunction:

MaNw *əlen ulut starik δönü kuβa* 'Es lebte [einst; Ö. B.] ein alter Mann und eine alte Frau' (Beke 1957: 48)

The postpositions formed with the element *δe* are in all likelihood very old in Mari (see Galkin 1964: 178–179). The postposition *δene* 'at, with' can denote the instrument, place or means by use of which an action takes place, e.g. *poyezd δene* 'by train', *korno δene* 'along the road'. It can also denote the person together with whom the action is performed, e.g. *tuδən δene* 'together with her' or the time at which something takes place, e.g. *kastene* 'in the evening'. In certain cases, the postposition *δene* occurs also in connection with the postposition *pərľa* and the construction then has the essential meaning of 'together with'. This postpositional construction will be discussed in section 5.2.5.

The use of the morpheme *δen* as a copulative conjunction can perhaps be connected to Turkic influence, possibly Chuvash. In Chuvash, there is no postpositional element entirely comparable to the Mari postposition *δen* but the functions of the Mari postposition are rendered in Chuvash by use of what Krueger (1961: 108) refers to as the "instrumental relational morpheme". Krueger (1961: 108–110) describes this morpheme, with the suffix *-pa, -pe*, as a case in Chuvash. One of its functions is to denote the instrument or means by which an action is carried out, e.g. *părajutpa kiltĕm* 'I came by steamer' (Krueger 1961: 109). It can also denote the person with whom something is done, e.g. *manpa pĕrle kilčĕ* 'he came together with me'(Krueger 1961: 109).

Apart from these functions, this Chuvash case can also be used to denote the place or time at which an action takes place, e.g. *irpe* 'in the morning' or *kaśpa* 'in the evening' (Krueger 1961: 109). According to Krueger (1961: 109), the "instrumental relational morpheme is often used to mean 'and', especially in titles", e.g. *kaχalpa puyan* 'The Lazybones and the Rich Man'. Apparently, there is a strong connection between the Mari postposition *δene* and the Chuvash "instrumental relational morpheme'. The functions of the Mari postposition and the Chuvash case suffix are practically identical. For this reason, I find it very likely that the instances in which the postposition *δen* is used as a copulative conjunction in Mari are the result of the selective copying of the copulative function of the Chuvash case suffix. Given the fact that there were no conjunctions (at least not according to Décsy 1990: 82) in the Uralic protolanguage and that many of the Mari conjunctions have been copied from the Turkic languages or from Russian, this conclusion seems feasible.

In Chuvash, the suffix *-pa, -pe* is used as a copulative conjunction in the same way as in Mari:

ChuvA *ĕlĕk pĕr karčăkpa starik purănaśśĕ tet* 'Einst lebten eine alte Frau und ein alter Mann' (Paasonen 1949: 158)

ChuvA *kaččaka takipe surăχ tus pulnă* 'Ein Ziegenbock und ein Schafbock waren Freunde' (Paasonen 1949: 210)

The selective copying of the copulative function of the Chuvash suffix has been facilitated by the fact that the Mari postposition and the Chuvash suffix have had basically identical functions. Also the instances in which the postposition *δene* is used to denote the time or place at which an action takes place are in all likelihood examples of selective copying. Both *er* 'morning' and *kas* 'evening' are global copies of Chuvash substantives, *ir* and *kaś* respectively (Räsänen 1920: 126, 143).

Forms such as *er δene* 'in the morning' and *kastene* 'in the evening' can be classified as mixed copies since they combine global copying of a Chuvash noun with the selective copying of one of the functions of the Chuvash suffix *-pa, -pe*.

Krueger (1961: 109) states that the suffix of the "instrumental relational morpheme" in Chuvash has several, archaic and dialectal allomorphs, i.a. *pala, palan, pele, pelen*, possibly etymologically related to the Tatar postposition *belän* 'together with, by means of' (Poppe 1963: 151). This postposition can be used to denote the person together with whom an action is performed:

TatM *taz šunda katïnï bilän dürt ay turdïlar-da soñra üylärenä kaytïp kittelär* 'Hier wohnte der kahle Junge vier Monate mit seiner Frau, dann kehrten sie heim' (Kakuk 1996: 61)

Apparently, the postposition *belän* can also function as a copulative conjunction:

TatM *Taz bilän katïnï, haywanlarï bolgan mäce kücük izläp yürüp taba-almadïlar* 'Seine Tiere die Katze und der Hund suchten den kahlen Jungen und seine Frau und konnten sie nicht finden' (Kakuk 1996: 62)

To conclude, it might be stated that there are great resemblances between the Mari postposition *δene*, the "instrumental relational morpheme" of Chuvash and the Tatar postposition *belän*. As for the copulative conjunction *δen* in Mari, I argue that it is a result of Turkic influence, mainly Chuvash and that it is an example of a selective copy in Mari. There are other morphosyntactic means of connecting sentences in Mari, for instance by use of particles with a copulative function, e.g. *...ak...ak,* Ma *izak-soľak* 'big brother and little brother' and this perhaps represents an older copulative construction in Mari.

5.2 Postpositions

According to Kangasmaa-Minn (1966: 131), the postpositions form a limited category in Mari and can be divided into two groups. The first group consists of words with a defective declination of old local case forms that rarely can occur as independent substantives. The second group consists of local case forms of nouns where the base forms can occur as independent substantives. To the first group belongs inter alia the postposition MaMe, MaE *pelen* 'at, with' and to the second inter alia the postposition MaMe *ončəl*, MaMo *anzə̂l* 'front'. A word can thus be defined as a postposition only on a syntactic basis. Many of the postpositions in Mari have according to Kangasmaa-Minn (1966: 131) retained what she refers to as an individual "meaning" whereas others are semantically quite colourless. In Mari there are both simple and compound postpositions. The head word of a postposition is normally in the nominative case with the exception of pronouns that are in the genitive case (Bereczki 1971: 52).

5.2.1 The postposition MaMe, MaE *köra, körä* 'according to, because of'

The postposition *köra* 'according to, because of' occurs in MaMe and MaE but not in MaMo and MaNw. It differs from most of the other postpositions in Mari in that it governs the dative case. Räsänen (1923: 40) and Anduganov (1991: 118) connect it to the Tatar postpostion *kürä*. It is especially frequent in what appears to be lexicalized expressions of the type *tuδlan köra* 'because of this, for this reason' but also in proverbs in which it has a meaning similar to that of the German 'wie...so...'

MaE *kajə̂kšlan körä muružo, jeŋžə̂lan körä omašə̂že* 'Wie der Vogel, so sein Gesang, wie der Mann, so seine Hüttel' (Beke 1961b: 158)

MaE *pörtšə̂lan köra oknaže* 'Wie das Haus, so die Fenster (eig. Sing.) (eig. dem Haus gemäss)' (Beke 1961a: 52)

MaE *marižlan köra βatə̂že* 'Wie der (Ehe)mann, so die Frau' (Beke 1961a: 44)

The postposition *köra* occurs also in texts published in the eastern literary language:

MaEL *olašte šuko kučaltmə̂lan köra [...] Pajašlan una-γuδə̂š malaš puraš loγaleš* 'Because of his being in town so often [...] Pajaš had to check in to a hotel' (Izhboldin 1994: 34)

The postposition *köra* is of an undisputable Tatar origin. In Tatar, the postposition *kürä* means 'according to, because of' (Poppe 1963: 229) and it occurs also in Turkish where it has the form *göre* and governs the dative case. Originally, this form is a converb meaning 'seeing', of the verb *gör* 'to see'. In Tatar too, the postposition governs the dative case:

TatK *Patša: ejjė, babaj, min sinė načar išlegen dip čakėrmadėm, jaχšėlėγėña küre čakėrdėm* 'Der Padischah sagte: "Hei, Väterchen, ich habe dich nicht darum gerufen, weil du böses getan hast, ich habe dich wegen deiner Güte gerufen"' (Kakuk 1989: 30)

TatM *bek kėzlarnė bik sevebėz bėtė kėzėlga küre* 'Die Töchter von Bäk lieben wir sehr wegen der Röte ihrer Wangen' (Paasonen 1953: 6)

In Chuvash, the postposition occurs in the form *kura* 'in hinsicht, gemäss, wegen' (Paasonen 1974: 77). The Chuvash postposition too governs the dative case:

Chuv *śüpšĕne kura χupalči* 'like the trough, so the roof' (Paasonen 1974: 77)

The Mari postposition *köra* has a formal and functional similarity to the Tatar postposition *kürä* and it is evident that *köra* is a global copy of the Tatar *kürä*. The possibility that the Chuvash *kura*, etymologically the same as the Tatar *kürä*, has exerted a certain influence on Mari can however not be excluded. That the postposition *köra* governs the dative case is the result of selective copying. The combinatorial property of the Tatar dative suffix *-gÄ, -kÄ* has been transferred to its Mari counterpart, the dative case suffix *-lan, -län*. Constructions of the type *tuδlan köra* 'because of this, for this reason' are therefore mixed copies, combining the global copying of a postposition with the selective copying of a combinatorial property.

A parallel to this development is present in Mordvin. Mordvin too has a postposition MoE *kořa*, MoM *kořä* 'considering, compared to' (Bartens 1999: 165) and the Mordvin postposition is evidently also of Turkic origin. Whether it is Tatar or Chuvash that has been the model code, is not possible to determine. Formally, the Mordvin postposition is close to the Chuvash *kura* but according to Johanson (2000: 168) the contacts between Chuvash and Mordvin have been limited and words of Turkic origin in Mordvin are often copied from neighbouring Tatar dialects, which probably means TatM. In Mordvin, the functions of the Mari dative are rendered by use of the illative case. Given the fact that Mordvin generally is considered a language that has had more limited contacts with the Turkic languages than Mari, the existence of a postposition of Turkic origin in Mordvin is a fact that should stimulate further studies of the impact the Turkic languages have had on Mordvin. In Mordvin, there is also another postposition copied from Tatar, e.g. MoE *baška*, MoM *paška* 'except' (Bartens 1999: 165). This postposition, like the Tatar postposition *baška* 'without, besides, with the exception of' (Poppe 1963: 52) governs the ablative case. The Tatar postposition is etymologically related to the Chuvash postposition *puśne*, to be discussed in 5.2.4.

The Mari postposition can be classified as a conventionalised copy of a Turkic postposition since it occurs not only in dialect texts representing the eastern dialects but also in the eastern literary language.

5.2.2 The postposition MaMo, MaNw, *βerc(ə)*, MaMe, MaE *βerč* 'for the sake of'

The postposition *βerc(ə), βerč* 'for the sake of' occurs in all dialects of Mari. It normally governs the nominative case, but in connection with pronouns, it governs the genitive case. Occasionally it can also govern the dative case. Gordeev (1983: 91) has discussed the etymology of this particle and compares it to the Finnish *varteen*, e.g. *varteen ottaa* 'to take into consideration'. A Finnish equivalent not discussed by Gordeev is the postposition *varten* 'for the sake of'. Gordeev seems to prefer an explanation that connects the Mari particle with a similar form in Ossetic. However, the postposition originates in the noun *βer* 'place' (UEW 569). The final *č* is the ending of a no longer productive directional case.

In certain cases, this postposition governs the dative case. Kangasmaa-Minn (1966: 167) mentions the dialects in which the postposition governs the dative case and from her data it is possible to conclude that this is characteristic of the eastern dialects. According to Kangasmaa-Minn, the dative case always represents the 3rd person singular, noun or pronoun:

MaE *tuδlan βerčə̂n raiš βereštə̂nat* 'Darum bist du in Paradies geraten' (Beke 1995: 184)

MaE *tuδlan βerčə̂n puren tul-rə̂βə̂ž δene* 'Deshalb kehrte er bei ihm mit dem Feuerfuchs ein' (Beke 1995: 178)

MaE *tuδlan βerčə̂n kə̂rkeδə̂lna* 'Deswegen raufen wir uns' (Beke 1995: 18)

MaE *jumulan βerč lijže!* 'Es sei [dein; Ö. B.] in Gottes Namen! (Beke 1961b: 188)

The postposition *βerc(ə), βerč* occurs in all dialects of Mari and its meaning and use apparently coincide with those of the postposition *köra* 'according to, because of'. I find it plausible that the postposition *köra* has been inserted into an equivalence position earlier reserved for the postposition *βerc(ə), βerč* 'for the sake of'. The fact that the postposition *βerc(ə), βerč* occasionally can govern the dative case is in my opinion the result of selective copying. Some of the combinatorial properties of the Tatar postposition *kürä* have been transferred to the Mari postposition *βerc(ə), βerč,* and this copying has probably been enhanced by mixed copies of the type *tuδlan köra* 'because of this, for this reason'. The copy can further be classified as a conventionalised copy in the eastern dialects since it occurs also in the eastern literary language:

MaEL *aram mo Jakterlan βerčə̂n pojan mariemə̂m, Keremetə̂m, puštə̂nam?* 'Did I kill my rich husband, Keremet, in vain for Jakter's sake?'

5.2.3 The postposition *toreš* 'towards'

The postposition *toreš* normally governs the nominative case in Mari. Kangasmaa-Minn (1966: 167) gives one example in which the postposition *toreš* governs the dative case:

MaMe *uβer ojla: mə̂ń, maneš, šoγalam kornə̂lan toreš* 'Der uβer [βuβer: A being or spirit in Mari traditional belief; A. H.] sagte: "Ich stelle mich auf (eig. quer über) den Weg (sagt er)"' (Beke 1957: 322)

There are, however, examples in which the postposition governs the dative case also in the material I have examined:

MaE *pečə̂ pečaš moštə̂tə̂mə̂ kornə̂lan toreš pečaleš* 'Wer es nicht versteht, einen Zaun zu machen, der macht ihn quer über die Strasse' (Beke 1961a: 504)

That the postposition *toreš* governing the dative case occasionally is used in the eastern literary languages is evident from the following example:

MaEL *Ikta-kölan toreš mutə̂m pelештaš* 'to give somebody an answer' (Moisio 1994: 305)

The instances in which the postposition *toreš* governs the dative case are rare and can probably be seen as the copying of combinatorial properties of the Tatar postposition *taba* 'towards, in the direction of' (Poppe 1963: 52) which also governs the dative case:

Tat *awılga taba* 'in the direction of the village' (Poppe 1963: 52)

5.2.4 The postposition *lec pasna, δeč posna, γə̑č posna* 'without, besides'

The postposition *lec pasna, δeč posna, γə̑č posna* 'without, besides' is used in its various forms in all dialects of Mari. This postposition governs the ablative case ending in *-lec* or, if the case suffix itself is not present in a certain dialect, the postpositional elements *δeč* and *γə̑č*. Anduganov (1991: 119) gives no details on its etymology but is apparently of the opinion that the postposition was present in Mari prior to its separation into dialects. According to Räsänen (1920: 181), the Mari postposition is of Chuvash origin. Several examples occur in the material I have examined:

MaNw *a kuδum ərestə pəštəmlec pasna pua, tüδüm kackə̑t jüt* 'Was er [ihnen: Ö. B.] aber gab (eig. gibt), ohne sich zu bekreuzigen, das assen [und; Ö. B.] tranken sie' (Beke 1957: 38)

MaMe *tə̑j čə̑la šüľetə̑m užalen pə̑tarə̑: uke γə̑n šüľə̑ δeč posna koδat* 'Verkauf all deinen Hafer, tust du das nicht, bleibst du ohne Hafer!' (Alhoniemi & Saarinen 1983: 102)

MaE *üštə̑leč posna kočkaš šinčat kiń, šeret o tem, manə̑t* 'Wenn du dich ohne Gürtel zum Essen setzt, wirst du nicht satt werden, sagt man' (Beke 1961a: 453)

The Mari postposition is surely of Chuvash origin, as was stated by Räsänen. According to Krueger (1961: 169) the postposition *puśne* is a postposition which can not be declined and which governs the ablative case. This postposition occurs in the material that I have examined:

ChuvA *unta purănnă čuχ arśın χĕr pulnaskĕr uray šălsa śüp tăkasran puśne urăχ ĕś nimĕnte tăva pĕlmen* 'Während er dort lebte, konnte der zum Mädchen gewordene Mann keine andere Arbeit ausführen als nur den Fussboden ausfegen und den Kehricht auf den Schutthafen schütten' (Paasonen 1949: 187).

The Chuvash postposition is etymologically related to the Tatar postposition *baška* 'without, besides, with the exception of, excluding' (Poppe 1963: 52–53) which also governs the ablative case. The Chuvash and Tatar postpositions originate in a dative-accusative form of the word Tat *baš*, Chuv *puś* 'head'. A Chuvash *u* in the first syllable corresponds to MaMe, MaE *o*, MaMo, MaNw *a* (Räsänen 1920: 77–81) which explains the allomorphs MaMe, MaE *posna*, MaMo, MaNw *pasna*. The Mari postposition can be classified as a mixed copy since it combines a global copy of a Chuvash postposition with the selective copying of combinatorial properties so that the Chuvash ablative is rendered by its Mari equivalent. The postposition further occurs in texts published in the eastern literary language (and probably also in the western, although I have no instances of this in the material I have examined) which is an indication of its being a conventionalised copy.

MaEL *teβak aβat δeč posna koδat, Janaktaj!* 'In this way you will be left without a mother, Janaktay!' (Boyarinova 1991: 32)

5.2.5 The postposition *(δen) pərľa* 'together with'

The postposition *(δen) pərľa* 'together with' constitutes a doubled postposition in Mari, combining the postposition *δene*, the function of which was discussed in 5.1.2.1 with the postposition *pərľa*. This postposition has the meaning 'together with' according to Moisio (1994: 257). From the examples given by Moisio it is also evident that the postposition can function as an adjective, e.g. *pərľa paša* 'co-operation, common work'. In the material I have examined a few examples of this double postposition occurs:

MaMe *ik kasten surt oza šajtan ten pərľa mutlanaš šinčeš* 'Eines Abends setzt sich der Hausherr mit dem Teufel zum Erzählen' (Alhoniemi & Saarinen 1983: 188)

It also occurs in texts published in the eastern literary language:

MaEL *Memnan δene pərľa kaja* 'Go together with us' (Taygiljdin 1993: 56)

The postposition *(δen) pərľa* 'together with' has a close resemblance to a Chuvash morpheme that in all likelihood is a postposition, *pěrle* 'zusammen' (Paasonen 1974: 96). Krueger (1961: 226) gives the meaning of *pěrle* as "having one = as one, together". Krueger (1961: 169) describes *pěrle* as a postposition that can not be declined. In Chuvash, this postposition governs the "instrumental relational morpheme" with the suffix *-pa, -pe*:

ChuvA *atya epirte śavsempe pěrle kayar* 'lass uns zusammen mit diesen reisen' (Paasonen 1949: 294–95)

In Tatar too there is a postposition with similar form and function: *birle* 'since; from the time of (postp. with the abl.)' (Poppe 1963: 205) but the Mari form suggests Chuvash rather than Tatar origin since Tatar *i* in the first syllable normally corresponds to Mari *e* or *i* (Räsänen 1923: 16). The postposition *(δen) pərľa* can be classified as a mixed copy in Mari, combining a global copy of a Chuvash postposition with the selective copying of semantic and combinatorial properties transferred to a native counterpart. The reasons for the copying of the postposition *pərľa* are probably connected with the identification of the Mari postposition *δen* with the Chuvash suffix *-pa, -pe*. The similar functions of the Mari postposition *δene* and the instrumental relational morpheme in Chuvash discussed in section 5.1.2.1 have probably facilitated the copying. The copy is apparently also possible to classify as a conventionalised copy since it occurs not only in the eastern dialects but also in the eastern literary language.

5.2.6 The postposition *δeč βara, leč βara, šeč βara* 'after this, then'

The morpheme *βara* and its functions as an adverb and an interrogative particle were discussed in section 4.1.6. It was argued that both the adverbial use of the morpheme and its function as a particle were the results of the copying of a Chuvash morpheme and its properties. In Mari, the morpheme *βara* can also function as a postposition with the essential meaning of 'then, after this'. While most postpositions in Mari govern the nominative case—apart from the small number of postpositions governing the ablative or the dative case—the postposition *βara* frequently governs the ablative case, especially when occurring with the demonstrative pronoun *tu* 'that, that one', e.g. *tuleč βara* 'then, after that':

MaMo *təšec βara βätəžə ńi-γə̂nam-at ńi-γə̂šk-at koltə̂δe, so ške-ok kaštə̂n* 'Nach diesem Erregnisse trug ihm die Frau nicht wieder auf, sondern machte alles selbst' (Ramstedt 1902: 186)

MaNw *no, erγəm, təlec βara teγe it ləštə!* 'Schon gut, mein Sohn, tu das nie wieder! (Beke 1957: 13)

MaMe *tleč βara maska δen meraŋ roδə̂ kučə̂mə̂m čarnen ulə̂t* 'Danach hörten Bär und Hase mit ihrer Freundschaft auf' (Alhoniemi & Saarinen 1983: 182)

MaE *tuleč βara apsatə̂m o lištə̂* 'Seitdem verrichtet [der Junge Schmied; Ö. B.] keine Schmiedearbeit mehr' (Beke 1961a: 472)

In my opinion, the cases in which the morpheme *βara* is used as a postposition are the result of the copying of yet another combinatorial property of the Chuvash morpheme *vara* 'then'. Bereczki (1971: 52) makes the same suggestion. In Chuvash, a similar postpositional construction is formed by adding the morpheme *vara* to an ablative form, *untan*, of a personal pronoun *văl* 'he, she, it, that, this' (Krueger 1961: 133), e.g. *untan vara* 'after this, then'. In Chuvash, this is a very common expression and several examples can be found in the material I have examined:

ChuvA *untan vara ača tură χĕrĕsene šɪrama kaynă* 'Dann ging der Jüngling, um nach den Töchtern Gottes suchen' (Paasonen 1949: 180)

ChuvA *untan vara ăslă kaškărsem uχmaχne vărmantan upana čĕnme yană* 'Da schickten die verständigen Wölfe den Dummen, um aus dem Walde den Bären herbeizurufen' (Paasonen 1949: 212)

ChuvA *untan vara upa pɪšak śerem kassa χăpatsa ilnĕte vĕrenpe śɪχsa iki-uran tărsa yar-yar sullană* 'Da nahm der Bär einen grossen Rasen, band ihn mit einer Schnur, stellte sich auf zwei Füsse und schwang (den Rasen) in verschiedene Richtungen' (Paasonen 1949: 213)

It seems possible to classify the Mari postposition *δeč βara, leč βara, šeč βara* as a copy of a Chuvash postpositional construction. The copy is a mixed copy, combining global copying of a Chuvash morpheme with the selective copying of semantic content, the ablative form of a personal pronoun. The copy is also conventionalised since it occurs in all dialects and in both literary languages of Mari:

MaWL *təlec βara Moskvaštə̂ arχitekturij institutə̂m pətärəš* 'After this he graduated from the Moscow Institute of Architecture' (Gornij & Korolyeva 1996: 9)

MaEL *tiδδeč βara Jə̂βanə̂n iləšə̂žə̂ kojə̂n sajemaš tüŋaleš* 'After this, Ivan's life improved considerably' (Taygiljdin 1993: 63)

There are no examples of a Tatar postposition similar in form and function. Above, I have suggested that the Chuvash *vara* and the Mari *βara* can be connected to the Tatar converb *bara* 'going'. This converb can follow upon an ablative form of a substantive:

TatK *Malay šul sukmaktan bara turγač barėp kire br üyge* 'Der Junge schritt immer noch auf diesem Pfad und trat in ein Haus' (Kakuk 1989: 118)

These constructions are quite similar to the Mari and Chuvash postpositions formed with the ablative form of a substantive to which the morpheme Ma *βara*, Chuv *vara* is added, although the Tatar *bara* is not a postposition. However, converbs can develop into postpositions, like the Tatar postposition *kürä*, originally a converb meaning 'seeing', see section 5.2.1.

5.3 Copied forms and functions of cases

According to Johanson (1999: 53) certain postpositions and affixes such as tense and case endings are among the elements in a language least inclined to be replaced by copies. These endings can thus be used to determine the basic code even in very complex contact situations. There are no examples of copied modal or tense endings in Mari, which rather has preserved ancient features in that respect. The tense endings in Mari are clear examples of this, for instance the ending for the second preterite case. In Mari, the original PFU ending **j* (Bereczki 1988: 345) has been preserved in the declination of verbs belonging to the *am*-conjugation. In the declination of verbs belonging to the *em*-conjugation, the ending *-š* is a continuation of a PU perfect ending **ś* (Bereczki 1988–345)

Similarly, the case system of Mari has preserved case endings of considerable age. According to Bereczki (1988: 342) the accusative case suffix *-m* is a continuation of the PFU accusative suffix **-m*. The genitive case suffix *-n* in Mari corresponds to the PFU genitive suffix **-n* according to Bereczki (1988:342).

In present-day Mari, there are 9 cases in the eastern dialects and 10 in the western. In table 3, the case system of modern Mari is shown.

With the possible exception of the modal case, also labelled the comparative case, to be discussed below in 5.3.1, the case suffixes in Mari are comparable to the cases in other Finno-Ugric languages. Bereczki (1979) has discussed the modal case suffix along with a small number of other case endings that according to him are examples of case suffixes of Chuvash origin in Mari. With the exception of the modal case, the suffixes discussed by Bereczki are characterized by a limited geographic distribution.

The fact that the copying of case suffixes in the form of the copying of a morpheme is something unusual in language contact situtations does not exclude other types of copying. The functions of a certain case can be copied and transferred to a corresponding case in the basic code. In Mari, the dative case has acquired certain specialised functions by the selective copying of functions of the Tatar dative case. This will be discussed in 5.3.2.

5.3.1 The modal case MaMe, MaE *-la*, MaMo, MaNw *-la, -lä*

In Mari, the modal case, also labelled the comparative case, has the suffixes MaMe *-la*, MaMo, MaNw, MaE *-la, -lä*. It is used throughout the entire language area.

MaMo *pə̂ra eδemlä kajə̂n* 'In menschlicher Gestalt (eig. als Mensch scheinend) geht er hinein [zu ihr; Ö. B.] (Beke 1951: 44)

MaNw *mäskät keleśen: "irlä tolam"* 'Der Bär antwortet: "Ich komme morgen"' (Beke 1957: 59)

MaMe *mari-šamə̂č oβδam južə̂žə̂ "jumə̂n uštə̂mə̂ üδə̂r" manə̂t, a južə̂žə̂ "ala mo ajδemə̂la lin koššə̂" manə̂t* 'Einige Tscheremissen nennen oβδa [a being in traditional Mari mythology; A. H.] 'die verrückte Tochter Gottes', aber andere 'irgendeinen menschenähnlich gewordenen Vagabunden'' (Alhoniemi & Saarinen 1983: 40)

MaE *ik jeŋ mijen unala ik jalə̂ške* 'Ein Mann ging einst in ein Dorf zu Gaste' (Beke 1961b: 29)

According to Alhoniemi (1985: 59–60), the modal case has several functions in Mari. It can, for example, be a predicative adverbial which is added to auxiliary verbs, e.g. MaMo *kəδərtəšlä čučeš* 'it feels like thunder'. It can also serve as a loose adverbial expressing the specific properties of the object, subject or any other part of speech, e.g. MaMe *omsam tümə̂rla perkalaš tüŋgalə̂t* 'They began to knock on the door as if it were a drum'. The modal case can also be used as an adverbial expressing the price of a commodity or even abstract concept, e.g. MaMe *oγeš lij tuδə̂m oksala nalaš* 'You cannot buy it (= love) for money'. The modal case can also be used to denote a game played or a language spoken, e.g. *Süanla moδə̂t* 'they play wedding' and *marla ojlaš* 'to speak Mari'. The modal case is frequent in lexicalised expressions of the type *erla* 'in the morning'. A similar suffix *-la, -lä* is also added to demonstrative pronouns and substantives declined in the directional illative case, e.g. *čoδəraškəla* 'to the forest'. In constructions of this type, the suffix *-la, -lä* denotes unspecified direction. Saarinen (1993: 149) seems inclined to connect these constructions with similar ones in Chuvash, e.g. *Šupăškaralla* 'to Cheboksary'.

Different explanations exist for the origin of the modal case (c.f. Saarinen 1993: 149–50) but Saarinen is apparently of the opinion that its Turkic origin is indisputable. In Chuvash, the suffix *-la* has functions mainly corresponding to the functions of the Mari case according to Saarinen (1993: 149). In Chuvash, *-la* can have a temporal function:

ChuvA *χĕlle măntărlanat. śula ırχanlanant—pusă-valaški* 'Im Winter wird es dick, im Sommer wird es mager—Der Trog am Brunnen (der sich im Winter mit Eis belegt)' (Paasonen 1949:95)

In Chuvash, the suffix *-la, -le* which Krueger (1961: 132) describes as an adjective-forming suffix, can denote a language spoken:

ChuvA *timuk tutarla pĕlmen, śavănpa ănlanayman* 'Timuk verstand nicht tatarisch, darum verstand er nichts' (Paasonen 1949: 152)

A similar suffix can also be added to nouns in the dative-accusative case, and in such constructions the suffix expresses directionality, e.g. *vărmanalla* 'to the forest'. Krueger (1961: 111) states that the morpheme *-(A)llA* is a case ending, the so-called directive morpheme with the meaning 'towards, to, at, in the direction of, -wards' but he does not connect this morpheme with the Mari suffix *-la, -le*. Instead he draws attention to the existence of a similar morpheme in what he calls "the Finnic languages", probably referring to the allative case in Finnish ending in *-lle*, e.g. *metsälle* 'to the forest'.

I find it likely that Saarinen is correct in assuming a Chuvash origin for the Mari suffix *-la, -lä*. The formal similarity and the almost identical combinatorial properties make the assumption very probable. Saarinen (1993: 148) points to the fact that similar suffixes occur also in other Turkic languages but that the Chuvash suffix has the most widespread distribution. In Chuvash, the suffix is held to be an adverbial ending and not a case ending. According to Saarinen (1993: 148), the Mari suffix *-la, -lä* can often be replaced by the adverb *γaj* 'way' a circumstance that makes one wonder whether the Chuvash suffix *-la, -le* in some way is connected to the Tatar adverbial suffix *-lÄy, -lEy*, discussed above in 4.1.3. The Tatar suffix has been copied into Mari and inserted into a position originally occupied by the Mari morpheme *γańe, γaj* 'way'. If this is the case then Mari has copied what with respect to Turkic historical linguistics is one and the same suffix from two different model codes, Chuvash and Tatar. In 4.4.1.2 I have demonstrated that such instances of double copying are possible since the so-called nomen agentis of the Turkic languages has been copied into Mari both from Tatar and from Chuvash. It is reasonable to assume that the Mari morpheme *-la, -lä* originally was a part of global copies such as Ma *kajəkla* 'like a bird', Chuv *kayăkla* 'id.', and that they later became parts of mixed copies of the type Ma *teŋela* 'like this, in this way', Chuv *śapla* 'such, thus, how, then' (Krueger 1961: 230). It is also reasonable to assume that the suffix *-la, -lä* is an even earlier copy than the suffix *-laj, -läj* copied from Tatar since it occurs throughout the whole Mari language area.

However, I am not convinced that the suffix *-la* occurring with demonstrative pronouns and nouns in the illative case is really the same suffix as the modal case suffix *-la, -lä*. In constructions of this kind, the suffix is used to express unspecified direction and thus seems to be a copy of the Chuvash "directive morpheme" with the suffix *-(A)llA*. The Chuvash morpheme contains a geminated *ll*, generally rendered as *l* in copies of Chuwash words in Mari (Räsänen 1920: 49) since long consonants do not occur within the same syllable in Mari. In Chuvash, this suffix is added to postpositions and substantives in the dative-accusative case:

ChuvA *apăšĕ tata malalla χăvalană* 'Die älteste Schwester verfolgte weiter' (Paasonen 1949: 131)

ChuvA *timuk śapaχ śites śĕre śitse tıräne sutnăta kilelle tavrănnă* 'Timuk kam dennoch an dem vorgesehenen Ort an, verkaufte das Getreide und kehrte nach Hause um' (Paasonen 1949: 152)

It could be argued, that the morpheme *-(A)llA* is an allomorph to the suffix *-la, -le* in Chuvash and that it is added to stems ending in vowels. This is apparently not the case since the suffix *-la, -le* in temporal expressions in Chuvash often is added to vowel-ending stems, e.g. *śula* 'in the summertime' < *śu* 'summer'. In my opinion, this makes it probable that we are actually dealing with two different Chuvash suffixes. The instances in which the morpheme *-la, -lä* in Mari are added to adverbs and substantives inflected for case can be described as mixed copies in which a Chuvash directive case and its combinatorial properties have been transferred to an equivalent of the base code, e.g. Ma *čoδəraškəla* 'to the forest', Chuv *vărmanalla* 'id.'.

The Mari morpheme *-la, -lä* is thus possible to describe as a copy of two different Chuvash morphemes, an adverbial suffix *-la, -lä* with counterparts in Tatar and a case morpheme *-(A)llA*. These formally identical morphemes can be classified as conventionalised copies since they occur in texts published in both literary languages of Mari:

MaEL *tə̂j δeket unala mijem manən* 'I come to you as a guest, he said' (Izhboldin 1994: 46)

MaEL *kumətənat βes βekə̂la kuržə̂t* 'All three of them ran in another direction' (Boyarinova 1991: 15)

MaWL *ma tiδe teŋela šokta* 'What is it that sounds like this?' (Petukhov 1994: 209)

MaWL *χalə̂k βekə̂la särnal ken* 'He has gone back to the people' (Petukhov 1994: 204)

5.3.2 The dative case MaMe, *-lan*, MaMo, MaNw, MaE *-lan, -län*

In Mari, the dative case has the endings MaMe *-lan*, MaE, MaMo, MaNw *-lan, -län*. The morpheme is a compound morpheme and according to Bereczki (1988: 342) it originates in a suffix *-l* denoting locality and a PFU lative suffix **-ń*. Bereczki states that a similar morpheme, the adessive case ending *-len*, exists in Finnish and certain dialects of Ingrian. Bereczki furthermore gives examples which according to him prove that the Mari dative case ending originally was *-lə̂n*, MaNw *molə̂n*, MaMo *malə̂n* 'warum'.

A somewhat different explanation is given by Luutonen (1997) who in an investigation of the morphotactic variation in Mari had reason to deal comprehensively with the origin of the dative case ending in Mari. Luutonen's discussion about the origin of the suffix is concentrated around the question of whether it is an ancient or fairly recent suffix. The suffix occurs in combination with plural and possessive endings and the order between the suffixes in question can vary without resulting in any diferences in meaning—which is what Luutonen calls morphotactic variation—and this indicates that it is a recent suffix in Mari. Luutonen (1997: 73), however, points to the fact that what he refers to as the morphological independence of an older suffix can increase and according to Luutonen (1997: 73–74) it is possible to assume several suffixes in *l* to which the PFU lative ending **-ń* is added.

Irrespective of whether it is an ancient or recent suffix in Mari, the dative case ending has a very large amount of functions in Mari. These are listed and exemplified by Alhoniemi (1985: 52–54) who gives a detailed account of the different ways in which the suffix is used. Among the functions of the dative case in Mari discussed by Alhoniemi, there are some that are especially interesting. Above, I have suggested that the copying of a postposition that governs a certain case, e.g. *köra* 'because of' can influence the choice of case even when it comes to original postpositions with the same meaning so that they too start to occur with the dative case. When a postposition governing the dative case is copied into Mari, this can make way for the selective copying of the combinatorial properties of the Tatar dative. In Mari, there are apart from mixed copies of the type *-lan köra* 'according to, because of' also other kinds of mixed copies in which the dative occurs. In Turkic languages, some verbs require an object in the dative case, e.g. Tu *inanmak* 'to believe in'. The copying of a verb that requires the dative can affect the choice of case marker in the basic code (Johanson 1999: 45). In Mari there are copies of Tatar verbs that require the dative case, e.g. Ma *inanem* 'believe in' < Tat *inan* 'believe in' and Ma *kuanem* 'to be happy about something' < Tat *kuan* 'id'.

MaMo *təńə jə̂mə̂lan əńänet kəńə, kolə̂mə̂ket ergəc taja* 'Wenn du dich auf Gott verlässt, wird nach deinem Tod dein Sohn dich begraben' (Beke 1951: 144)

MaMe *mə̂j, maneš, nö-γölan inanen omə̂l ə̂l'e, maneš* 'Er spricht: Ich habe niemandem geglaubt' (Beke 1961a: 153)

MaE *jeŋlan inanaš ok jörö—maneš suas* 'Es ist nicht gut, einem anderen zu glauben—sagt der Tatare' (Beke 1995: 100)

MaE *jeŋən pojanžəlan it kuane: škańet jumo pužo*! 'Freue dich nicht des Reichtum anderer (Sing.), Gott gebe dir selbst Reichtum!' (Beke 1961b: 158)

In Mari, the dative case can be used as an adverbial expressing the price of a commodity:

MaE *ik tenŋelan kńiγam naľəm* 'I bought this book for one ruble' (Alhoniemi 1985: 53)

MaE "*kürlə̂nam, maneš, latkut koŋam šüδö kandašlu teŋgelan*" 'Sechzehn Öfen für hundertachtzig Rubel [zu setzen: Ö. B.] habe ich mich verdungen—sagt er' (Beke 1995: 102)

In this respect, there is a close correspondence between Mari and Tatar where the dative is used to express the price of a commodity:

Tat *bu kıtapnı öč sumga aldım* 'I bought this book for three rubles' (Poppe 1963: 36)

TatM *min sine yüz sumga baka dip satïp aldïm, sin kïz buldïñ dide* 'Ich kaufte dich—sagte der Kahlkopf—für einhundert Rubel als einen Frosch, aber du bist nun ein Mädchen geworden' (Kakuk 1996: 58)

In Mari, the dative case can also be used as an adverbial of time denoting the time during which an action takes place:

Ma *kə̂zə̂t kok minutlan kanəmašəm əštena* 'Now we take a break for two minutes' (Alhoniemi 1985: 53)

MaE "*tə̂šte šonet, maneš, tiδe sβetə̂šte kum časlan sajə̂n jumə̂m, sulə̂ket pə̂ta*"—*maneš* 'Wenn du hier, auf dieser Welt—sagt er—drei Stunden (Sg.) lang Gottes schön gedenkst, werden deine Sünden (Sg.) erlöschen"—sagt er' (Beke 1995: 234)

In Tatar too, the dative case can be used as an adverbial to express the time at or during which an action takes place:

Tat *ber sägatkä* 'for one hour' (Poppe 1963: 36)

The same applies to Chuvash in which the dative case is used to denote the moment at or during which an action takes place:

ChuvA *ukspa arăměpe kenral kanašlanăta vunike časra karapa tapratsa kayma χušnă karap śüretekenne* 'Die Kaufmansfrau und der General trafen eine Verabredung, und um zwölf Uhr befahlen sie dem Schiffer, das Schiff in Bewegung zu setzen' (Paasonen 1949: 295)

Bereczki (1983: 13) has discussed these functions of the Mari dative, as well as the fact that it can be used to express direction:

Ma *čoδǝralan münδǝr oγǝl* 'It is not far to the forest' (Bereczki 1983: 213)

This use of the dative case is characteristic also for the Turkic languages:

TatM *bolar ber as könnär kitkännän soñ ber urmanγa kirgännär* 'Nachdem sie einige Tage gewandert waren, kamen sie in einen Wald' (Paasonen 1953: 115)

TatM *"Tsigan, sin urmanγa barıp büre tutup kayt, pišerip ašik", digän* 'Er sagte: "Zigeuner, geh in den Wald, fange einen Wolf und bringe ihn her, so werden wir ihn kochen und essen"' (Paasonen 1953: 49)

According to Kuznetsova, (1996: 235) many of the functions of the dative in eastern Mari are expressed by use of the lative case in western Mari. With eastern Mari, Kuznetsova refers to both MaMe and MaE while western Mari in a similar way refers to both MaMo and MaNw. It is very likely that some of the functions —to express the price of a commodity, to denote the time during which an action takes place and to express direction—of the MaE and MaMe dative have been copied from Tatar. It also seems as if, if one is to believe Kuznetsova, it is mainly in MaMo and MaNw that the lative is used in the same functions as the dative in MaMe and MaE. But apparently the lative can be used to express the price of a commodity also in MaMe:

MaMe *ala tiδe βakšǝm užalet. moš puet?* 'Du verkaufst doch sicher diese Mühle. Für wieviel gibst du sie? (Alhoniemi & Saarinen 1983: 198)

MaMe *pop joδeš: moš tiδe munet šoγa* 'Der Pfarrer fragt: Was kostet dieses Ei? (Alhoniemi & Saarinen 1983: 184)

MaNw *βara ik jeŋǝ̂m mum, tärlǝšǝm šǝm teŋeš kuδo jatke kandaš* 'Da begegnete ich einem Mann [mit einem Wagen; Ö. B.], gab ihm 7 Rubel (eig. dingte ihn für 7 Rubel), damit er mich nachhause fahre' (Beke 1957: 11)

It seems as if both the dative and lative cases are acceptable choices in some instances. Occasionally, the same noun can occur with both cases in the same text, which is evident from the following example:

MaMe *kupeč erγǝ̂ tiδǝ̂m βitľǝ̂ teŋkeš* [lat.] *naleš ta jülalta. lomǝ̂žǝ̂m βaržǝ̂š opta ta aδak kaja. βes βere tuδǝ̂ aδak tǝ̂γaj šančaš tüškam užeš, tiδǝm aδak βitľǝ̂ teŋkelan* [dat.] *naleš ta jülalta* 'Der Sohn des Kaufmanns kauft ihn für fünfzig Rubel und verbrennt ihn. Die Asche tut er auf den Kahn und fährt weiter. An einem anderen Ort sieht er wieder einen solchen Haufen Späne. Auch den kauft er für fünfzig Rubel und verbrennt ihn' (Alhoniemi & Saarinen 1983: 120)

In my opinion, the Mari dative is a parallel to the particles *γǝ̂na* and *laj* discussed above, particles identified with the native Mari mophemes *βele* and *γańe, gaj*. With respect to the functions it can fill, the Mari dative is a selective copy of combinatorial patterns of the Tatar dative, patterns transferred to an equivalent of the basic code. It is evident that the dative in the eastern parts of the Mari language area has acquired functions of the Tatar dative, functions earlier expressed by use of the lative case and—in the western part of the language area—still expressed with the lative case. The different functions and their geographic distribution thus form a pattern with respect to the integration of code-copies from the Turkic languages into the basic code, and are comparable to the copying and distribution of particles.

5.4 Infinite verb forms

In Mari, the use of infinite verb forms is fairly extensive and this is also the case in the Turkic languages. The infinite verb forms in Mari have recently attracted the attention of turcologists, and Johanson (2000: 168) explicitly states that the use of infinite verb forms in Mari is the result of contact-induced change. In Finno-Ugric linguistics, there are several detailed accounts of the infinite verb forms in Mari, among them being Alhoniemi (1970) and Bartens (1979). Kokla (1986) has also studied the infinite verb forms in Mari. However, opinions differ when it comes to the question of how many infinite verb forms there are in Mari and different scholars give different numbers, see Bartens (1979: 92).

5.4.1 MaMe, MaE *-šaš(lə̑k)*, MaMo, MaNw *-šaš(lə̑k), -šäš(lək)*

The suffix MaMe, MaE *-šaš(lə̑k)*, MaMo, MaNw *-šaš(lə̑k), -šäš(lək)* is the ending for the so-called future participle (Alhoniemi 1985: 138). It is a compound suffix, consisting of a morpheme *-šaš, -šäš* and the derivational ending *-lə̑k* discussed above in section 4.4.2.1. The existence of a longer form with the suffix *-lə̑k* thus points to Turkic influence. It seems as if the longer form is more frequent in the western dialects, but according to Alhoniemi (1985: 138) it occurs also in the eastern dialects. In the same way, the shorter form occurs also in the western dialects. In the material I have examined, both forms occur:

MaMo *noβə̑j γot βatə̑ əδər nälšäšlək mə̑lojec jäl amalaš βacmə̑kə̑ pərcəm kəšänešəžə pištä δä keä nə̑rə̑škə̑* 'Am Neujahrsabend geht der heiratslustige Bursch, wenn die anderen schlafengelegt haben, aufs Feld' (Beke 1951: 36)

MaMo *äťäž δon äβäžə manə̑t nälšäš* 'Seine Eltern sagen ihm: heirate (eig. [ein Mädchen; Ö. B.] ist zu nehmen)! (Beke 1951: 56)

MaMe *pojə̑ktaršašlə̑kə̑m pojə̑ktarem ə̑ľə̑ aδak čot* 'Du bist reich geworden, aber ich hätte dich noch mehr reich gemacht' (Alhoniemi & Saarinen 1983: 172)

MaE *kuβa: "temə̑šaš", maneš* 'Die Alte: "Er soll gefüllt werden", sagt sie (Paasonen 1939: 221)

According to Galkin (1964: 167), the Mari participle *-šaš, -šäš* is also a compound ending, originating in a combination of the active participle and an adjective suffix *-aš*. Both suffixes are of Finno-Ugric origin. Alhoniemi (1985: 138–40) discusses the functions of this participle and states that it has a "future-necessitive" meaning. The suffix can function as an attribute in which function it can be passive as well as active, for example *tolšaš una* 'a coming guest, a guest who is to come". It can also take a predicative function in a sentence, often in combination with personal forms of the verb *ulam* 'to be' and in this case it forms a sort of compound predicate, e.g. *me tutlan čəla semənat polšəšaš uləna* 'We have to help her in every way' (Alhoniemi 1985: 139). In Mari, this participle can also function as the subject of a sentence. In this context it frequently occurs with a predicate in the form of the existential verb *ulo* 'there is' or its negative counterpart *uke* 'there isn't', e.g. *χalaš kešäšləkem ulo* 'I have to go to town' (Alhoniemi 1985: 140). The participle can also occur as a participial subject, e.g. *kešäšləkšə keźə!* 'May he go, he who has to go!' (Alhoniemi 1985: 140). The participle can also occur as an object, e.g. *məń təδən kešäšəžəm koľəm* 'I heard, that she had to go' and finally this participle can serve as the main word for postpositions and also as an adverbial. According to Alhoniemi, a final adverbial can take the dative case ending *-lan*, e.g. *taza lijšašlan jüštələna* 'We swim in order to get healthy' (Alhoniemi 1985: 140).

A comparison between the Mari participle in *-šašlək* and participles in the Turkic languages gives interesting results. In Tatar, the so-called "second future participle" (Poppe 1963: 73) has the suffixes *-r, -Är, -Er*. In section 4.1.3. it was observed that the particle *laj, läj,* copied from Tatar, occasionally can occur added to the Mari participle in *-šaš, -šäš,* e.g. MaE *čaj jüjšašlaj paγət šuəldən* 'Die Zeit des Teetrinkens ist gekommen' (Paasonen 1939: 176). In Tatar, the adverbial suffix *-dÄy, -dEy* can be added to the so-called second future participle, e.g. Tat *belerdey* 'as if he knows' (Poppe 1963: 106). The Mari participle thus has other connections with the Tatar participle in *-r, -Är, -Er*, something that can explain why a suffix *-lək*, copied from Tatar can be added to the Mari participle. The Tatar participle denotes actions that are to take place sometime in the future, e.g. *al* 'to take' → *alır* 'one who will take'. If the dative ending *-gÄ, -kÄ* is added to the participle, the goal of the action is expressed, e.g. *al* 'to take' → *alırga* 'in order to take'. Personal endings can be added to this participle, the forms functioning essentially as a tense expressing actions that will take place in the future, e.g. *eślärmen* 'I shall work' (Poppe 1963: 75). Derivational endings can be added to the participle, among them the suffix *-lEk: birešer* 'to surrender, to yield' → *birešerlek* 'the surrendering, yielding' (Poppe 1963: 205). In Tatar, the second future participle can also occur as part of what Poppe (1963: 103) refers to as "participle compounds", often in combination with the verb *i-* 'to be' in the following way: *adresın belsäm, χat yazar idem* 'if I knew his address, I would write [him] a letter' (Poppe 1963: 104).

In my opinion, the Mari participle in *-šaš* has beeen identified with the Tatar participle in *-r, -Är, -Er*. The possibility of adding the particle *laj, läj* copied from Tatar to the participle *-šaš, -šäš* speaks in favour of this. Both the Mari and the Tatar participles refer to actions which are to take place in the future and the Tatar participle can, as its Mari counterpart, occur in compounds with person-forms of a verb meaning 'to be'.

In Tatar, the ending *-r, -Är, -Er* can take the suffix *-lEk*. Participial forms in Mari containing the suffix *-lək* are therefore easily explained. The suffix *-lək* has been added to the participle because it is this position the originally Tatar suffix occupies in Tatar forms with the "second future participle". There is a clear equivalence position in Mari, the Tatar suffix *-r, -Är, -Er* has been identified with the Mari participle in *-šaš*. The longer form, *-šašlək*, in Mari can be said to be a mixed copy since it combines material copying of a morpheme with the selective copying of one of its combinational properties. In all likelihood, also the cases in which the dative case ending is added to the participle, e.g. *taza lijšašlan jüštələna* 'We swim in order to get healthy', can be described as the result of copying since it is possible to add the dative case ending *-gÄ, -kÄ* to the second future participle in Tatar, e.g. *alırga* 'in order to take'. In this case, the copying is selective because the Mari dative ending has taken over functions of the Tatar original. Semantically, the Mari example corresponds to the Tatar example since the dative ending in both cases expresses the goal of the action.

However, the possibility that Chuvash influence can be detected in this particular instance can not be excluded. In Chuvash too there is a future participle with the suffix *-(A)s* added to the stem of the verb, *vulas* 'one who will read, that which is to be read, which will be read'. Krueger (1961: 155–56) gives several examples of the use of this participle, predicatively with or without a pronoun, e.g. *epĕ pĕles* 'I will know, I should know', *kayas, atte* 'I'll go, father'. According to Bereczki (1988: 348), the derivational ending *-lăχ, -lĕχ* can be added to the Chuvash participle in *-(A)s*, e.g. *ĕśĕslĕk ĕś* 'die zu machende Arbeit'. Furthermore the so-called purposive case ending in *-šăn, -šĕn* can be added to the participle. This case has the essential meaning of 'for, for the purpose of' (Krueger 1961: 156), e.g. *appana kurasšăn epĕ kunta kiltĕm* 'I came for the seeing of my sister, to see my sister'. According to Krueger (1961: 156) the combination fills the same functions as "the infinitive of the European languages in many ways" and it is comparable to the Mari example *taza lijšašlan jüštələna* 'We swim in order to get healthy' (Alhoniemi 1985: 140)

Lavrentyev (1971: 193–196) is of the opinion that the future participle in Mari originates in a combination of the ending for the present participle *-še* and an adjective suffix *-aš* (see Alhoniemi (1985: 157, note 1, according to whom the suffix is a compound suffix). According to Lavrentyev, the Turkic languages have played an important role in this matter, because these languages had a participle that was phonetically identical and semantically comparable to the Mari future participle. Lavrentyev does not have a surfeit of examples from the Turkic languages (to put it mildly) but judging from the discussion it seems as if he has the Chuvash participle in *-(A)s* in mind. In Tatar, there is a "participle of necessity" ending in *-ÄsE* or *-ysE* and this can be the Tatar participle Lavrentyev refers to. According to Poppe (1963: 70), this participle is a compound suffix, combining a suffix *-lÄ, -y* to which the possessive suffix of the 3rd person singular, *-sE*, has been added. In Tatar, this participle can be used predicatively, e.g. *kunaklar irtägä kiläse* 'the comrades must come tomorrow' (Poppe 1963: 71). If the Mari participle is a necessitive-future participle as Alhoniemi claims, it is possible that the necessitive meaning originates in the Tatar and Chuvash participles and that its function as a future participle has been influenced by the second future participle in Tatar.

The view that the longer variant in *-šašlə̑k, -šäšlək* is more frequent in the western dialects of Mari is held by Alhoniemi. It is difficult to determine whether this is actually the case but judging from the material I have used, both forms are equally frequent in the collection of MaMo texts published by Beke in 1951, at least in the fairy-tale and proverb sections (Beke 1951: 10–315). The longer form occurs a total of nine times, often with the same verb, while the shorter form occurs eight times. Below, examples of both forms are given:

MaMo *noβə̑j γot βatə̑ əδər nälšäšlək mə̑lojec jäl amalaš βacmə̑kə̑ pərcəm kəšänešəžə pištä δä keä nə̑rə̑škə̑* 'Am Neujahrsabend geht der heiratslustige Bursch, wenn die anderen schlafengelegt haben, aufs Feld' (Beke 1951: 36)

MaMo *məńə popazenäm ə̑l'ə̑ jamšašlə̑k βäreškə* 'Ich kam an [so; Ö. B] einen Ort, dass ich fast umkam' (Beke 1951: 301)

MaMo *äťäž δon äβäžə manə̑t nälšäš* 'Seine Eltern sagen ihm: heirate (eig. [ein Mädchen; Ö. B.] ist zu nehmen)!' (Beke 1951: 56)

In the section of Beke's collection that contains folk-songs (Beke 1951: 316–359) the frequency of the short and the long forms of the participle is totally different. The short form occurs no less than 23 times whereas the longer form occurs only once. In Beke's collection of songs, a modal verb, *ə̑l'ə̑* 'was', of the verb *ulam* 'to be', is often added to the participle in *-šaš*:

MaMo *sarə̑ jažo limeškəžə,*
Mə̑tə̑k χuža lišäš ə̑l'ə̑
βätə saγa-ok ələšäš ə̑l'ə̑
βätə saγa-ok ələšäš ə̑l'ə̑

'Statt ein blonder [und; Ö. B.] schöner Bursche zu sein
Wäre ich lieber klein und hässlich
Und würde lieber mit meiner Frau leben,
Und würde lieber mit meiner Frau leben' (Beke 1951: 325)

In Tatar too a modal verb is often added to the second future participle:

TatK *uramlardın uzγan čakta*
Nige bizge kirmedıñ
Karšı čıγıp alır-idim
Sin ikeniñ bilmedim

'Als du die Strasse entlang gingst,
warum kamst du bei uns nicht vorbei?
Dir entgegengehend hätte ich dich empfangen,
Aber ich wusste nicht, dass es du warst.' (Kakuk 1980: 95)

The conclusions that can be drawn are that the Mari participle in *-šašlə̂k* strongly resembles similar verbforms in the Turkic languages and that it occurs in the same contexts. The copying of the suffix *-lə̂k* and the emergence of a longer form of the Mari participle are closely connected to the Tatar and Chuvash participial forms with the same suffix. The opinion that the longer form is more frequent in the western dialects, is not supported by the material I have examined.

5.4.2 MaMe, MaE *-δə̂maš, -tə̂maš,* MaMo, MaNw, *-δə̂maš, -δəmäš, -tə̂maš, -təmäš*

The suffix MaMe, MaE *-δə̂maš, -tə̂maš,* MaMo, MaNw, *-δə̂maš, -δəmäš, -tə̂maš, -təmäš* is according to Alhoniemi (1985: 156) made up of the negative gerund *-te, -δe* and a deverbal suffix *-maš*. Forms of this kind constitute verbal nouns referring to unfinished actions. Alhoniemi further states that the suffix is a productive suffix in Mari. Alhoniemi's example, *lijδə̂maš* 'impossibility, that which will not happen in the future' makes it possible to draw the conclusion that the suffix also has a temporal meaning and that it functions as the negative counterpart of the future participle discussed above in 5.4.1. There are very few examples of this suffix in the material I have examined and the discussion about the suffix and its relation to corresponding features in the Turkic languages is therefore not based on sufficient evidence.

Apparently, the suffix *-lə̂k* can be added to this suffix, e.g. *lijδə̂mašlə̂k* 'impossibility' (Moisio 1994: 147) and this form is seemingly a parallel form to *lijδemaš* 'id' (Moisio 1994: 147). *lijδə̂mašlə̂k* evidently has the function of a negative counterpart of the form *lijšašlə̂k* discussed above and the fact that a derivational ending *-lə̂k* of Tatar origin has been added to the Mari derivational ending MaE *-δə̂maš, -tə̂maš,* MaW *-δə̂maš, -δəmäš, -tə̂maš, -təmäš* is in all likelihood the result of Tatar influence.

In Tatar, negatives of the second future participle *-r, -Är, -Er* are formed by adding the negative suffix *-mÄs* (Poppe 1963: 74) to the stem of the verb, e.g. *yatmas* 'one who will not lie down' ← *yat-* 'to lie down', *kermäs* 'one who will not come in' ← *ker-* to come in'. Below is an example of the use of the negative future participle in Tatar.

TatK *sin anardan razi bolsañ bolmas-mė?* 'würdest du ihm nicht versichten?' (Kakuk 1989: 170)

These negative forms can take the dative case ending *-gÄ, -kÄ* and then refer to something that will not take place in the future, or something that has to be done in order to avoid a certain future event, e.g. *kurkmaska* 'in order not to be afraid' (Poppe 1963: 74). Since it is a noun, the negative second future participle can also take different derivational endings such as *-lık,* e.g. *bulmaslık* 'impossibility, that which will not happen in the future'. Examples of both the affirmative and negative second future participles to which the derivational ending *-lık* is added are given below.

TatK *Kart: ey patša, nė süzigėz bar, süylep karaγės, eger-de bulurlėk bulsa, ǯavab birėrmėn, bolmazlėk bolsa, minė γayėb itmessėz* 'Der Alte meinte: Hei Padischah, was du hast zu sagen, sag es, wenn es möglich sein wird, werde ich antworten, wenn nicht, wirst du mich nicht beschuldigen' (Kakuk 1989: 32)

There are probably several reasons as to why the suffix *-lə̂k* can be added to the ending MaE *-δə̂maš, -tə̂maš,* MaW *-δə̂maš, -δəmäš, -tə̂maš, -təmäš*. First, the suffix is the negative counterpart of the Mari participle *-šaš, -šäš* to which the suffix *-lə̂k* is also added. Forms such as *lijδə̂mašlə̂k* thus have counterparts in forms like *lijšašlə̂k*. Second, the formal resemblance between the Mari suffix *-maš* and the negative second future participle *-mÄs* in Tatar can be of importance. In Mari, the suffix *-te,- δe* gives the compound suffix a negative meaning while *-maš* is a deverbal suffix that gives the compund suffix an abstract meaning, *-maš* thus corresponds to the Tatar suffix *-lık* and can possibly be one of the suffixes with which the Tatar *-lık* has been identified. On the other hand it is not impossible that the compound suffix MaE *-δə̂maš, -tə̂maš,* MaW *-δə̂maš, -δəmäš, -tə̂maš, -təmäš* is perceived as an equivalent to the Tatar suffix *-mÄs* to which the suffix *-lık* is added. Relatively homophonous "false friends" can according to Johanson (1999: 49) lead to copying.

5.4.3 The affirmative instructive gerund *-en, -n*

The so-called affirmative instructive gerund (Alhoniemi 1985: 141) in Mari has the endings *-en* and *-n*. The suffix *-en* is added to verbs in the *em*-conjugation whereas the suffix *-n* is added to verbs belonging to the *am*-conjugation. As far as the verbs in the *am*-conjugation are concerned, sometimes the stem of the verb is used as an affirmative instructive gerund. In Mari, the gerund is used as a complementary to certain verbs, e.g. *tuδo muren mošta* 'he knows how to sing, he can sing' (Alhoniemi 1985: 142) and *lin keteš* 'it can happen, perhaps'. Usually, the gerund is used as an adverbial. According to Alhoniemi (1985: 142) the gerund can express different semantical concepts such as way, cause and intention and its connection to the main verb can be varied. According to Alhoniemi (1985: 142), the semantics of the gerund are not always clear.

The action that the gerund refers to takes place at the same time as the action that the main verb expresses. The gerund and the main verb thus have the same agent which also is the subject, e.g. *tuδo kuržə̂n toleš* 'he comes running' (Alhoniemi 1985: 142). It is also possible to form sentences in which several gerunds are serialized and they then refer to actions that follow each other, e.g. *tuδo kuržə̂n tolə̂n puren lektə̂n kajə̂š* 'he came running, stepped in, went out and left (coming running, stepping in, going out he left)' (Alhoniemi 1985: 143).

According to Alhoniemi (1985: 143), sometimes the gerund can refer to conditions around the action rather than to the action itself, e.g. *ala-moγaj ajδeme, kužu šińežə̂m čijen, kartužə̂m komδə̂k upšalə̂n, jalə̂š purə̂š* 'some man, putting on an overcoat, turning his cap backwards, came in to the village'. The affirmative instructive gerund can also function as an attribute, e.g. *šužen ij* 'hunger year' (Alhoniemi 1985: 143). These are cases of lexicalised expressions. Occasionally, the gerund can be geminated in Mari, e.g. *muren, muren kaja* 'singing and singing she goes'. In these cases, the geminated gerund expresses durativity.

The affirmative instructive gerund in Mari can also occur in what has been referred to as aspectual converb structures (Bartens 1979: 147–148). These verb constructions are combinations of one or more gerunds and a finite verb expressing different types of actionality. In Turkic linguistics, these finite verbs are generally referred to as postverbs. Since this is a syntactical way of expressing the actionality of the verb, these verb constructions in Mari with direct equivalents in the Turkic languages will be discussed below in 5.5.

The affirmative instructive gerund in Mari closely resembles verbforms in other Finno-Ugric languages, among them the so-called instructive of the second infinitive in Finnish. This infinitive in Finnish is formed by adding an ending *-n* to the stem of the verb, e.g. Fi *lapsi tuli itkien kotiin* 'the child came home crying' (Karlsson 1978: 187). The instructive of the second infinitive rarely occurs in Finnish and according to Karlsson is mainly found in lexicalized expressions. It has been suggested that the ending of the affirmative instructive gerund in Mari is identical to the ending of the genitive case in *-n* and that the gerund thus can be assumed to be a genitive form of the verb (c.f. Korhonen 1981: 213). In North Saami, the so-called verbal genitive can be used as an adverbial, often in connection with verbs of motion and then expresses the way in which one moves or travels, e.g. SaN *Láśśe båđii vázzi* 'Lasse came walking' (Ruong 1974: 83).

It is reasonable to assume that the affirmative instructive gerund in Mari is formed with an ending *-en, -n* closely connected to, or perhaps identical with, the genitive case ending in *-n*. It is thus a suffix of high age in Mari. In my opinion, there are nevertheless examples of Turkic influence in the use of this gerund, especially when it comes to auxiliary verb constructions. Also in other respects there are resemblances between the use of the Mari gerund and corresponding verb forms in the Turkic languages.

The existence of several infinite verb forms is one of the characteristic features of the Turkic languages. Among the more prominent of these are the so-called converbs, abundant in both Tatar and Chuvash. According to Krueger (1961: 162), Chuvash converbs are verbal forms not marked for person, number or tense. They are used to express that the action they refer to is in a certain relation to the action expressed by a finite verb and thus correspond to the gerunds or participles in English. According to Krueger, the thought is "held in abeyance by use of a converb until the concluding verb". Converbs are thus verb forms of what Krueger refers to as "a suspensory nature" and they express "a secondary action coordinate to or complementary to the main action". According to Krueger, converbs can not finish a statement or sentence.

In Chuvash, but not in Mari, there is a morphological distinction between subordinate and coordinate converbs. The subordinate converbs in Chuvash take the ending *-a, -e* (Krueger 1961: 162) and they refer to an action completely subordinate to that of the finite verb:

ChuvA *karăm, karăm, kaś pula puślarě* 'Ich wanderte und wanderte, es begann, Nacht zu werden' (Paasonen 1949: 117)

According to Krueger (1961: 162), the subordinate converb in Chuvash can "be reduplicated to show continuation". In Paasonen's collection of Chuvash texts, reduplicated subordinate converbs are fairly common:

ChuvA *epě payan kuněpe ulma śiye śiye tură χěrěsene širasa śürěp* 'Heute werde ich den ganzen Tag hindurch nach den Töchtern Gottes suchen und Äpfel essen' (Paasonen 1949: 180; the same example is given by Krueger (1961: 163) although in an abridged version)

ChuvA *śapla üke üke starik pětěmpe śěměrělse pětně* 'Indem er so sprang und sprang, wurde der Alte ganz müde (Paasonen 1949: 158)

The coordinate converbs in Chuvash take the ending *-sa, -se* and are very frequent. According to Krueger (1961: 163), they can "be found in nearly every Chuvash sentence". These converbs refer to actions of what Krueger calls "equal value" and according to the author (1961: 163) some of the most common combinations have "become stylized into equivalents of single verbs". In reality, these verb constructions are the Chuvash counterparts of the auxiliary verb constructions to be discussed below in 5.5.

In Chuvash, the coordinate converbs can be serialized so that sentences in which several converbs follow each other are possible:

ChuvA *kaχalě kulkalasa šăχărkalasa larsa pırat tet* 'Der faulenzer fährt lachend und pfeifend' (Paasonen 1949: 109)

ChuvA *yătti věrse tulasa χusa yană văpărlă karččăka* 'Der Hund jagte bellend und beissend die Hexe hinweg' (Paasonen 1949: 291)

The Chuvash coordinate converb in *-sa, -se* closely resembles the verbal adverb in *-sa* in Udmurt and according to some scholars it is an originally Udmurt feature in Chuvash. Other scholars are of the opinion that it is rather the Udmurt verbal adverb that is of Chuvash origin (for a detailed discussion, see Bartens 1979: 178). However, the Chuvash coordinate converb is doubtlessly identical to a Volga Bulgar verb form with the suffix *-sA* discussed by Erdal (1993: 70–75). This suffix has been seen as connected to an Old Turkic conditional suffix and according to Erdal (1993: 75), there is little reason not to connect this Volga Bulgar (and consequently also the Chuvash) suffix with the Old Turkic conditional suffix. Erdal cautiously does not exclude Finno-Ugric influence and points to the fact that common linguistic features are often the result of convergence. Given the fact that the language contact between Udmurts and Chuvash is more scant and short than that between Chuvash and Mari, it is hardly probable that the existence of a Chuvash converb *-sa, -se* and a verbal adverb *-sa* in Udmurt could be the result of convergence. It is more likely that the formal resemblance is the result of coincidence. Admittedly, there are features in Chuvash which could be the result of Udmurt substratum influence, for instance the negative imperative forms in *an*, but—as far as substratum influnces are concerned—when code-copies are carried over from one language to another, they are more often phonological code-copies such as pronunciation habits or syntactic code-copies such as sentence-forming patterns whereas lexical and morphological copies are much more unusual.

Infinite verb forms labelled as converbs are characteristic also of Turkic languages in the Kipchak group, to which Tatar belongs. According to Poppe (1963: 75), the converbs, which he refers to as gerunds, function as adverbs, verbal attributes or adverbial complements. In Tatar there are two converbs with connections to the affirmative instructive gerund in Mari. As in Chuvash, there is a morphological distinction between subordinate and coordinate converbs. According to Poppe (1963: 76), the so-called "first present gerund" (formally and functionally equivalent to the Chuvash converb in *-a, -e*) has the endings *-Ä* and *-y* respectively. In Tatar, this is also the form of the present participle. In Tatar, this gerund (or converb) refers to actions simultaneous to the action expressed by the finite verb and in this way they express actions "merging into one combined action" (Poppe 1963: 76).

TatM *Malay cïgïp agacka balta bilän caba bašlagan ide* 'Der Junge ging und begann mit dem Beil Bäume abzuhauen' (Kakuk 1996: 77)

TatK *Ebi bilen malay brge-brge tura bašlilar* 'Die Alte Frau und der Junge begannen gemeinsam zu leben' (Kakuk 1989: 94)

According to Poppe (1963: 76), the gerund can express frequently occurring actions and it can be reduplicated to show continuation:

TatM *Ulusu bara bara ber šähärgä barïp ǯitte, ul šähärdä padša saylïlardï* 'Der Grössere, als er lange seines weges gezogen war, kam zu einer Stadt, wo das Volk eben einen Padischah wählte' (Kakuk 1996: 69)

In Tatar, the so-called second present gerund with the suffix *-p* or *-Ep* after consonant stems corresponds to the coordinate converb *-sa, -se* in Chuvash. According to Poppe (1963: 76), this converb denotes actions starting before the action expressed with the finite verb and continuing together with it. In Tatar too, serialization of the gerund is quite frequent:

TatM *Mune kürep kïz Yusïpnï ber kucaklak suwurïp üpte-dä katïn bilän ikäwläp küterep alïp barïp kïznïñ üz kumnatïna saldïlar* 'Als das Mädchen das gesehen hatte, umarmte sie Jusuf und küsste ihn, dann hob sie ihn mit der Frau zu zweit und sie trugen ihn in die Wohnung des Mädchens' (Kakuk 1996: 91)

Alhoniemi (1985: 143) points to the fact that the affirmative instructive gerund in Mari can refer to conditions around the action rather than to the action itself. There are examples of this also in the material I have examined. The following two examples are representative for the sub-dialect of MaMe that Bereczki (1985: 191) calls the Volga dialect and which according to him is characterized by both western and eastern dialectal features:

MaMe *šužarže əmńəžəm pokten nöröp türškö namija* 'Seine Schwester führt die Pferde an den Brunnen' (Beke 1957: 582)

MaMe *kas peleš mijen kuγəžan olaš pura* 'Gegend Abend gelangt er in die Stadt des Kaisers' (Beke 1957: 628)

In this respect, the affirmative instructive gerund in Mari has a point in common with the second present gerund *-p* in Tatar which apparently also can be used to denote circumstances around the action rather than the action itself:

TatM *Malay cıgıp agacka balta bilän caba bašlagan ide* 'Der Junge ging und begann mit dem Beil Bäume abzuhauen' (Kakuk 1996: 77)

The thought that the affirmative instructive gerund in Mari and the second present gerund in Tatar describe circumstances around the action rather than the action itself is perhaps not straightforward. It is rather so that the Tatar and Mari gerunds denote actions preceding the action expressed by the main verb but that "the thought is held in abeyance by use of a converb until the concluding verb" (Krueger 1961: 162)

An interesting feature that deserves a detailed study is that there are examples in which the affirmative instructive gerund in Mari is used as an adverbial complement to a finite verb, but then in a final position:

MaMo *pə̂ra eδemlä kajə̂n* 'In menschlicher Gestalt (eig. als Mensch scheinend) geht er hinein [zu ihr; Ö. B.] (Beke 1951: 44)

MaMe *tə̂retmə̂ γoδə̂m küδə̂rčan jür toleš muren* 'Bei der Ernte bricht mit [grossem; Ö. B.] Getöse ein Gewitter aus (eig. kommt der Regen mit Donner)' (Beke 1961a: 156)

This corresponds well with Saami in which the so-called verbal genitive usually is preceded by a finite verb and Finnish in which the instructive of the second infinitive is preceded by a finite verb to which it is an adverbial complement:

SaS *Aehtjie bööti vaedtsien* 'Father came walking' (Bergsland 1982: 70)

Fi *lapsi tuli itkien kotiin* 'The child came home crying' (Karlsson 1978: 187)

In Finnish, the reverse order between the instructive of the second infinitive and the finite verb is possible only in relative clauses, e.g. *minä pelästyin, kun tyttö itkien tuli kotiin* 'I got frightened, when the girl came home crying'

The existence of infinite verb forms such as the affirmative instructive gerund in Mari and the converbs in Tatar and Chuvash with partly similar functions is interesting with respect to code-copying. In this particular case, I would like to stress the fact that all similarities probably not can be analyzed as the result of code-copying and that some of them deserve a more detailed study. The affirmative instructive gerund in Mari has parallels in other Finno-Ugric languages (Bereczki 1988: 348), and in languages like North Saami there are infinite verb forms that express the same as an adverb of manner, one of the functions of the gerund in Mari. There are however clearly equivalence positions that can make code-copying possible. This mainly concerns the postverbs to be discussed in 5.5 but the possibility of Turkic influence on other uses of the gerund can not be excluded. An example of this is the reduplication of the gerund to express continuation and durativity. Although the possibility of reduplicating gerunds in this way can have existed theoretically in Mari, it is not impossible that it has increased in frequency in the wake of the contacts between Mari and the Turkic languages. In this way, it can be analysed as selective copying because frequential patterns and combinatorial properties are among the features that can be copied in language contact situations. A characteristic feature of both Mari and the Turkic languages is the serialization of gerunds. Verb serialization occurs in many languages (among them many languages in Africa) but it can not be excluded that this characteristic feature of the Turkic languages in the Middle Volga region has exerted an influence on Mari. The serialization of the affirmative instructive gerund in Mari could thus in all likelihood be analysed as the selective copying of combinatory and frequential properties of Tatar and Chuvash converbs.

5.5 Auxiliary verbs

One of the features that distinguish Mari from other Finno-Ugric languages, with the exception of Udmurt, are the auxiliary verbs. These are combinations of the affirmative instructive gerund ending in *-en* or *-n* and a finite verb that expresses different kinds of actionality, momentarity, frequentativity or durativity. The finite verb can partly or totally lose its lexical meaning and only serve to describe the way in which the action is carried out. The gerund gives the construction its semantical content (Alhoniemi 1985: 143–144), e.g. Ma *ija šortə̂n kolta* 'the devil bursted out crying' (lit. the devil crying sent). In Mari, there is also a large number of derivational endings filling the same function and many of them occur mainly in global copies of Tatar or Chuvash lexemes. This system is according to Saarinen (1997b: 394) partly overlapping with what she refers to as "aspectual converb constructions", that is the combinations of gerunds and finite verbs. These verb constructions have only developed in Mari and to a smaller extent in Udmurt and are seen as the result of Turkic influence (Saarinen 1997b: 393–394). The term "aspectual converb" goes back to Bartens (1979: 147) and these verb forms have been been studied in detail also by Čhaidze (1960; 1968) and Driussi (1995). However, the term "aspect" is less appropriate in the case of Mari, mainly because the combinations of a gerund and a finite verb in Mari do not always have an aspectual meaning in the sense that they refer to the perfect or imperfect aspect of an action. It is true that some of the verbs in Mari that can be used as auxiliaries in verb combinations of this type sometimes also can describe completed actions but more often they denote the way in which an action is carried out and express momentarity or durativity. A more appropriate term would thus be auxiliary verb constructions. As I intend to discuss these verb forms within the framework of a more exhaustive study, here I will limit myself to a desription of them and their relationship to similar verb forms in the Turkic languages.

There is a large number of verbs in Mari that can be used as finite verbs in auxiliary verb constructions (c.f. Alhoniemi 1985: 144; Bartens 1979: 147–148). Among the more frequently occurring of these are the verbs *kajem* 'to go' which according to Alhoniemi (1985: 144) refers to momentary, completed actions and *koltem* 'to send' which also refers to momentary actions. The system of auxiliary verb constructions covers the entire Mari language area:

MaMo *marə̂ βaštəl γolta* 'Der Mann lacht' (Beke 1951: 150)

MaNw *popet anzal kolten* 'Der Geistliche schaute sie an' (Beke 1957: 40)

MaMe *kunam βatə̂žə̂ pisman mariž δeč naln, luδən ta βik šortə̂n kolten* 'Als die Frau von ihrem Mann den Brief bekam, las sie ihn und brach direkt in Weinen aus' (Alhoniemi & Saarinen 1983: 96)

MaE *śüjän-marij kalə̂k šaulaten oŋə̂r δene lektə̂n kajat* 'Die Hochzeitsgäste gehen hinaus und machen sich auf den Weg' (Beke 1961b: 210)

In Chuvash, the auxiliary verb constructions are made up of combinations of a coordinate converb with the suffix *-sa, -se* and a finite verb, e.g. *χusa yar* 'to send and dispatch = to send' (Krueger 1961: 164). In Tatar they are combinations of a gerund ending in *-p, -Ep* (Poppe 1963: 76) and a finite verb, e.g. *min yazıp beteräm* 'I am finished writing' (Poppe 1963: 77). Wintschalek (1993: 129) claims that these auxiliary verb constructions are restricted to the languages of the Middle Volga region and that they constitute what he calls an "areale Erscheinung", or a typological feature characteristic of the Finno-Ugric and Turkic languages of the area. This is however not correct since similar verb constructions exist also in numerous other Turkic languages (c.f. Schönig 1984: 292–323).

In Tatar and Chuvash, several different verbs can serve as finite verbs in constructions of this type and express actionality. Krueger (1961: 164) only discusses this briefly in his description of the functions of the coordinate converb in *-sa, -se*, but there is a slightly more elaborate description in Benzing (1959b: 715–716). Schönig (1984: 318) is of the opinion that the Chuvash auxiliary verb constructions are inspired by the Tatar, by which one possibly can conclude that they have been copied from Tatar into Chuvash.

The Tatar and Chuvash auxiliary verb constructions have so many features in common with the Mari ones that it hardly can be the result of coincidence. In Mari, global copies of Tatar or Chuvash verbs can be used as finite verbs in auxiliary verb constructions, e.g. Ma *pə̂tarem* 'to finish' and *pə̂tem* 'to end' < Chuv *pĕter* 'to end, use up', *pĕt* 'to end, finish, lose, give out, run out' (Krueger 1961: 226), < Tat *beter-* 'to finish, destroy; abolish; ruin; spend', *bet* 'end; perish; go' (Poppe 1963: 205). According to Räsänen (1923: 53), both verbs are of Tatar origin in Mari and probably also in Chuvash. The Mari verb *kajem* 'to go' formally resembles the Chuvash *kay* 'to go' which also occurs in auxiliary verb constructions, e.g. Chuv *tuχsa kay* 'to go out, leave (to go emerging)' (Krueger 1961: 164). In most cases, the finite verbs occurring in this context seem to be selective copies of Tatar or Chuvash verbs and where only semantic properties have been copied onto a verb in the basic code, e.g. Ma *koltem* 'to send', Chuv *yar* 'id.', Tat *ğibär* 'id.'. Somewhat surprisingly, the number of verbs used as auxiliary verbs appears to be slightly higher in Mari than in Tatar or Chuvash. It is worth noting again that code-copying can lead to changes in frequential patterns so that a copy can become more frequent in the code into which it is copied. I find it more than likely that the auxiliary verb constructions in Mari are the result of Turkic linguistic influence and that it is Tatar that has been the model code. The reason for this copying is probably the functional similarities between the Mari affirmative instructive gerund in *-en, -n* and the Tatar and Chuvash converbs in *-Ep, -p* and *-sa, -se* discussed above in 5.4.3. In cases where these auxialiary verb constructions are made up of a gerund and a global copy of a Tatar or Chuvash verb used as a finite verb, the forms can be classified as mixed copies since they combine material copying of a lexeme with the selective copying of combinational properties. However, most of the auxiliary verb constructions in Mari can be classified as selective copies in which only semantic and combinatory copying has taken place, e.g. Ma *šortə̂n kolta* 'to burst out crying', Tat *yï(γ)lap ğibär* 'losweinen, in Tränen ausbrechen' (Schönig 1984: 175). The auxiliary verb constructions can furthermore be classified as conventionalised copies since they occur in both literary languages of Mari:

MaEL *kočkə̂t-jüt, malaš βozə̂t, erγat malen kolta* 'They ate and drank and went to bed, the son too fell asleep' (Taygildin 1993: 51)

MaWL *ma lin kolten βara?* 'What was it that had happened?' (Petukhov 1994: 11)

Verbforms similar to the ones in Mari and the Turkic languages in the Middle Volga region exist also in Indic languages. These have been studied in detail by Masica (1976) who uses the term "explicator compound verbs". They are made up of what Masica (1976: 141) calls a "conjunctive participle immediately followed by a finite verb". In these constructions the finite verb partly or totally loses its semantic content and becomes grammaticalized. The verbs used as auxiliaries are "generally described as belonging to limited sets" (Masica 1976: 142). Often included in these limited sets are verbs with meanings such as 'go', 'come', 'give', 'take', 'rise', 'fall', 'throw', 'put' and 'sit'. These are thus mainly verbs of state or motion. Masica (1976: 142) points to the fact that if these limited sets are extended, then the verbs included in the set are only variations on the same theme. Verbs that can become grammaticalized auxiliaries in compound verbs of this type are, apart from the ones mentioned also verbs like 'emerge', 'move', 'run away', 'descend', 'arrive', 'lie', 'stand', 'send', release' and 'lift up' (Masica 1976: 142). Quite a few of the verbs used as auxiliary verbs in Mari have meanings identical or similar to these.

"Explicator compund verbs" exist in all Indic languages according to Masica

(1976: 144) and have been connected with Dravidian substratum influence. One problem with this explanation is that the system seems more elaborate for instance in Hindi than in Dravidian languages. However, as was indicated above, code-copying can result in a higher frequency in the language into which a particular feature is copied than in the language serving as the model code.

5.6 The morpheme *uke* 'there/it is not'

The free morpheme *uke* 'there/it is not' is the negative counterpart of the verb *ulo* 'there is' (Kangasmaa-Minn 1998: 231). The morpheme occurs in all dialects of Mari.

MaMo *təńəm pukχšə̂šə̂ ikt-ät uke. kolə̂mə̂ket-ät ik-ät tajə̂šə̂ uke* 'Du hast niemand der dir zu essen geben würde, du hast niemand, der dich nach deinem Tod bestatten würde' (Beke 1951: 144)

MaNw *kəźət kuδo uke, ažnə̂ ulmašen* 'Heute haben wir keine Sommerhütte[n; Ö.B] [mehr; Ö.B], früher gab es [welche; Ö.B]' (Beke 1957: 27)

MaMe *šińčə̂n šalšə̂ šuk[o; Ö.B] ulo, šoγal šalše uke* 'Es gibt viele (Sing.), die sitzend pissen (eig. sitzend pissende, d.h. Weiber), [doch; Ö.B] keine (Sing.), die stehend pissen (d.h. Männer)' (Beke 1961a: 53)

MaE *βujž[o; Ö.B.] uke, kitš[e; Ö.B] uke* 'Es hat keine Füsse (Sing.), (hat) keine Hände (Sing.)' (Beke 1961b: 364)

The etymology of *uke* is uncertain. According to Kangasmaa-Minn (1998: 231), it is a "negative noun", possibly of Turkic origin. Honti (1997: 162) claims that it originates in a verb form *ok* 'es ist nicht'. But he also seems to be of the opinion that the vowel *u* in the Mari morpheme *uke* can be the result of influence from Kazan Tatar in which *yuk* 'es gibt nicht' according to him is a negative particle. The Mari morpheme *uke* does have a formal resemblance with morphemes in Tatar and Chuvash, Tat *yuk* 'non-existent; absent; there is not; no' (Poppe 1963: 261) and Chuvash *śuk* 'there is not, there are not; there does not exist' (Krueger 1961: 232). Poppe (1963: 126) states that *yuk* is a negative noun in Tatar, the functions of which closely resemble those of the Mari *uke*. In my Tatar material there are several examples:

TatK *üzė kul jaulėγė bilen baldaγėn alim dip kisesėne tėγėlγan idė, ǯauluk-ta yuk, baldak-ta yuk* 'Er steckte die Hand in die Tasche und sagte: "ich will mein Tuch und meine Pfeife herausnehmen", doch weder das Tuch noch die Pfeife war da' (Kakuk 1989: 84)

In other respects too there are corresponding features in the Mari *uke* and the Tatar *yuk*. In Tatar, the conditional ending *-sA* can be added to *yuk* and *yuksa* takes the meaning of 'sonst, im anderen Fall' (TDW 1989). The fact that a conditional ending can be added to *yuk* in Tatar implies that *yuk* is balancing on the border between nouns and verbs, as is the case with *uke* in Mari. In Mari, a construction with the same meaning as *yuksa* in Tatar is formed by adding the conjuction *γə̂n* 'if' to *uke*:

MaMe *jeŋən motoržəlan it kuγane, ške motoret uke γə̂n!* 'Freue dich dessen nicht, das der Besitzt des anderen schön ist, wenn das Deine nich schön ist!' (Beke 1961a: 38)

In Mari, *uke* can be used as an adjective attribute:

MaE *pojanə̂n βülnümüžüm ot šińče, uke jeŋən kolmə̂žə̂m ot šińče* '[Wenn: Ö.B.] der Reiche verarmt, erführst du es nicht, [wenn; Ö.B.] der Arme stirbt, erführst du es nicht' (Beke 1961b: 20)

In Mari, *uke jeŋ* has the meaning 'poor'. In Chuvash, the morpheme *śuk* can have the same function, as in *śuk-śin* 'a man who has nothing' (Krueger 1961: 231).

Another characteristic feature of *uke* in Mari is that it according to Alhoniemi (1985: 112), can be combined with the denominal verb form *ulmaš* 'the being, it was':

MaMe *tuδə̂n pə̂rčə̂ ik kormə̂ž uke ulmaš* 'Er hatte nicht einmal eine handvoll haferkörner' (Alhoniemi & Saarinen 1983: 100)

The possibility of combining *yuk* and *śuk* respectively with verb forms is characteristic also of Tatar and Chuvash:

TatM *Yurtta baška χaywanlarï yuk-ide* 'Im Hause hatten sie kein anderes Vieh' (Kakuk 1996: 58)

TatM *Wäzir bilän padša-ulï: minda äwäldä yurt yuk ide, üydä barïp karïyik dide* 'Früher hat hier kein Haus gestanden—sprach der Vezir und der Padischah-Sohn. Gehen wir hinein und sehen wir es uns an' (Kakuk 1996: 79)

ChuvA *akă teprine pĕtertĕm, urăk śuk pulă tenĕ* 'Sieh, einen anderen tötete ich, etwas anderes ist das gewisst nicht, sagte er' (Paasonen 1949: 154)

There are other similarities between the Mari morpheme *uke* and corresponding morphemes in the Turkic languages. *uke* often occurs with the interrogative particle *mo* (see below, 5.8). To it, the dative case ending *-lan* can be added and *ukelan* has the meaning 'in vain, for no reason'. This is characteristic also of Tatar where the dative case ending *-gA, -kA* can be added to *yuk* and *yukka* has the meaning 'umsonst; zwecklos; grundlos' (TDW 1989). In Mari, *uke lijaš* means 'to be gone' and in Tatar the infinitive form of a verb meaning 'to be, become' can be combined with uke to form *yuk bulu* 'verschwinden' (TDW 1989). Above in 4.4.3.1 I have suggested that the adjective forming suffix *-le, lo, -lö, -lə̂, -lə* of Turkic origin has an equivalent in the Mari suffix *-an, -än*. In Mari, *ulan-ukean* means 'insignificant, a little' and this corresponds fully to Tatar *barlı-yuklı* 'sehr wenig; unbedeuted' (TDW 1989).

There are thus both formal and functional similarities between Mari *uke* and the Tatar *yuk* and the Chuvash *śuk*, similarities that hardly can be accidental. I believe that Kangasmaa-Minn is right in assuming a Turkic origin of the Mari morpheme *uke*. It is however probably not possible to determine which of the Turkic languages has been the model code. Etymologically, Tatar *yuk* and Chuvash *śuk* are related since an initial *ś* in Chuvash corresponds to *y* in other Turkic languages (Krueger 1961: 59). The form of the Mari morpheme is problematic since initial *ś* in global copies of Chuvash lexemes normally is kept unchanged (Räsänen 1920: 29–31). It is however worth noting that code-copies can be highly creative formations with respect to their phonological and morphological adaption to the basic code. As was discussed above in 4.1.7, the Mari particle *aδak* most likely is a copy of the Chuvash *tataχ* 'again' in spite of the fact that an initial *t* in global copies of Chuvash lexemes in Mari usually remains unchanged.

The copies in which *uke* is part can be classified in different ways; *uke* itself is a global copy of a Turkic morpheme, whereas copies such as *ulan-ukean* 'insignificant' and *uke γə̂n* 'if not' are mixed copies of Turkic models since combinatorial properties in the model code have been applied on morphemes in the basic code, e.g. Tatar *barlı-yuklı* 'sehr wenig; unbedeutend', Tat *yuksa* 'sonst; im anderen Falle'. Furthermore, *uke* is a conventionalised copy since it occurs in both literary languages of Mari:

MaEL *kapka βiš, oralat uke* 'The door is open, there isn't any guard' (Izhboldin 1994: 127)

MaWL *təńən ikmańarə̂ oksaet uke?* Don't you have any money' (Petukhov 1994: 291)

5.7 The use of *maneš* 'says' and *manə̂n* 'saying'

In my material, the verb forms *maneš* 'says' (3rd person singular, present tense of the verb *manam* 'to say') and *manə̂n* 'saying' (affirmative instructive gerund of the same verb) fill an important function. This is especially characteristic of the material representing MaE. It seems as if these verb forms can be seen as particles with a narrative function:

MaE *Temə̂r βatə̂r kaja. mijen šueš pörtöškö. "mo somə̂l δene koštat, šol'ə̂m?" maneš. "osalə̂m kə̂čal koštam" maneš. "šə̂m βujan βuβer," maneš. "ot kert, šol'ə̂m, maneš, seŋen."—"kertam, maneš, seŋen."—"kertat kə̂n, jörä, maneš. βüδüm konδem, maneš, ik šišam"* 'Held Temə̂r macht sich auf den Weg. Er geht und gelangt an ein Haus. "Was für eine Sache gehst du nach, mein Junge (eig. mein jüngerer Bruder)?" (sagt sie). "Ich suche den Bösewicht," sagt er. "Der βuβer hat sieben Köpfe (eig. ist siebenköpfig) (sagt sie), du kannst ihn nicht besiegen, mein Junge", sagt sie. "Ich kann ihn besiegen," sagt er. "Wenn du das kannst, ist's gut," sagt sie. "Ich bringe [dir; Ö.B.] eine Flasche Wasser," sagt sie' (Beke 1961b: 418).

MaMo *βätəžə: ti ü ak sitə βara, manən. i melenäeš-ät čəδə, manən. keok, eče šukərakəm kandok, manən* 'Das Weib sagte: dieser Butter genügt nicht, kaum für einen Kuchen, sagte sie. Geh, hole mir viel mehr dazu, sagte sie' (Ramstedt 1902: 180)

In MaE, these verb forms are very frequent and the number of examples could easily have been increased. The frequent use of these two forms of the verb *manam* in this context has parallels in the Turkic languages and these are explicitly given as examples of a characteristic feature of the Turkic languages by Johanson (1992: 191). "In den Türksprachen dienen Gerundien der verba dicendi te-, de- usw. 'sagen', d.h. teyän, dep, deyü, diye, tese usw. 'sagenderweise', als postpositive Zitierpartikeln, die Einbettung von direkter Rede und gedankenwiedergabe markieren, sowie als freie postpositive Subjunktoren (gliedsatztausleitende Konjunktionen) zur Markierung von Finalsätzen und Handlungsbegründenden Kausalsätzen (Erklärung von Handlungen durch fingierte Wiedergabe von Gedanken des Handelnden)."

In the Tatar material I have examined, the use of different forms of a verb with the meaning 'to say' strongly resembles the use of forms of a verb with the same meaning in Mari:

TatM *kuyan buz üstünä tüšüp "diñ diñ" sikergän. "buz, sin batïrmï?" digän. buz "batïr" digän. "batïr bulsañ, sine kuyas nik iretä?" digän. "kuyas, sin batïrmï?" digän. "batïr" digän. "batïr bulsañ, sine bulut nigä kaplï?" digän. "bulut, sin batïrmï?" digän. "batïr" digän. "batïr bulsañ, sine yil nik aktara?" digän. "yil, sin batïrmï?" digän. "batïr" digän. "batïr bulsañ, nigä tawnï tašnï tišmiseñ?" digän. "taw, sin batïrmï?" digän. "batïr" digän. "batïr bulsañ, sine tïškan nigä tišä?" digän. "tïškan, sin batïrmï?" digän. "batïr" digän. "batïr bulsañ, mačï sine nigä tuta?" digän* 'Der Hase ging auf das Eis hinab und hüpfte (so dass das Eis) "ding ding" (klang). "Eis, bist du stark?" fragte er. "Stark (bin ich)", sagte das Eis. "Wenn du so stark bist, wieso schmeltzt dich denn die Sonne?" sagte er. "Sonne, bist du stark?"fragte er. "Stark", sagte sie. "Wenn du stark bist, wieso verhüllt dich denn die Wolke?" sagte er. "Wolke, bist du stark?" fragte er. "Stark", sagte sie. "Wenn du stark bist, wieso, treibt dich denn der Wind?" sagte er. "Wind, bist du stark?" fragte er. "Stark", sagte jener. "Wenn du stark bist, warum durchborst du nicht Berg und Stein?" sagte er. "Berg, bist du stark?" fragte er. "Stark", sagte jener. "Wenn du stark bist, wieso durchgnagt dich denn die Maus?" sagte er. "Maus, bist du stark?" fragte er. "Stark", sagte sie. "Wenn du stark bist, wieso fängt dich denn die Katze?" sagte er' (Paasonen 1953: 66)

In the Chuvash material too, there are examples of this use of forms of a verb meaning 'to say':

ChuvA *unta kĕśĕn ıvălĕ tuχnăta, "atya, atte, śime, mĕšĕn χuyχăratăn?" tenĕ. aššĕ kalană: "mana payan śapla, śapla pulččĕ. esĕ kayăni?" tenĕ. ıvălĕ kalană: kayas atte, esĕ kirek ăśta yarsanta kayăp", tenĕ. aššĕ vara śime kĕnĕ, śise tăransan kĕśĕn ıvălĕ kalană: "χaleχ kaymalla-i?" tenĕ. aššĕ: "χaleχ kaymalla" tenĕ. ıvălĕ kalană: "atte sănččăr yĕven tutarsa kil", tenĕ* 'Darauf kam sein jüngster Sohn heraus und sagte: "Komm, Vater, essen, warum weinst du?" Sein Vater sprach: "Soeben hat mich solches (und solches) betroffen. Gehst du vielleicht?" Sein Sohn sagte: "Ich werde gehen, Vater, wohin auch immer du mich senden willst, werde ich gehen." Darauf kam der Vater herein zu essen. Nach dem Essen sagte der jüngste Sohn: "Hat man sofort zu gehen?" Sein Vater sagte: "Sofort hat man zu gehen." Sein Sohn sagte: "Vater, lass eine Halfterkette machen und bring sie her" (Paasonen 1949: 176–177)

The use of the present tense and gerundial forms of a verb with the meaning 'to say' in Mari is possible to classify as a selective copy of a model in the Turkic languages. The selective copying has been facilitated and preceded by other types of copying such as the global copying of a Chuvash verb *kalasa* 'to say, to tell' and different types of mixed copies. The gerund *manən* 'saying' of the verb *manam* 'to say' often occurs in combination with the verbs *kalasam* 'to say, to tell' and *joδam* 'to ask':

MaNw *"a mam təńəm pukχšə?" manən jaδən ulut* '"Und was gab er dir zu essen?" fragten sie' (Beke 1957: 36)

MaE *könena šüδö lu teŋge okśalan, ik teŋge aβa-γumδurlan, ik βedra arakalan tolźa! manən kalaśəšt, maneš* 'Wir geben unsere Einwilligung, der Brautpreis sei altso: hundertzehn Rubel (Geld), ein Rubel Stillungspreis, ein Eimer Branntwein: komm dann zu uns! sag(t)en sie' (Beke 1961b: 248).

The use of the different forms of the verb *manam* 'to say' as narrative particles is a selective copy of Tatar and/or Chuvash verba dicendi *di-* and *te-*. In the same way, the instances in which the gerund *manən* 'saying' occurs with finite forms of the verbs *kalasam* and *joδam* are also copies of models in the Turkic languages; in all likehood it is Chuvash that has been the model code:

ChuvA *"san patna pĕr-pĕr śın kimeri?" tese ıytnă yămăkinččen* 'Ist nicht zu dir ein Mann gekommen? fragte sie ihre Schwester' (Paasonen 1949: 131)

ChuvA *ăna χirĕś: "mĕn tese kalanĕ"* 'Ihr zugewandt fragte er: "Was sagst du?"'(Paasonen 1949: 221)

The verb *joδam* is not included in Räsänen's (1920) list of words of Chuvash origin in Mari. Still, it can be argued that the Mari verb *joδam* 'to ask' is a copy of the Chuvash verb *ıyt-* 'to ask, inquire' (Krueger 1961: 220) since the Chuvash verb formally resembles the Mari verb. The fact that the Mari verb belongs to the so-called *am*-conjugation and not to the *em*-conjugation like most other verbs copied from the Turkic languages, can possibly be explained by assuming that it is a fairly old copy. The verb *sižam* 'to feel' also belongs to the *am*-conjugation but is undoubtedly copied from Tatar, Tat *siz* 'to feel' and a comparatively old copy as well. The metathesis in the Mari verb is probably due to the fact that the combination of a vowel and *j* in the beginning of words is unusual in Mari and mainly occurs in copies of Tatar words, e.g. Ma *ayə̂k* 'nüchtern' < Tat *ayık* 'nüchtern' (Räsänen 1923: 18). Since the Chuvash verb has equivalents in other Turkic languages (see Paasonen 1974: 18), it is my opinion that the Chuvash verb can not be of Mari origin.

5.8 The interrogative particle MaMe, MaE *mo*, MaMo, MaNw *ma*

A characteristic feature of Mari is the existence of an interrogative particle *mo, ma*. This particle does not occur in the dialect texts representing MaMo published by Beke (1951) and as far as I have been able to tell not in the material representing MaNw either. In these dialects, the particle *βara* seems to fill the function of an interrogative particle. Ramstedt (1902: 76), however, states that *ma* "drückt eine Frage aus" and this makes it possible to conclude that an interrogative particle *ma* exists, or at least has existed, in subvarieties of this dialect. The particle seems, judging from the material, restricted to the eastern dialects:

MaMe *tə̂j mə̂jn joltašem kočkə̂nat ta, mə̂jə̂mat kočnet mo?* 'Hast du meinem Kameraden gefressen und auch mich möchtest du fressen?' (Alhoniemi & Saarinen 1983: 138)

MaE *šüδə̂ralaš nele mo?* 'Ist es schwer, zu spinnen?' (Beke 1961b: 207)

The interrogative particle *mo* of the eastern dialect is frequently used in combination with the morpheme *uke* (see section 5.6):

MaE *Temə̂r βatə̂r ške uke mo?* 'Lebt (eig. ist) Held Temə̂r nicht mehr?' (Beke 1961b: 422)

The particle is also relatively frequent in combination with the negative verb *oγə̂l* 'is not'.

ME *mə̂jə̂n βatə̂lə̂kə̂m oγə̂l mo?* 'Ist sie nicht meine Zukünftige?' (Beke 1961b: 244)

Several scholars have pointed to the existence of an interrogative particle *mo, ma* in Mari (Johanson 2000: 168; Erdődi 1979). Often singled out for mention of characteristic features of the Turkic languages is the use of an interrogative particle in yes-or-no questions (Johanson 1992: 193). In Turkish, the particle has the allomorphs *mu, mü, mı* and *mi*. The Turkic languages of the Middle Volga region also make frequent use of various interrogative particles. According to Krueger (1961: 171) the particles *-i, -ši, -i-mĕn* and *-im* are used as interrogative particles in Chuvash. Poppe (1963: 85) states that *-mE,-meni* and *-mını* are interrogative particles in Tatar. The first occurs in yes-or-no questions of the type *bügen lektsija bulamı* 'will there be a class today?' (Poppe 1963: 85), whereas the latter according to Poppe is an interrogative particle with a shade of doubt, e.g. *ul kilgänmeni* 'has he really come?'

In my opinion, the formal difference between the interrogative particles in Chuvash and the Mari *mo, ma* and the fact that the particle is most frequent in the eastern dialects of Mari excludes Chuvash influence in this respect. In Tatar, however, the particle *-mE* is an interrogative particle in yes-or-no questions. It occurs in my material:

TatM *ayaksïz: kïznï alasïz-mï dide* 'Da fragt der Fusslose: "Wollt ihr das Mädchen heiraten?" ' (Kakuk 1996: 102)

It is often used in connection with the negative verb *yuk* 'no; there is not':

TatM *miña χizmätkä barasïñ-mï yuk-mï, alaysa min sine mïnda üterem digän* 'Willst du bei mir den Dienst antreten oder nicht? wenn nicht dann töte ich dich' (Kakuk 1996: 109)

In Tatar, the particle often occurs in combination with the verb *tügel* 'is not':

TatK *Bügülmedin kilgen tügül-mė?* 'Sind sie wohl as Buguljma?' (Kakuk 1980: 57)

The combinatorial properties of the Mari particle *mo* thus corresponds to the combinatorial properties of the Tatar particle *-mE*. According to Erdődi (1979: 221) the Mari particle is etymologically the same as the interrogative pronoun *mo, ma* 'what?' but this pronoun has taken over functions of a similar particle in Tatar. In the instances in which *mo* functions as an interogative particle in yes-or-no questions, we are dealing with the selective copying of semantic and combinatorial properties of a Tatar morpheme. The same applies to the cases in which *mo* is combined with the verb *oγə̑l* 'is not', e.g. *oγə̑l mo* 'isn't it?' which corresponds to Tatar *tügül-mė* 'isn't it?' As for *uke mo* 'is there not?' the question of whether the copy is a selective or a mixed copy is dependent on whether *uke* is a global copy of a morpheme Tat *yuk*, Chuv *śuk* or not. I argue that *uke* is a copy of a Turkic original and that *uke mo* is possible to classify as a mixed copy combining the globally copied Tat *yuk* or Chuv *śuk* with the selective copying of combinatorial properties of the Tatar interrogative particle *-mE* transferred to the interrogative pronoun *mo, ma* in Mari.

The particle *mo, ma* can further be classified as a conventionalised copy since it occurs in both literary language of Mari:

MaEL *βüt uke mo?* 'Isn't there any water? (Taygildin 1993: 57)

MaWL *teŋge aγə̑l ma?* 'Is it not like this?' (Petukhov 1994: 259)

6 Summary

The analysis in Chapters 3–5 of the Tatar and Chuvash features in Mari has shown that the Code-copying Framework of Johanson is a good tool for the analysis and classification of these features. When the influence that Mari has undergone as a result of its contacts with the Turkic languages is analysed as code-copies, an interesting picture emerges concerning the factors underlying linguistic change, and also the direction, kind and distribution of these changes. The social factors, which were discussed in Chapter 2, are characterized by the social, political, numerical and cultural dominance of the Turkic peoples vis-à-vis the Mari, and also by the fact that the dominance relations have been changing. The Volga Bulgar empire was a world power in medieval Europe, and exerted a political and cultural influence far beyond its borders. The Golden Horde and later on the Khanate of Kazan took over the dominating position of the Volga Bulgar empire and as a result of this the descendants of the Volga Bulgars, the Chuvash, became a socially, politically and culturally dominated people. The demographic changes that occurred in the Middle Volga region as a result of the establishment of the centralized states with a Turkic-speaking elite, and later on the changes in Russian politics towards the different peoples that were integrated into the growing Muscovite empire, has led to the emergence of mixed settlements and a qualified bilingualism which has further increased the structural changes in the dominated languages. The Mari and their language in particular have been subject to large-scale influence.

This influence has furthermore been facilitated by the structural similarities between the languages in question. Typologically, the Finno-Ugric and Turkic languages are close, which has been shown in Chapter 2. Structural and social factors combine to produce contact-induced change and with respect to this, the structural changes in Mari as a result of the contacts with the Turkic languages Tatar and Chuvash seem less surprising. When the Tatar and Chuvash features in Mari are analysed as code-copies, it is also evident that the number of global copies is considerable in Mari, far higher than in any other Finno-Ugric language exposed to Turkic influence. Words of Tatar or Chuvash origin are not restricted to one or two word classes but penetrate the Mari lexicon in a systematic way.

The number of mixed copies is also considerable, and there are examples of mixed copies in both lexicon and syntax in Mari, for example when a global copy of a derivational ending is added to a Mari stem which in turn is an example of the selective copying of semantic properties. The most evident examples are the many words formed with the originally Tatar derivational ending *-lək*, words that have direct counterparts in the Turkic languages. Another example is the copying of postpositions that in Tatar or Chuvash require a certain case and where the global copying of a postposition such as *köra* 'according to, because of', will influence the choice of case in Mari.

According to the Code-copying Framework, a large-scale selective copying is preceded by mixed copies, and selective copying of linguistic features is also a characteristic of Mari. An evident example of this is the copying of certain functions of the dative case in Tatar which have been transferred to the Mari counterpart. Nevertheless, it seems as if the number of global and mixed copies in Mari outnumbers the selective copies, and this can be interpreted in the way that the code-copying process has stopped, possibly as a result of the increased importance of Russian.

Further aspects of the Turkic features in Mari can be described with the help of the Code-copying Framework. First, it is evident that the Chuvash influence goes deeper than the Tatar since it is generally detectable in every dialect of Mari. This concerns not only words of Chuvash origin in the Mari lexicon, words that generally have a wider distribution than words of Tatar origin, but also particles such as *-at, -ät* 'and, too' < Chuv *ta, te* 'id' and certain syntactic copies such as postpositions that require a certain case, for example the postposition *pasna, posna* 'without, except' < Chuv *puśne* 'id'. Copies of Tatar particles and postpositions, such as the particle *γə̑na* 'only' and the postposition *köra* 'according to, because of' have a less extensive distribution and are concentrated to the eastern dialects of Mari. It is probable that the contacts between Mari and Chuvash have been longer lasting—but not necessarily more intensive—than the contacts between Mari and Tatar. Thus, the Chuvash impact on Mari has been considerable.

Secondly, it is also evident that the structural changes that Mari has undergone as a result of of the contacts with the Turkic languages can be described as systematic. Code-copies in Mari are subject to different kinds of restructuring to better fit into the morphological system of Mari, but they are not inserted into the basic code in a haphazard way but into an equivalence position reserved for a Mari counterpart. In certain instances, this equivalence position is identifiable: this is the case with the particle *laj* 'as, in...way' which apparently has been inserted into a position reserved for the Mari morpheme *γańe* 'id'. The copying of a certain particle and functions of this particle can lead to further copying so that all the functions of a particle are copied systematically. This is evidently the case with the originally Tatar particle *ala* 'perhaps, or' which in Mari can function as a disjunctive conjunction and also occur in the formation of indefinite pronouns, as in Tatar. This way of systematic copying of forms and functions of particles will lead to the emergence of new equivalence positions which will make further copying possible. This can also be described as an instance of convergence which was discussed in Chapter 1. The basic code, Mari, has been converging with the Tatar and/or Chuvash model codes and has become more similar to them.

Thirdly, code-copies are originally momentary copies. They are the result of an individual's momentary use of an item of the model code, but every momentary copy can become habitualised and conventionalised and have effects on the linguistic norms. As has been shown by the use of examples taken from both the literary languages of Mari, this is exactly what has happened. There is a large number of lexical, morphological and syntactic copies in Mari which are conventionalised copies and when they occur in texts published in the literary languages they will spread even further; they have become accepted linguistic norms. An example of this is the disjunctive conjunction *ja...ja...* 'either...or...' of Tatar origin which does not occur in the dialect material I have examined but is frequent in some texts published in the eastern literary language. Mari is a language in which not only a few traces of Turkic influence are to be seen. The Turkic impact on the formation of the Mari language has been pervasive. In my opinion, it is possible to find numerous other structural features in Mari which are a result of the contacts with the Turkic languages Tatar and Chuvash. This thesis is just a first attempt at a comprehensive description.

Abbreviations

Chuv	= Chuvash
ChuvA	= Anatri dialect of Chuvash
ChuvV	= Viryal dialect of Chuvash
CT	= Common Turkic
Fi	= Finnish
Hu	= Hungarian
Ko	= Komi
Ma	= Mari
MaE	= Eastern dialect of Mari
MaEL	= Eastern literary language of Mari
MaMe	= Meadow dialect of Mari
MaNw	= North-west dialect of Mari
MaMo	= Mountain dialect of Mari
MaWL	= Western literary language of Mari
MoE	= Erzha Mordvin
MoM	= Moksha Mordvin
Mong	= Mongolian
Osm	= Osman Turkish
PFU	= Proto-Finno-Ugric
PU	= Proto-Uralic
SamN	= North Saami
SamS	= South Saami
Swe	= Swedish
Tat	= Tatar
TatK	= Kazan Tatar
TatM	= Mishar Tatar
Tu	= Turkish
Udm	= Udmurt

Tables

Table 1. The vowel system of Mari

The vowel system of Eastern Mari		
i	*ü*	*u*
e	*ö*	*o*
		a
		ə̂

The vowel system of Western Mari		
i	*ü*	*u*
e	*ö*	*o*
ä		*a*
ə		*ə̂*

Table 2. The consonant system of Mari

The consonant system of Eastern Mari			
p	*t*		*k*
		č	
	s	*š*	
	z	*ž*	
β	*δ*		*γ*
m	*n*	*ń*	*η*
	l	*l′*	
	r		
			j

The consonant system of Western Mari			
p	*t*	*t′*	*k*
	c	*č*	
	s	*š*	
f	*z*	*ž*	*χ*
β	*δ*		*γ*
m	*n*	*ń*	*η*
	l	*l′*	
	r		
			j

Table 3. The case endings in Mari

Case	MaMe, MaE	MaMo, MaNw
Nominative	*ø*	*ø*
Genitive	*-n*	*-n*
Accusative	*-m*	*-m*
Dative	*-lan*	*-lan, -län*
Lative	*-š, -eš*	*-eš*
Illative	*-ške,- ško, škö*	*-š(kə̂), -š(kə)*
Inessive	*-šte, -što, -štö*	*-štə̂, -štə*
Modal	*-la*	*-la, -lä*
Comparative	*-γe, -ke*	*-γe, -ke*
Caritive	-	*-δe, -te*

Maps

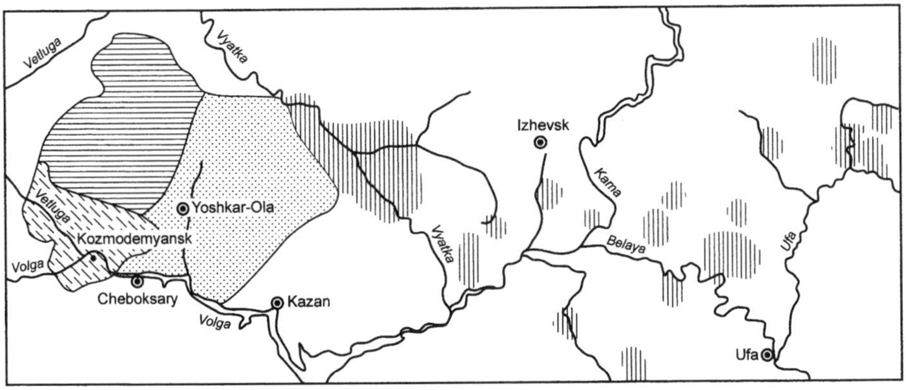

Map 1. The Mari dialects

(Map based on: Kovedyayeva 1976 & Luutonen 1997)

1 MaMe   2 MaE   3 MaMo   4 MaNw

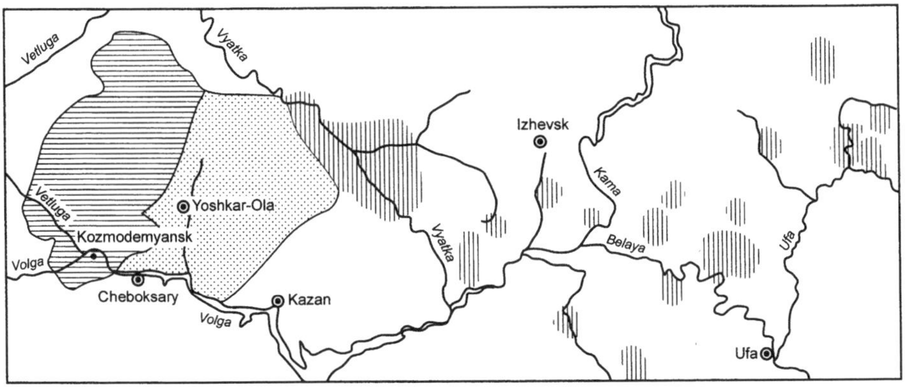

Map 2. Distribution of plural morphemes

(Map based on: Kovedyayeva 1976 & Luutonen 1997)

1 -šamâč   *2 -βlak*   *3 -βlä*

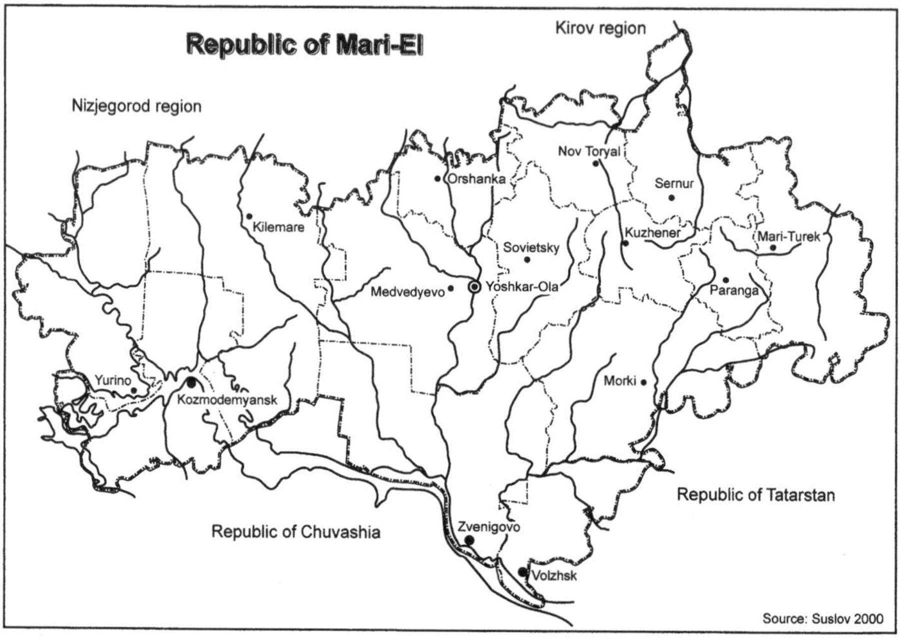
Republic of Mari-El
Kirov region
Nizjegorod region
Nov Toryal
Orshanka
Sernur
Kilemare
Kuzhener
Sovietsky
Mari-Turek
Medvedyevo
Yoshkar-Ola
Paranga
Yurino
Kozmodemyansk
Morki
Republic of Tatarstan
Republic of Chuvashia
Zvenigovo
Volzhsk
Source: Suslov 2000

Literature

Abondolo, D., 1998. Introduction. In: The Uralic Languages. Pp. 1–42.

Adamovič, M., 1983a. Das Tschuwaschische im Lichte der Substrattheorie. In: Symposium Saeculare Societatis Fenno-Ugricae. (MSFOu 185.) Helsinki. Pp. 9–24.

Adamovič, M., 1983b. Der Tschuwaschische Plural -sem. In: FUM 7. Pp. 21–27.

Adamovič, M., 1985. Umstrittene tschuwaschische Etymologien. In: UAJb. Neue Folge. Band 5. Pp. 74–97.

Agyagási, K., 1997. The Theoretical Possibilities of the Chronological Interpretation of Cheremiss Loanwords in Chuvash. In: Historical and Linguistic Interaction between Inner-Asia and Europe. Proceedings of the 39th Permanent International Altaistic Conference (PIAC). Szeged, Hungary: June 16–21, 1996. (Studia uralo-altaica 39.) Szeged. Pp. 1–10.

Agyagási, K., 1998. On the characteristics of Cheremiss linguistic interference on Chuvash. In: The Mainz Meeting. Proceedings of the Seventh International Conference on Turkish Linguistics. Edited by Lars Johanson. (Turcologica 32.) Wiesbaden. Pp. 667–682.

Alhoniemi, A., 1970. Über die Formen des Objekts im Tscheremissichen. In: FUF 38. Pp. 1–136.

Alhoniemi, A., 1985. Marin kielioppi. (Apuneuvoja suomalais-ugrilaisten kielten opintojen varten X.) Helsinki.

Alhoniemi, A., 1986. Marin kielen lukemisto. (Apuneuvoja suomalais-ugrilaisten kielten opintojen varten XI.) Helsinki.

Alhoniemi, A., 1988. Das Tscheremissische. In: Sinor 1988. Pp. 84–95.

Alhoniemi, A. & S. Saarinen, 1983. Timofey Yevseevs Folklore-Sammlungen aus dem Tscheremissischen. I. Märchen, Sagen und Volkserzählungen. (MSFOu 184.) Helsinki.

Ahlqvist, manuscript = Ahlqvist, A. Manuscript in the Archives of the Finno-Ugric Society. Heksinki.

Alvre, P., 1996. Über einige Pluralbildungen in den uralischen Sprachen. In: Larsson, L-G. (ed.). Lapponica et Uralica. (Studia Uralica Upsaliensia 26.) Uppsala. Pp. 153–157.

Anduganov, Y. V., 1991. Istoricheskaya grammatika marijskogo jazyka. Sintaksis. Yoshkar-Ola.

Ayplyatov, G. N., 1965. O marijskij sobstvennykh imenakh XVII veka. In: SFU 1. Pp. 90–93.

Ariste, P., 1969. Über die Dreisprachigkeit unter einigen finnisch-ugrischen Völkern. In: SFU 5. Pp. 245–254.

Baldauf, I., 1993. Schriftreform und Schriftwechsel bei den muslimischen Russland- und Sowjettürken (1850–1937): ein Symptom ideengeschichtlicher und kulturpolitischer Enbtwicklungen. (Bibliotheca Orientalis Hungarica 40.). Budapest.

Bartens, R., 1979. Mordvan, tšeremissin, ja votjakin konjugaation infiniitisten muotojen syntaksi. (MSFOu 170.) Helsinki.

Bartens, R., 1997. Zur Beschreibung der Sprachgeschichte des Tscheremissischen (Review of Bereczki, G.: Grundzüge der tscheremissischen Sprachgeschichte I–II). In: FUF 54. Pp. 325–336.

Bartens, R., 1999. Mordvalaiskielten rakenne ja kehitys. (MSFOu 232.) Helsinki.

Beke, Ö., 1911. Cseremisz nyelvtan. Budapest.

Beke, Ö., 1914/15. Türkische Einflüsse in der Syntax finnisch-ugrischer Sprachen. In: Ksz XV. Budapest. Pp. 1–77.
Beke, Ö., 1951. A cseremiszek (marik) népköltészete és szokásai. Budapest.
Beke, Ö., 1957. Mari szövegek. I kötet. Budapest.
Beke, Ö., 1961a. Mari szövegek. III kötet. Budapest.
Beke, Ö., 1961b. Mari szövegek. IV kötet. Budapest.
Beke, Ö., 1995. Mari szövegek. II. (Bibliotheca Ceremisica I). Savariae.
Benzing, J., 1959a. Das Baschkirische. In: Philologiae Turcica Fundamenta. Göttingen. Pp. 421–434.
Benzing, J., 1959b. Das Tschuwassische. In: Philologiae Turcica Fundamenta. Göttingen. Pp. 695–751.
Benzing, J., 1993. Bolgarisch-tschuwaschische Studien. Herausgegeben von Claus Schönig. (Turcologica 12.) Wiesbaden.
Bereczki, G., 1968. W. Steinitz és E. Itkonen finnugor vokalizmuselmélete és a cseremisz nyelv. In: NyK 70. Pp. 23–34.
Bereczki, G., 1971. Cseremisz (Mari) nyelvkönyv. (Finnugor Jegyzetek XIX.) Budapest.
Bereczki, G., 1977. Permi-cseremisz lexikális kölcsönzések. In: NyK 79. Pp. 57–78.
Bereczki, G., 1979. Tschuwaschische Kasussuffixe im Tscheremissischen. In: Festschrift für Wolfgang Schlachter zum 70. Geburtstag. (Veröffentlichungen der Societatis Uralo-Altaica 12.) Wiesbaden. Pp. 65–69.
Bereczki, G., 1983. A Volga-Káma vidék nyelveinek areális kapcsolatai. In: Areális nyelvészeti tanulmányok. Budapest. Pp. 207–236.
Bereczki, G., 1985. Kriterien zur Aufteilung der tscheremissischen Mundarten. In: Dialectologia Uralica. (Veröffentlichungen der Societatis Uralo-Altaica 20.) Wiesbaden. Pp. 187–193.
Bereczki, G., 1988. Geschichte der wolgafinnischen Sprachen. In: Sinor, D. (ed.). The Uralic Languages. Description, History and Foreign Influences. (Handbuch der Orientalistik, achte Abteilung Vol. 1.) Leiden. Pp. 331–350.
Bereczki, G., 1994. Grundzüge der tscheremissischen Sprachgeschichte I. (Studia uralo-altaica 35.) Szeged.
Bereczki, G., 1999. Die Entstehung der tscheremissischen „Sprachen". In: Hasselblatt, C. & P. Jääsalmi-Krüger (eds.). Europa et Siberia. Beiträge zu Sprache und Kultur der kleineren finno-ugrischen, samojedischen und paläosibirischen Völker. Gedenkband für Wolfgang Veenker. (Veröffentlichungen der Societatis Uralo-Altaica 51.) Wiesbaden. Pp. 67–79.
Bergsland, K., 1982. Sydsamisk gramatikk. Tromsø–Oslo–Bergen.
Berta, Á., 1998a. Middle Kipchak. In: The Turkic Languages. Pp. 158–165.
Berta, Á., 1998b. Tatar and Bashkir. In: The Turkic Languages. Pp. 283–300.
Boeschoten, H., 1998. The Speakers of Turkic Languages. In: The Turkic Languages. Pp. 1–15.
Boyarinova, V., 1991. Oβδa. Yoshkar-Ola.
Borisov, T. K., 1991. Udmurt kylljukam. Izhevsk.
Castrén, M. A., 1845. Elementa Grammatices Tscheremissae. Kuopio.
Čchaidze, M., 1960. Sparennye glagoly v marijskom jazyka. Yoshkar-Ola.
Čchaidze, M., 1968. Paired verbs in some east Uralic and other Oriental Languages. In: SFU 4. Pp. 285–297.
Clark, L., 1998. Chuvash. In: The Turkic Languages. Pp. 434–452.
Collinder, B., 1960. Comparative Grammar of the Uralic Languages. (Handbook of the Uralic Languages, part 3.). Stockholm.
Collinder, B., 1962. Introduktion till de uraliska språken. Finskan och dess frändespråk. Stockholm.
Comrie, B., 1988. General Features of the Uralic Languages. In: Sinor 1988. Pp. 452–477.

COTD = Alderson, A. D. & Fahır Iz, 1959. The Concise Oxford Turkish Dictionary. Oxford.
Décsy, G., 1990. The Uralic Protolanguage: A Comprehensive Reconstruction. (Bibliotheca Nostratica 9.) Bloomington.
Doerfer, G., 1996. Eine čeremissisch-čuvašische Gemeinsamkeit: das Pluralsuffix. In: FUM 20. Pp. 35–43.
Donnelly, A. S., 1968. The Russian Conquest of Bashkiria 1552–1740. (Yale Russian and East European Studies 7.). New Haven.
Driussi, P., 1995. Paired verbs—serial verbs in Cheremis. In: FUM 16/17. Pp. 59–105.
Erdal, M., 1991. Old Turkic Word Formation, Vol. 1. A Functional Approach to the Lexicon. (Studia Turcologica 7.). Wiesbaden.
Erdal, M., 1993. Die Sprache der wolgabolgarischen Inschriften. (Studia Turcologica 13.) Wiesbaden.
Erdődi, J., 1979. Die Fragepartikel *mo* des Tscheremissischen. In FUF 43. Pp. 213–221.
Fedotov, M. R., 1965. Marijskie zaimstvovanija v chuvashkom jazyke. In: SFU 1. Pp. 255–266.
Fokos-Fuchs, D. R., 1959. Syrjänisches Wörterbuch. Band II. Budapest.
FUF = Finnisch-ugrische Forschungen. 1–. Helsinki 1901ff.
FUM = Finnisch-ugrische Mitteilungen. 1–. Göttingen. 1977ff.
FUS = Fenno-ugrica Suecana. 1–. Stockholm 1978ff.
Galkin, I. S., 1964. Istoricheskaja grammatika marijskogo jazyka. Morfologija. Chast' I. Yoshkar-Ola.
Galkin, I. S., 1966. Istoricheskaja grammatika marijskogo jazyka. Morfologija. Chast' II. Yoshkar-Ola.
Galkin, I. S., 1977. Nekotoroe voprosy kontaktirovanija jazykov. In: SFU 13. Pp. 107–110.
Gordeev, F. I., 1976. Tatarizmy v leksike marisjkogo jazyka. In: SFU 12. Pp. 94–103.
Gordeev, F. I., 1979. Etimologicheskij slovar' marijskogo jazyka. Tom. 1. Yoshkar-Ola.
Gordeev, F. I., 1983. Etimologicheskij slovar' marijskogo jazyka. Tom. 2. Yoshkar-Ola.
Gornij, I.I. & J. J. Korolyeva, 1996. Mämnän täŋgnä γišän šamak. Gen. Matyukovskij γišän äšənδärəšβlä. Yoshkar-Ola.
Gruzov, L. P., 1969. Istoricheskaja grammatika marijskogo jazyka. Vvedenie i fonetika. Yoshkar-Ola.
Hajdú, P., 1987. Die uralischen Sprachen. In: Hajdú, P. & P. Domokos. Die uralischen Sprachen und Litteraturen. (Bibliotheca Uralica 8.). Budapest.
Halperin, C. J., 1985a. Russia and the Golden Horde: the Mongol impact on medieval Russian history. Bloomington.
Halperin, C. J., 1985b: The Tatar Yoke. Columbus.
Haugen, E., 1950. The Analysis of Linguistic Borrowing. In: Lg 26. Pp. 210–231.
Heikel, A. O., 1888. Die Gebäude der Čeremissen, Mordwinen, Esten und Finnen. (JSFOu 4.) Helsingfors.
Hesselbäck, A., 1996. Review of Wintschalek, Walter, (1993). Die Areallinguistik am Beispiel syntaktischer Übereinsstimmungen im Wolga-Kama-Areal. In: LU 32. Pp. 294–296.
Holmberg, U., 1914. Tsheremissin uskonto. Helsingfors.
Honti, L., 1992. Phonetische Angleichung von Lehnwörtern aus indogermanischen Sprachen im Ungarischen und im Finnischen. In: Honti, L. (ed.). Finnisch-ugrische Sprachen zwischen dem germanischen und dem slavischen Sprachraum: Vorträge des Symposiums aus Anlass des 25–jährigen Bestehens der Finnougristik an der Rijksuniversiteit Groningen. Amsterdam. Pp. 65–75.
Honti, L., 1996. Überwucherung von Suffixen in der U/FU Grundsprache? In: Larsson, L-G. (ed.). Lapponica et Uralica. (Studia Uralica Upsaliensia 26.) Uppsala. Pp. 201–210.

Honti, L., 1997. Numerusprobleme. (Ein Erkundungszug durch den Dschungel der uralischen Numeri.) In: FUF 54. Pp. 1–125.
Isanbaev, N. I., 1978. Vlijanie tatarskogo jazyka na padezhnuju sistemu vostochnomarijskij govorov. In: SFU 14. Pp. 172–177.
Isanbaev, N. I., 1979. Strukturno-slovoobrazovatelynij analiz tatarskikh zaimstvovannykh sushchestvitelynykh v marijskom jazyke. In: SFU 15. Pp. 76–83.
Isanbaev, N. I., 1988. Bashkirskie zaimstvovanija v marijskom jazyke i problema otgranichenija ikh ot tatarizmov. In: SFU 24. Pp 168–173.
Isanbaev, N. I., 1989. Marijsko-tjurkskie jazykovye kontakty. Yoshkar-Ola.
Isanbaev, N. I. & L. S. Arslanov, 1984. K voprosy o marijskikh zaimstvovanijakh v tatarskom jazyke. In: SFU 20. Pp. 104–114.
Itkonen, E., 1954. Zur Geschichte des Vokalismus der ersten Silbe im Tscheremissischen und in den permischen Sprachen. In: FUF 31. Pp. 149–345.
Itkonen, E., 1955. A finnugor nyelvek hangsúlyviszonyairól. In: NyK 56. Pp. 1–12.
Ivanov, I. G., 1975. Istorija marijskogo literaturnogo jazyka. Joshkar-Ola.
Ivanov, I.G., 1985. Marij dialektologij. Joshkar-Ola.
Ivanov, I. G. & G. M. Tuzharov, 1970. Severo-zapadnoe narechie marijskogo jazyka. Yoshkar-Ola.
Ivanov, I. G. & A. Moisio, 1998. Marin kielen sanaston kehitys 1900–luvulla. (Publications of the Department of Finnish and General Linguistics of the University of Turku 57.). Turku.
Izhboldin, V., 1994. Pajaš. Marij mə̂skara-ßlak. Yoshkar-Ola.
Johanson, L., 1992. Strukturelle Faktoren in türkischen Sprachkontakten. Stuttgart.
Johanson, L., 1998a: The History of Turkic. In: The Turkic Languages. Pp. 81–125.
Johanson, L., 1998b. The Structure of Turkic. In: The Turkic Languages. Pp. 30–66.
Johanson, L., 1999. The dynamics of code-copying in language encounters. In: Brendemoen, B., E. Lanza & E. Ryen (eds.). Language Encounters across Time and Space. Oslo.
Johanson, L., 2000. Linguistic Convergence in the Volga Area. In: Gilbers, D. G., J. Nerbonne & J. Schaeken (eds.). Languages in Contact. (Studies in Slavic and General Linguistics 28). Amsterdam–Atlanta. Pp. 165–178.
Johanson, L., 2001. Discoveries on the Turkic Linguistic Map. (Swedish Research Insitute in Istanbul. Publications 5.) Stockholm.
JSFOu = Journal de la Société Finno-Ougrienne. 1–. Helsinki 1886ff.
Kakuk, Z., 1980. Kasantatarische Volkslieder. Auf Grund der Sammlung von Ignác Kúnos. (Keleti Tanulmányok 4.). Budapest.
Kakuk, Z., 1989. Kasantatarische Volksmärchen: Auf Grund der Sammlung von Ignác Kúnos. (Keleti Tanulmányok 8.). Budapest.
Kakuk, Z., 1996. Mischärtatarische Texte mit Wörterverzeichnis. Aufgrund der Sammlung von Ignác Kúnos. (Studia uralo-altaica 38.). Szeged.
Kangasmaa-Minn, E., 1966. The syntactical distribution of the Cheremis genitive I. (MSFOu 139.). Helsinki.
Kangasmaa-Minn. E., 1998. Mari. In: The Uralic Languages. Pp. 219–248.
Kappeler, A., 1982. Russlands erste Nationalitäten. Das Zarenreich und die Völker der mittleren Wolga vom 16. bis 19. Jahrhundert. Köln & Wien.
Karlsson, F., 1978. Finsk grammatik. (Suomalaisen Kirjallissuuden Seuran Toimituksia 339.). Helsingfors.
Karpova, L., 1995. Chastitsy srednecheptskogo dialekta udmurtskogo jazyka. In: LU 31. Pp. 196–202.
Kelmakov, V. K., 1985. K voprosy o bulgarskom substrate v jazyke besermjan. In: Voprosy dialektologij tjurkskikh jazykov. Pp. 114–22. Ufa.

Kokla, P., 1986. Das System der infiniten Formen in der marischen Sprache. In. FUM 10. Pp. 207–217.
Korenchy, É., 1988. Iranischer Einfluss in den finnisch-ugrischen Sprachen: Sinor, D. (ed.). The Uralic Languages. Description, History and Foreign Influences. (Handbuch der Orientalistik, achte Abteilung Vol. 1.). Leiden. Pp. 665–681.
Korhonen, M., 1981. Johdatus lapin kielen historiaan. Helsinki.
Korhonen, M., 1986. History of the Uralic languages and the principle of lateral areas. In: FUF 47. Pp. 156–162.
Kovedyaeva, E. I., 1976. Marijskij Jazyk. In: Lytkin & al (eds.). Osnovy finno-ugorskogo jazykoznanija. Marijskij, permskij i ugorskie jazyki. Moskva. Pp. 3–96.
Krueger, J. R., 1961. Chuvash Manual (UAS 7.). Bloomington.
KSz = Keleti Szemle (Revue Oriental. 1–21. Budapest 1900–1932.
Kuznetsova, M., 1996. Wiesentscheremissisch und Bergtscheremissisch—zwei Dialekte oder zwei Sprachen? In: Larsson, L-G. (ed.). Lapponica et Uralica. (Studia Uralica Upsaliensia 26.). Uppsala. Pp. 231–240.
Larsson, L-G., 1990. The origin of Mordvin M *šaba*, E *žaba* 'child' and Cheremis *šuβo*. In: NyK 91. Pp. 147–153.
Larsson, L-G., 1999. Fränder genom språket: den finsk-ugriska språksläktskapen. In: Kultur och samhälle i språkets spegel. En essäsamling från Språkvetenskapliga fakulteten. Uppsala. Pp. 65–78.
Larsson, L-G., 2001. Baltic influence on Finnic languages. In: Dahl, Östen & Maria Koptjevskaja Tamm. Circum-Baltic Languages. Volume 1: Past and Present. Studies in Language Companion Series. Amsterdam–Philadelphia. pp. 237–251.
Lavrentyev, G. I., 1971. Prichastie budushchego vremeni v volzhkom govore marijskogo jazyka. In: SFU 7. Pp. 193–196.
Lazar, O., 1975. The Formation of Abstract Nouns in the Uralic Languages. (Studia Uralica et Altaica Upsaliensia 10.) Uppsala.
Levzion, N. & R. L. Pouwels, 2000. Introduction. Patterns of Islamization and Varieties of Religious Experience among Muslims of Africa. In: Levzion, N. & R. L. Pouwels (eds.). The History of Islam in Africa. Athens–Oxford–Cape Town. Pp. 1–18.
Lg = Language. Journal of the Linguistic Society of America. 1–. Baltimore 1925ff.
LU = Linguistica Uralica. 26–. Tallinn 1990ff.
Luutonen, J., 1997. The Variation of Morpheme Order in Mari Declension. (MSFOu 226.) Helsinki.
Luutonen, J., 1999. The history of Permian, Mari and Chuvash plural suffixes in the light of Indo-Aryan parallels. In: JSFOu 88. Pp. 73–101.
Masica, C. P., 1976. Defining a Linguistic Area: South Asia. Chicago–London.
Menz, A., 1999. Gaugasische Syntax. Eine Studie zum kontaktinduzierten Sprachwandel. (Turcologica 41.). Wiesbaden.
Moisio, A., 1993. Marin kielen konjunktio. In: Virittäjä 1993. Helsinki. Pp. 69–80.
Moisio, A., 1994. Marla-finnla muter. Yoshkar-Ola.
MRS = Serebrennikov, B. A. (ed.), 1956. Marijsko-russkij slovar'. Moskva.
MSFOu = Mémoires de la Société Finno-Ougrienne. 1–. Helsinki 1890ff.
Munkácsi, B., 1896. A votják nyelv szótára. Budapest.
Mägiste, J., 1959. Gibt es im Tscheremissischem baltische Lehnwörter? In: UAJb 31. Pp. 169–176.
Nurse, D. & T. Spear, 1985. The Swahili. Reconstructing the History and Language of an African Society 800–1500. Philadelphia.
NyK = Nyelvtudományi közlemények. 1–. Budapest 1860ff.
Oδar, I., 1993. Targəltəš. Yoshkar-Ola.
Paasonen, H., 1902. Die sogenannten Karataj-Mordvinen oder Karatajen. In: JSFOu 21. Pp. 1–51.

Paasonen, H., 1939. Tscheremissische Texte. Herausgegeben von Paavo Siro. (MSFOu 78.). Helsinki.
Paasonen, H., 1949. Gebräuche und Volksdichtung der Tschuwassen. (MSFOu 94.). Helsinki.
Paasonen, H., 1953. Mischärtatarische Volksdichtung. Übersetzt und herausgegeben von Eino Karahka. (MSFOu 105.). Helsinki.
Paasonen, H., 1974. Tschuwaschisches Wörterverzeichnis. (Studia uralo-altaica IV.). Szeged.
Pelenski, J., 1974. Russia and Kazan. Conquest and Imperial Ideology. The Hague–Paris.
Petukhov, V., 1994. Äkram. Yoshkar-Ola.
Pihlström, Anders = Anders Pihlströms dagbok. (Historiska Handlingar 18.) Stockholm 1903.
Poppe, N., 1963. Tatar Manual. (UAS 25.). Bloomington–The Hague.
Poppe, N., 1964. Bashkir Manual. (UAS 36.). Bloomington–The Hague.
Pritsak, O., 1959. Das Karaimische. In: Philologiae Turcica Fundamenta. Göttingen. Pp. 318–340.
Pugh, S., 1999. Systems in Contact, System in Motion. (Studia Uralica Upsaliensia 30.). Uppsala.
Raag, V., 1998. The Effects of Planned Change in Estonian Morphology. (Studia Uralica Upsaliensia 29.). Uppsala.
Ramstedt, G. J., 1902. Bergtscheremissische Sprachsstudien. (MSFOu 17.). Helsingfors.
Ramstedt, G. J., 1922. Zur Frage nach der Stellung des Tschuwassischen. In: JSFOu 38. Pp. 1–34.
Ramstedt, G. J., 1952. Einführung in die altaischen Sprachwissenschaft II. Formenlehre. (MSFOu 104:2.). Helsinki.
Ravila, P., 1938. Über die entstehung des tscheremissischen konjugationssystems. In: FUF 25. Pp. 1–25.
Róna-Tas, A., 1975. Some problems of Uralic vocalism from an Altaist's point of view. In: CIFU 3. Tallinn. Pp. 139–143.
Róna-Tas, A., 1988. Turkic Influence on the Uralic Languages. In: Sinor, D., 1988. Pp. 742–780.
Róna-Tas, A. & S. Fodor, 1973. Epigraphica Bulgarica. A volgai bolgár-török feliratok. (Studia uralo-altaica I.) Szeged.
Rorlich, A-A., 1986. The Volga Tatars. A Profile in National Resilience. Stanford.
Ruong, I., 1974. Min Sámigiella. Samisk Grammatik av Israel Ruong. Uppsala.
Räsänen, M., 1920. Die tschuwassischen Lehnwörter im Tscheremissischen. (MSFOu 48.) Helsinki.
Räsänen, M., 1923. Die tatarischen Lehnwörter im Tscheremissischen. (MSFOu 50.) Helsinki.
Saarinen, S., 1985. Die Dialekte des Tscheremissischen: Einteilung und Klassifizierungskriterien. In: Dialectologia Uralica. (Veröffentlichungen der Societatis Uralo-Altaica 20.) Wiesbaden. Pp. 195–199.
Saarinen, S., 1986. Über einige tscheremissische Enklitika. In: UAJb. Neue Folge 6. Pp. 37–46.
Saarinen, S., 1991. Karakteristiska drag i tjeremissiskan. In: FUS 10. Pp. 97–105.
Saarinen, S., 1993. Ns. marginaaliset sijat marin kaasussysteemissä. In: Systeemi ja poikkeama. Juhlakirja Alho Alhoniemen 60-vuotispäiväksi 14.5 1993. (Publications of the Department of Finnish and General Linguistics of the University of Turku 42.) Turku. Pp. 145–157.
Saarinen, S., 1994. Volgalaiskielten sanaston nykytilasta. In: Volgalaiskielet muutoksessa. (Turun yliopiston suomalaisten ja yleisen kielitieteen laitoksen julkaisuja 45.) Turku. Pp 213–223.

Saarinen, S., 1997a. Borrowed Vocabulary in Mari and Udmurt Dialects. In: Finnisch-ugrische Sprachen in Kontakt. Vorträge des Symposiums aus Anlass des 30-jährigen Bestehens der Finnougristik an der Rijksuniversiteit Groningen 21.-23. November 1996. Maastricht. Pp. 191–196.
Saarinen, S., 1997b. Language Contacts in the Volga region: Loan Suffixes and Calques in Mari and Udmurt. In: Language in Time and Space. Studies in Honour of Wolfgang Viereck on the Occasion of his 60th Birthday. Ed. by Heinrich Ramisch and Kenneth Wynne. Stuttgart. Pp. 388–396.
Saarinen, S., 1999. Tjurko-tatarskie zaimstvovanija v marijskom i udmurtskom jazyke. In: Problemy udmurtskoj i finno-ugorskoj filologia. Izhevsk. Pp. 250–250.
Sarhimaa, A., 1999. Syntactic transfer, contact-induced change and the evolution of bi-lingual mixed codes: focus on Karelian-Russian language alternation. Helsinki.
Schönig, C., 1984. Hilfsverben im Tatarischen. Wiesbaden.
Sebeok, T. & F. J. Ingemann, 1961. An Eastern Cheremis Manual. Studies in Cheremis Vol. 9. (UAS 5.) Bllomington.
Serebrennikov, B. A., 1976. O nekotorykh vozmozhnykh putyakh utgraty garmonij glas-nykh v permskikh jazykakh i lugovom dialekte marijskogo jazyka. In: SFU 12. Pp. 35–40.
SFU = Sovetskoe Finnougrovedenie. 1–25. Tallinn. 1965–1989.
Sinor, D. (ed.), 1988. The Uralic Languages. Description, History and Foreign Influences. (Handbuch der Orientalistik, achte Abteilung Vol. 1.). Leiden.
Spuler, B., 1965. Die Goldene Horde. Die Mongolen in Russland 1223–1502. 2nd revised edition. Wiesbaden.
Steinitz, W., 1944. Geschichte des Finnisch-ugrischen Vokalismus. Stockholm.
Stipa, G., 1977. Schilderung der Volkstraditionen der Bergtscheremissen in dem Reise-bericht A. von Haxthausens aus dem Jahr 1843. In: FUM 1. Pp 27–42.
Strahlenberg, P. J. von, 1730. Das Nord- und Ostliche Theil von Europa und Asia, in so weit solches das gantze Russische Reich mit Siberien und der grossen Tartarey in sich begreiffet [...]. Stockholm.
Suhonen, S., 1988. Baltische Lehnwörter der finnisch-ugrischen Sprachen. In: Sinor, D. (ed.), 1988. The Uralic Languages. Description, History and Foreign Influences. (Hand-buch der Orientalistik, achte Abteilung Vol. 1.). Leiden. Pp. 596–614.
Suslov, E. V., 2000. Mari-El. Kraj Marisjkij. Yoshkar-Ola.
Taygiljdin, G., 1993. Izi patə̂r. Finn-ugor kalə̂k jomak-ßlak. Yoshkar-Ola.
TDW = Dawletschin, T, I. Dawletschin & S. Tezcan, 1989. Tatarisch-Deutsches Wörter-buch. (Turkologie und Türkeikunde, band 2.) Wiesbaden.
The Turkic Languages, 1998. Eds. L. Johanson & É. Á. Csató. London–New York.
The Uralic Languages, 1998. Ed. D. Abondolo. London–New York.
Thomason, S. G. & T. Kaufmann, 1988. Language Contact, Creolization and Genetic Lin-guistics. Berkeley.
Thomsen, K., 1959. Das Kasantatarische und die westsibirischen Dialekte. In: Philologiae Turcica Fundamenta. Göttingen. Pp. 407–421.
UAJb = Ural-Altaische Jahrbücher. Fortsetzung der Ungarischer Jahrbücher. (Societatis Uralo-Altaica.) 24–52. Wiesbaden 1952–1982.
UAJb. Neue Folge. = Ural-Altaische Jahrbücher. Neue Folge. 1–. Wiesbaden 1981ff.
UAS = Uralic and Altaic Series. 1–. Bloomington 1960ff.
UEW = Rédei, Karoly, 1986–91. Uralisches Etymologisches Wörterbuch. Wiesbaden, Harrasowitz. Budapest, Akadémiai kiadó.
Volodin, A. P., 1997. Finnisch-ugrische (uralische) Sprachen in Kontakt. Zur allgemeinen Fragestellung. In: Finnisch-ugrische Sprachen in Kontakt. Vorträge des Symposiums aus Anlass des 30-jährigen Bestehens der Finnougristik an der Rijksuniversiteit Groningen 21.-23. November 1996. Maastricht. Pp. 35–43.

VTD I = Radloff, W., 1960. Versuch eines Wörterbuches der Türkdialekte. Erster band. The Hague.

VTD II = Radloff, W., 1960. Versuch eines Wörterbuches der Türkdialekte. Zweiter band. The Hague.

VTD III = Radloff, W., 1960. Versuch eines Wörterbuches der Türkdialekte. Dritter band. The Hague.

Weinreich, U., 1953. Languages in Contact. New York.

Wichmann, Y., 1903. Die tschuwassischen Lehnwörter in den permischen Sprachen. (MSFOu 21.) Helsingfors.

Wichmann, Y., 1924. Die türkischen Lehnwörter im Tscheremissischen. In: FUF 16. Pp. 32–53.

Wichmann, Y., 1931. Volksdichtung und Volksbräuche der Tscheremissen. (MSFOu 59.) Helsinki.

Wichmann, Y., 1987. Wotjakischer Wortschatz. Herausgegeben von M. Korhonen. (Lexica Societatis Fenno-ugricae XXI.) Helsinki.

Wickman, Bo. 1962. Some remarks on the problem of Fenno-Ugric vocalism. In: Commentationes Fenno-ugricae in honorem Paavi Ravila. (MSFOu 125. Helsinki. Pp. 671–679.

Wiedemann, F. J., 1847. Versuch einer Grammatik der tscheremissischen Sprache nach dem in der Evangeliumübersetzung von 1821 gebrauchte Dialekte. Reval.

Wintschalek, W., 1992. Areallinguistische Betrachtungen im Wolga-Kama-Areal. In: Festschrift für Károly Rédei zum 60. Geburtstag. (Studia Uralica 6. Institut für Finno-ugristik der Universität Wien.) Wien. Pp. 451–456.

Wintschalek, W., 1993. Die Areallinguistik am Beispiel syntaktischer Übereinstimmungen im Wolga-Kama-Areal. (Veröffentlichungen des Instituts für Finno-Ugristik der Universität Wien. Band 7). Wiesbaden.